ADVANCE

IF THESE STONES COULD TALK

Organized around the stories of men and women buried in the African-American Stoutsburg cemetery near Hopewell, New Jersey, this extraordinary book narrates the history of black communities in the Hopewell Valley and Sourland Mountains over a period of nearly three centuries. The authors place these stories in the larger context of American history in the eras of slavery, the Civil War, freedom, and civil rights. Part genealogy, part history, and part personal memoir, rooted in an amazing amount of research, and written with grace and flair, this book brings to light a rich past that had almost been lost.

— James M. McPherson, author of
Battle Cry of Freedom: The Civil War Era

Since the founding of our country, the recorders of history have not accurately transcribed the African American experience. Much of the African American history has been deleted, misconstrued and / or misinterpreted. Elaine Buck and Beverly Mills have taken the difficult steps to change the false narrative and provide clarification for generations to come.

— Marion T. Lane, Ed.D., Organizing Secretary General,
National Society of Colonial Daughters of the Seventeenth Century

An honest and thorough unveiling of this slice of American history has been long overdue. This is a wonderful read – a veritable page-turner. Elaine Buck and Beverly Mills are, at once, dedicated researchers and masterful story tellers. They have skillfully woven their personal experiences into a compelling multi-generational story of the formidable challenges faced and remarkable feats achieved by one localized African American community. It has broad implications for American society as a whole.

— Peter Moock, former Professor of Economics and Education,
Teachers College, Columbia University,
and former Lead Education Economist, The World Bank,
Africa Region and East Asia and Pacific Region

Humanity is prone to the unfortunate habit of forgetting, avoiding and altogether rewriting history, particularly when it falls into uncomfortable territory. Yet history offers clarity for the present and allows us to plot a course for the future — and it does so with even greater force when that history is painful. If These Stones Could Talk has collected an important and often forgotten history of central New Jersey, preserving it permanently so that everyone can understand the diverse tapestry of our past.

It's easy to overlook the value of a place until presented with a need to recognize it. Here, the authors have sifted through family trees, maps, legal records, and all the memories of the past to present us with the undeniable value of this region to African American history through the threads that connect it to the most impactful events in our national conscience, from the Revolutionary War to the civil rights movement.

— Bonnie Watson Coleman, Congresswoman (NJ-12)

IF THESE STONES
COULD TALK

AFRICAN AMERICAN PRESENCE IN THE

HOPEWELL VALLEY, SOURLAND MOUNTAIN,

AND SURROUNDING REGIONS

OF NEW JERSEY

IF THESE STONES
COULD TALK

AFRICAN AMERICAN PRESENCE IN THE
HOPEWELL VALLEY, SOURLAND MOUNTAIN,
AND SURROUNDING REGIONS
OF NEW JERSEY

ELAINE BUCK &

BEVERLY MILLS

WILD
RIVER
BOOKS

Published by Wild River Books
PO Box 672
Lambertville, NJ 08530
www.wildriverconsultingandpublishing.com
Copyright ©2018 Wild River Books

Distributed by Wild River Consulting & Publishing, LLC.

Publisher's Cataloging-In-Publication Data
Buck, Elaine and Mills, Beverly
    If These Stones Could Talk: African American Presence in the Hopewell
    Valley, Sourland Mountain, and Surrounding Regions of New Jersey

Library of Congress Control Number: 2018953890

ISBN: 978-1-941948-08-8

Printed in the United States of America

First Edition

This book is dedicated to our children
as we leave this book as a legacy to the
Mills Family children
Jason & Drew and grandchildren

Charde', Aviel, Hayden, Jameson and Megan
Buck Family children
Aaron, Jason and Shaniqua Jenkins Kennedy

In loving memory to my Grandparents,
Robert and Queen Hester Coleman
and my son Joseph (JB) Buck 1979-2000

---

*"There are two great days in a person's life —
the day we are born
and the day we discover why."*
–William Barclay

CONTENTS

LIST OF ILLUSTRATIONS & TABLES

ILLUSTRATIONS

TABLES

FOREWORD

For much of the twentieth century "serious" archivists and scholars of American history cast a disparaging eye on "mere genealogists," belittling them for their seemingly uncritical ancestor worship.

But by the end of the century, many of these same scholars had awakened to the power and dynamism that can be wrought from interweaving "family history" into a larger narrative of trends and events. Such intertwining can enrich and enliven our understanding of culture and identity; can shed light on complex relationships between inhabitants and "place;" can demonstrate links between individual lives and the cultural matrix that shapes them; or can point to interactions between the perceptions, fantasies and misconceptions of one generation, and the choices, triumphs, fears, errors, and rigidities of their heirs.

Modern historians and journalists such as Herbert Gutman, Alan Taylor, Emily Bingham, Daniel Richter, and Edward Ball[1] are among the writers who have developed pathways that move personal stories through colonial times to the present, inviting readers to see larger national themes in the nuanced memoirs and interactions of black Americans, upper-class white Americans, Jewish-Americans, and Native American Indians. Other scholars, such as Dolores Hayden, have used oral histories, geography, and newspaper accounts to tease out details of the experiences of European immigrants, Asian newcomers, and the many African and Spanish-language emigrés and refugees that comprise the American patchwork.[2] Increasingly, with the modern techniques of DNA matching and online search tools, the possibilities for situating the "small" individual story in a larger context seem limitless. Historians, archaeologists, playwrights, psychologists, anthropologists, and novelists increasingly seek out the threads of such stories and use them to ply their craft of knitting together a drama.

But sometimes, circumstances drop the strands of a story onto the doorstep of someone who wasn't a knitter at all. So it was with Beverly Mills and Elaine Buck, whose detective-labor-of-love has led to *If These Stones Could Talk*. Neither Bev nor Elaine was a professional historian. However, led by their religious commitment to their ancestors, inspired by the local history of their families' birthright, and spurred by their respect for the dignity and patriotism of their region's past inhabitants, they found themselves called to *learn* to knit, to *learn* how to seek out the fibers and filament they needed to braid together an important drama, and to present their findings in a voice that will appeal to a wide audience. Scholars and amateur history enthusiasts, school students and their teachers, church members and their pastors, local-history buffs and followers of national news, will find here an engrossing read that will challenge, anger, surprise and stretch them, broadening not only their view of New Jersey's local history, but also their view of a complex national politics and economy.

Using a small central New Jersey community, Mills and Buck develop what they describe as one of the "overlooked national stories [to be found] in small towns all over the United States." And thus here, in a narrative that is partly memoir, partly detective story, the reader meets a fascinating parade of characters. One of the first in Buck and Mills' parade was Walter Niemeier, "an elderly white man," who—distressed when he heard about the possibility of a road being cut through a black cemetery—contacted Elaine. Niemeier, reports Buck, found it "inconceivable … that anyone with a modicum of decency would consider destroying the burial ground of someone's ancestors for the sake of a driveway. Niemeier was not about to let it happen."

And so, in 2006, the story begins. Tacking back and forth between the present and the past, between the particular/individual ancestors and the general "community" down through time, Buck and Mills draw readers into their story, offering permission and an invitation for others—Black or not, lofty or not—to see their own stories as part of a larger mosaic of a human story that stretches across time and across the world.

Both the tale of *what* these two determined sleuths uncovered and the narrative of *how* their findings were painstakingly unearthed make for riveting reading. Though theirs is a seemingly-familiar story about slavery and racial injustice in American history, it's also about much more. Elaine and Bev's story is about both race-based pain and interracial triumph; it's about pettiness and greed and prejudice and ignorance and exclusion. But it's also about teamwork and mutual human concern, and about the intricacies of family life among and between White and Black Americans, stretching from the eighteenth and nineteenth century into the twenty-first century.

It's a story about land-occupancy, community-building, and a sense of psychological ownership as European and African newcomers, displacing the native peoples, sank their roots and buried their bones in the soil of central New Jersey over many generations. We see these New Jerseyans welcome home their heroes from the American Revolution, the Civil War and two world wars, and develop industries and grounding institutions. And we learn how they lived in—and around the edges of—racial separation and racial integration. Like Florida-born Depression-era anthropologist/novelist Zora Neale Hurston,[3] Buck and Mills blended meticulous archives research with an intimate knowledge of the community of their birth to piece together their portrait of what we might see "if those stones could talk."

Similarly, describing her mission to locate the burial-place and to enrich the biography of Zora Neale Hurston, modern African-American philosopher/novelist Alice Walker said this: "We are a people. A people do not throw their geniuses away. And if they are thrown away, it is our duty as artists, as witnesses for the future, to collect them again for the sake of our children, and, if necessary, bone by bone."[4] Buck and Mills—artful witnesses for the future—have brought alive some three-centuries-worth of the European, African-American, and Native American inhabitants of New Jersey's Sourland Mountains. And they have done it, "bone by bone." Perhaps Mills and Buck will inspire you, the reader, to seek out the places where your family's bones intersect with a larger historical narrative?

— Emma J. Lapsansky-Werner,

Professor of History Emeritus, Haverford College,

Author, *Struggle for Freedom: A History of African Americans*

May 29, 2018

[1] Herbert Gutman, *The Black Family in Slavery and Freedom*, 1750-1925. (New York: Pantheon, 1976); Alan Taylor, *Divided Ground: Indians, Settlers, and the Northern Borderland of the American Revolution.* (New York: Knopf, 2006); Emily Bingham, *Mordecai: An Early American Family.* New York: Hill and Wang, 2003); Daniel K. Richter, *Facing East from Indian Country: A Native History of Early America.* (Cambridge: Harvard University Press, 2001); Edward Ball, *Slaves in the Family.* (New York: Ballantine Books, 2001).

[2] Dolores Hayden, *The Power of Place: Urban Landscapes as Public History.* Cambridge, MA: MIT Press, 1995. Though Hayden centers her exploration of variables such as race, gender, and ethnicity in an urban setting, the issues she raises about "place," and the changes therein over time, provide an informative context for *Stones*.

[3] Zora Neale Hurston, *Mules and Men.* (1935).

[4] Alice Walker, *In Search of Our Mothers' Gardens: Womanist Prose.* (New York: Harcourt, 1983).

ACKNOWLEDGEMENTS

As first-time authors we have so many people we would like to thank. We would first like to thank our husbands, Robert Mills and John Buck, for being put on the back burner while we delved into mounds of paperwork in search of every clue that made this book possible and for graciously sharing their time and energy to help as we gathered this information.

We would like to begin by thanking Kim Nagy, Hope Tillman, Joy Stocke, and the Wild River Publishing Team for believing in our work. From the beginning of this project Kim Nagy has been our cheerleader, mentor and confidant who encouraged us to stay the course when our exhaustion told us we could not go on. Thank you, Kim, for how you guided, nurtured and molded us into the writers you somehow knew we were capable of being. Thanks for helping our voices soar in ways we never knew possible because you believed in our dream. Our gratitude also goes to Emma J. Lapsansky-Werner of Haverford College for her unwavering support of our endeavor, her sage advice and words of wisdom!

A special acknowledgement also to our friend, Kate McGuire, who took on our project in the beginning stages by spending countless hours unearthing records and documents that made this story possible. Your tireless efforts have changed our lives. A special thank you goes to Ronnie Coleman, (Elaine's uncle in South Korea), who purchased a laptop for her capable of storing a terabyte of information. We want to acknowledge the hours of assistance we received from local historian Beverly Weidl who provided memories and records from her mother, Eva Kyle who lived on the Sourland Mountain and played the piano at Mt. Zion Church every Sunday. A special recognition goes to Lloyd "Junie" Tucker, husband of the late Beverlee Nevius Tucker (who was the keeper of the Black Nevius, Truehart, Stives family genealogy), to Bonnie Stills (Beverly's "little" cousin whose memory never failed), to Carol Nevius Waldron, Florence Case and Dolores Grover Varner for sharing family pictures, artifacts and information.

We would also like to extend a special thank you to Joe Klett, Chief of Archives at the State of New Jersey Department of Archives; Jim Davidson, President of the East Amwell Historical Society; and John Allen; Walter Niemeier and Ian Burrow for all their help with the West Amwell Rock Road project that started us on this journey.

We would also like to acknowledge Kevin Burkman for his award-winning creation of a local African American sites map, Jack Koeppel for his tireless work on our photos, Caroline Katmann, Executive Director of the Sourland Conservancy, Jamie Sapoch of the Bunbury Foundation and the Princeton Area Community Foundation and Amanda Blount Quay for spearheading our YouCaring fundraising site.

Further acknowledgements go to Katherine A. Ludwig and Patricia Romagna of the David Library of the American Revolution, Washington Crossing, Pennsylvania and Bonita Grant of the Hopewell Valley Historical Society and Rutgers Archival & Special Collections.

Our list of thanks continues with Mike Alfano of the Hunterdon County Historical Society and member of the Sons of the American Revolution, Sue Bennett from the Hunterdon County Hall of Records and the late David Blackwell from the Hopewell Valley Historical Society.

Additional acknowledgments go to Jack Davis and his mother, Elizabeth Blackwell Davis, of the Blackwell Memorial Home in Pennington, New Jersey who generously offered their businesses' book of burials for our research and to Charles Holcombe Fisher of the Holcombe Fisher Memorial Home in Flemington, New Jersey.

We will never forget the tender loving care we received from Susan Molnar (owner of the Hopewell Bistro), her mother and wait staff who helped us decompress with delicious food and drink after a day of tedious research.

To all of our supporters, you know who you are—especially to all our Friday Memory Facebook followers, we thank you!

Sincerely,
Elaine & Beverly

A SPECIAL THANK YOU

THE MERCER COUNTY CULTURAL & HERITAGE COMMISSION AND THE BUNBURY FOUNDATION AT THE PRINCETON AREA COMMUNITY FOUNDATION

This book would not have been possible without grants from the Mercer County Cultural & Heritage Commission and the Bunbury Foundation at the Princeton Area Community Foundation. It is because of these grants that we have been able to bring this story to our readers and see this project to fruition. We cannot thank the Mercer County Cultural & Heritage Commission and the Bunbury Foundation at the Princeton Area Community Foundation enough for their beliefs in our endeavor.

Stamp
50 ₵

Randolph Stout & Wife
To
Stacy Rivers, Moses Blew,
and Henry Lane

This Indenture, made this Seventh day of November in the year of our Lord, one thousand eight hundred and Fifty Eight. Between Randolph Stout and Carrie M. his Wife of the township of Hopewell in the County of Mercer and State of New Jersey party of the First part, and Stacy Rivers and Moses Blew, of the County of Hunterdon and Henry Lane of the County of Somerset, all of the State of New Jersey, party of the second part, Witnesseth that the said party of the First part, for and in consideration of the sum of Thirty Dollars lawful money of the United States to them the said party of the first part, in hand well and truly paid by the said party of the second part, before the sealing and delivery of these presents the receipt whereof the said party of the First part do hereby acknowledge, have granted, bargained, sold, aliened, released, conveyed, and confirmed; and by these presents do grant, bargain, sell, alien, release, convey and confirm unto the said party of the second part, their successors and assigns, all that certain lot or parcel of land situate in the Township of Hopewell, in the County of Mercer and State of New Jersey, and is bounded and described as follows, Beginning at the Northwest corner of the Burying Ground and in Charles W. Stout's line thence (1) along said Charles W. Stout's line North seventeen and three quarters degrees west one chain and seventy four links to a Stake for a corner, thence (2) with said Randolph Stout's land North seventy degrees East one chain and sixty eight links to a Stake for a corner, thence (3) with the same South nineteen and a half degrees East, one chain and Seventy four links to the North East corner of the said Burying ground, thence (4) along said burying ground South seventy degrees West, one chain and seventy one links to the place of Beginning, Containing thirty hundredths of an acre of Land be the same more or less, the said parties of the second part do hereby bind themselves, their heirs, Executors, administrators and assigns to Keep the said lot of land in good and lawful fence, also not to use or occupy the said lot of land for any other purpose than as a burying ground, also not to use any other road or drift way in going to or from said lot over the Lands of the said Randolph Stout than the road formerly and at present used, without the consent of the said Randolph Stout. Together with all and singular the buildings, improvements, ways, woods, waters, watercourses, rights, liberties, privileges, hereditaments and appurtenances to the same belonging or in any wise appertaining, and the reversion and reversions, remainder and ———————— remainders, rents, issues and profits thereof, and of every part and parcel thereof; and also all the estate, right title, interest, use, possession, property, claim and demand whatsoever both in law and Equity of them, the said party of the First part, in and to the said premises, with the appurtenances. To have and to hold the said lot of land, hereditaments and premises hereby granted and every part and parcel thereof with the appurtenances, unto the said party of the second part, their successors and assigns, to the only proper use, benefit and behoof of them the said party of the second part, their successors and assigns forever. And the said Randolph Stout party aforesaid of the First part, for himself his heirs, Executors, and administrators, doth hereby covenant, promise and grant to and with the said Stacy Rivers, Moses Blew and Henry Lane, party of the Second part their successors, heirs, and assigns. That at the time of the Sealing and delivery hereof, they the said party of the First part, are seized in their own right of an absolute and indefeasible estate of inheritance in fee simple of and in all and singular the premises hereby granted, with the appurtenances, and have good right, full power and sufficient authority in the law to grant, bargain, sell and convey the same unto the said party of the second part, their successors and assigns forever according to the true intent and meaning of these presents. And also, that it shall and may be lawful for the party of the second part their successors and assigns, at all times forever hereafter, peaceably and quietly to have hold, use, occupy, possess and enjoy the said premises, with the appurtenances, and every part and parcel thereof without the lawful let, suit, eviction, interruption, or disturbance of the said party of the first part their heirs and their heirs, and against all and every other person or persons whomsoever lawfully claiming or to claim the same, shall and will warrant and forever Defend. In Witness whereof, the said party of the First part, have hereunto set their hands and seals the day and year first above written. Randolph Stout (seal) Carrie M

INTRODUCTION
WRITTEN IN STONE

by BEVERLY MILLS

I have always enjoyed cemeteries. Altars for the living as well as resting places for the dead, they are entryways, I think, to any town or city, the best places to become acquainted with the tastes of the inhabitants, both present and gone.

—Edwidge Danticat, *After the Dance*

Cemeteries have stories to tell. Anyone who has gazed at the dates marking a carved headstone, memorializing one single life, knows the momentary wonder of thinking: Who is here? Who walked before me? What happened in their lives? If only these stones could talk.

This is a story of a community taking control of its past, its present, and its future. It's a story of what can happen when people of faith set out to protect and publicize important truths and stories gleaned from a few of the oldest African American cemeteries in Hunterdon and Mercer counties in central New Jersey—primarily the Stoutsburg Cemetery, the Pennington African Cemetery, the Elnathan Stevenson Family Burial Ground, and the Old School Baptist Church Cemetery. The maps we include will help you visualize the present locations and connect them to the past.

Our story centers on one particular African American cemetery, the Stoutsburg Cemetery in Hopewell, Mercer County, New Jersey. The land on which the cemetery is located was purchased by African Americans in the mid-nineteenth century to bury people of color with honor and dignity. On this journey, however, we will be referring to all of the above-mentioned cemeteries in the region, which are interconnected and have their own stories to tell. African American cemeteries, you might ask? Separate from White? People may not realize that for much of American history, Whites and Blacks were buried in separate locations.

This separation represented a stark division of privilege that can be traced back to legal restrictions that persisted in the period after abolition in our corner of central New Jersey. Because Blacks could not be buried with Whites until this practice was deemed illegal by New Jersey in 1884, there was a need for burial grounds where African Americans could be laid to rest respectfully. Some local cemeteries had a special area, separate from the White family plots, where people of color were buried. For instance, the Old School Baptist Church in Hopewell borough had a designated area for their Black parishioners situated not too far from the outhouse.

The Stoutsburg Cemetery has been overlooking the picturesque Hopewell Valley with its distinctly Norman Rockwell feel since the early nineteenth century. Straddling the East Amwell border, the cemetery is also a part of Montgomery Township. The Stoutsburg Cemetery has served as a burial ground for African American residents and many veterans. The graves there consecrate the collected lives of a minority Black community in a predominantly White region, a pattern of community that reflects a larger, deeply important but typical overlooked national story in small towns all over the United States.

I'm Beverly Mills. I was born a mere eighty-five years after Congress ratified the Thirteenth Amendment that abolished slavery in the United States, declaring that "Neither slavery nor involuntary servitude, except as a punishment for crime whereof the party shall have been duly convicted, shall exist within the United States." I was a Black baby girl born to parents who were descendants of remarkable people with deep roots in this part of New Jersey where the Delaware River separates us from Pennsylvania. This was the beginning of my story.

I was born in 1950, when Harry S. Truman was president of the United States, the Korean War had just begun, and Senator Joseph Mc-Carthy was ramping up his witch hunt that ultimately led to the black-listing of many Americans. For as far back as I can remember, I grew up knowing about the Stoutsburg Cemetery. My maternal grandmother, Herma Fields, whom we called "Mom" and who was the oldest daughter of Sarah Matilda and Herbert Albert Hubbard, was raised on the Sour-land Mountain. As the oldest granddaughter I was first to hear about what life has been like in those days there. Mom would tell me about how her family farmed and made all their food from scratch—a virtual miracle considering the reputation of the land's infertility. She described how they raised and killed their chickens and hogs, and how hog killing could be a multifamily affair in the fall. She also described the rich cakes and juicy pies the Black ladies made that would match the baking of any present-day gourmet cook.

The stories were endless, but what I remember most are the names she associated with the stories. Mom had a knack for associating a name or phrase with something we did as kids that reminded her of someone from the mountain. We never understood why we were suddenly being called Lottie Hooper, Sam Ridley, or Old Sam Schenck. What did we do that reminded her of one of these Stoutsburg folks? When she would call us a name she would simultaneously break into gales of laughter. We were never privy to the joke. Likening us to people who lived decades before us became part of the funny recollections we would recall later as adults. When visiting the Stoutsburg Cemetery with one of my cousins, if by chance we saw a gravestone with one of those familiar names that our grandmother called us, we would look at each other and laugh—our own inside joke.

One of the main reasons I frequently visited the Stoutsburg Cemetery was because of my mother, Jean Marie. In 1968 she died suddenly of a pulmonary embolism, less than one month after giving birth to my brother Travis who was born prematurely. At age eighteen I lost my forty-year-old mother to a blood clot that traveled to her lung, killing her as she napped one warm July afternoon. I later learned that on the morning of the day she died, she had called her mother, Herma, to ask if she would make her some corn fritters. It was the beginning of corn season and she had a taste for her mother's cooking. My grandmother, not hearing back from her, assumed she had changed her mind. Nor did she think it was odd when her kitchen clock stopped just before 2:30 p.m. It wasn't until later that we realized the clock had stopped right around the time of my mother's passing. One of the town's doctors whose responsibility was to care for maternity patients was dismissive of my mother's concern that she had continued to bleed heavily for days after giving birth. The doctor's advice to her had been to rest and simply keep her legs elevated. He never suggested that she come into the office nor did he make a house call, which was customary at the time. Meanwhile, my brother, born weighing only two pounds, three ounces, was still in the hospital in the neonatal ward. I found my mother's death unbearable, and making the trip to the Stoutsburg Cemetery to lay my beautiful young mother to rest was excruciating.

A year after my mother's death, I left the area to go to school in New York. I was young, single, and, in my mind, light years away from home and from the Stoutsburg Cemetery. I went home every other weekend for social events or to visit the relatives who became my lifeline after losing my mother. After a few years in the big city I moved back home to live with my fiancé, Robert. Even with all the excitement and glamour of New York, the bread trail still connected me home: the tastes, smells, and talk of the people and the love of my soon-to-be husband. After I returned, I got a job that merely paid the bills because I wasn't looking for a job that was too challenging or mentally taxing because we planned to start a family soon after marriage. My first child was born fifteen months after we married, and another son arrived a little shy of four years later. Added to our young family was my brother, eighteen years my junior, who had previously been living with my mother's sister, Bonnie, and her family. But once again a trip to Stoutsburg Cemetery would become necessary when, in 1983, Bonnie suddenly died from a heart attack in the prime of her life at the age of forty-eight. It seemed that attending burials at the Stoutsburg Cemetery was to become an all too familiar occurrence.

When I was a young mother it never occurred to me that my connection to the Stoutsburg Cemetery would expand into a leadership role, but that "rite of passage" would literally be thrust upon me. Unbeknownst to me, at one of the Stoutsburg Cemetery Association meetings, my uncle Fred Clark announced plans to draft me as the new secretary, which would relieve him of the duty he had had for a number of years. When the "passing of the baton" took place I was the youngest in a room of people a couple generations my senior. Uncle Fred placed a notebook on my lap and stated, "Here, it's time for somebody young to take over because us old-timers are not going to be here forever." That was four decades ago.

As I settled into my new role as secretary of the Stoutsburg Cemetery Association, I noticed how excited everyone got when we met to plan the cemetery's annual Memorial Day Service, a tradition observed for years that we continue to this day. Each year, on the last Sunday in May, the Stoutsburg Cemetery Association hosts descendants from in and out of state who come to participate in our memorial service to commemorate the veterans buried in Stoutsburg. We greet people with names that match those etched on the gravestones such as Hoagland, Grover, Nevius, True, and Stives, just to name a few. We gather to pray, sing, and teach what we have learned about our people, so they can take it home and share with others. We always laugh, because every year we have to remind everyone to bring along their chairs. Others who come join the service from colorful blankets they spread out on the freshly mowed grass. We generally keep our service to one hour because we need time to hug each other and talk about how we look forward to seeing one another again next year, God willing. We cherish this annual ritual because we strongly believe in carrying on the tradition of how our ancestors commemorated those who went before us.

I can't tell you exactly how many years I have known my coauthor, Elaine Buck, but it's been most of my life. She is not only my research partner in writing this book but also assistant secretary of the Stoutsburg Cemetery Association. Back in the 1980s we attended the same church, sang in the choir, and raised all boys who were about the same age. When I was a child, Elaine's biological father, Goldman Kidd, and my father, William Smith (who always went by the nickname Shud), were friends with very similar senses of humor. Whenever they would see each other you can be sure there was a lot of storytelling and laughing. No one really knew for sure what the joke or story was about because the possibilities were endless. You know the old saying that apples don't fall far from trees; Elaine and I are the same way together. When we were young mothers we would get together with a group of girlfriends whenever we could—without kids or husbands. We would talk about whatever we wanted without judgment or fear. We called ourselves the "Girls Club." Elaine was one of the main ringleaders who kept us in hysterics with her quick wit and comedic timing. We were our own support system and were there for each other when life presented inevitable challenges, which at times seemed to be many. Elaine was always there to dish out an extra dose of nurturing and would say, "If we don't take care of each other, who else will?"

One thing that fascinated me about Elaine was her interest in history and her knowledge of "old-timey" ways and customs. She was always open about being born to a fifteen-year-old girl and being raised by her grandparents whom she called Mom and Dad. Elaine liked to share what she learned from them and her old Aunties, concoctions her grandmother would whip up to cure whatever ailed you, she would tell us. One remedy I'll always remember Elaine telling us, though I never tried it myself, was to put raw onions on the soles of a baby's feet if the child had a fever. The next morning, when the socks were removed, supposedly the fever would be gone and the onions cooked! She would have our mouths watering as she would tell us about the delicious meals her grandmother Queen Hester would cook from picking right out of their garden. Their family lived "farm to table" long before this became trendy.

We clearly knew that Elaine and her family were spiritually yoked and that they worshipped at the same Baptist church for generations because God always came first in their home.

Elaine never hid the profound respect she had for how she was raised and gladly passed her knowledge on to others. When we were young mothers I particularly admired her attempt to preserve African American history long before any of us became interested or involved in researching and teaching the stories of our ancestors. In fact, Elaine often volunteered to speak to classrooms full of young White children during Black History Month, something she continued to do long after our children left the school system. I've always regarded Elaine as a teacher and a leader. Perhaps this is why she received the call that changed the course of our lives—but more on that in the next chapter.

The title of the book, *If These Stones Could Talk*, refers to four African American cemeteries that are all within close proximity of one another. To travel from one cemetery to the other, you'll be traveling through George Washington Country—the most direct route would be through the Village of Hopewell past the Old School Baptist Church and west onto Route 518, which is also known as the George Washington Turnpike. In 1778, Washington's army journeyed on that same route— what we now call Route 518—on their way to the Battle of Monmouth, roughly sixty miles to the east.

This little pocket in central New Jersey is ripe with history as our region played a pivotal role in the new country's struggle for freedom from the British. This area has been a home for artists, writers, a signer of the Declaration of Independence, a 120-year-old former slave woman, enslaved and freed Blacks, peach orchard workers and peach basket makers, farmers, miners, quarry and pottery workers, and so many others. For as long as the Sourland Mountain has been in existence many have feared its huge menacing rocks, slithering creatures, maze-like roads, impenetrable forests, and pitch-black nights.

When Elaine and I earnestly started collaborating in our research on central New Jersey African American cemeteries, we began with a few of the names we saw etched on tombstones in the Stoutsburg Cemetery; many of these births dated back to the eighteenth century when British settlers claimed and named the area as part of what they called "West Jersey," prior to the Revolutionary War. We noticed that many of the surnames on the tombstones were the same as those of prominent White men who had been the founding fathers from this area. How did this happen? Was it a mere coincidence? We had learned in school that slavery existed in the South and that it was not uncommon for slaves to take on the last name of their masters. But we thought, certainly this could not have happened in New Jersey? We couldn't have been more wrong.

What we had never been taught in school is that New Jersey had been a slave state along with all the other colonies that comprised the original thirteen. I wondered how it was possible that I had lived all these years and knew nothing about slavery in New Jersey. I had been taught in American history classes in school that slaves were a happy contented people who, for the most part, lived in the South and were always eager to be of service to their white families. I can recall one particular short film in which a Black Mammy was happily serving a White family seated at the table eagerly awaiting their meal. The mammy, grinning from ear to ear, bustled around in a headscarf as she served the family. I clearly remember how my White classmates turned to look at me while all I could do was to stare straight ahead while consumed with shame. The conservative 1950s and turbulent 1960s were particularly challenging times for a Black child to live not only in the United States but in Hopewell Township, New Jersey. One day I asked Elaine, who was a few years behind me in school, if she had learned anything about slavery in New Jersey. "Did you learn anything about slavery in Jersey?" No, she had never been taught anything about slavery in New Jersey. All through school, Elaine had always felt there was something missing from the school history lessons. In fact, in 1969 on her first day at Hopewell Valley Central High School in Pennington, she opened the assigned history book and after leafing through the chapters she recalled her blood pressure rising before she screamed, "I know Black folks did more than have babies and pick cotton! What gives?!" That was her first trip to the office to see the principal!

Elaine and I have had so many conversations about the curriculum that we would like to see taught not just in Hopewell Valley but in all schools. Since my days in school there have been valiant attempts by school districts, historians, and historical sites and institutions to change the narrative to include the significant influence African Americans have had on the development of American society and culture. Although these efforts should certainly be recognized for bringing potentially difficult conversations to the forefront, Elaine and I both feel the needle has not moved sufficiently for our local area or New Jersey as a state. We wanted to help make this happen.

But the vastness of our mission seemed overwhelming. How could two small-town, middle-aged, African American women make a difference in reshaping how our history is taught and perceived? We were willing to find out.

Chapter 1 is an introduction that officially welcomes you into a world Elaine and I have been researching for more than a decade. We recount how one phone call turned us into historical preservationists on a statewide mission. Come with us as we unravel a past that has been long dormant, a past with stories that are microcosms of the national experience that can be replicated throughout the country. In chapter 2 I unfold how nineteenth-century members of the African American community seized the opportunity to purchase land at the base of the Sourland Mountain outside of Hopewell, New Jersey—land that would expressly be used as a cemetery for Black residents.

I have devoted chapter 3 to introducing you to our region's earliest African American settlers. The chapter also provides more detail about how some of these local families have descended from an African American patriot of the Revolutionary War. From here I segue to chapter 4, which takes a deeper dive to familiarize you with these ancestors and how they came to settle in this region as former slaves or free people. In chapter 5 I share with you a story that circulated in my family for years—about Black landownership on the Sourland Mountain, where African Americans purchased land and struggled to keep it within their families. In chapter 6 Elaine brings you into the world of local houses of worship that spiritually fed the local African American community for over a century. In chapter 7 Elaine introduces you to some of our region's pioneers of liberty: African American men and women who rose to the challenge to serve in every theater of war on behalf of the country which, despite their service, continued to marginalize them as citizens. As we take a turn in chapter 8, both of us use oral histories to share inspirational and touching stories of the accomplishments of African American descendants and to chronicle life on the Sourland Mountain and surrounding region. Similar to the previous chapter, in chapter 9 we highlight stories from our local communities about places, people, and events that have been unknown, little known, or silenced. In chapter 10 Elaine invites you into the world of yesteryear; she recounts how her ancestors and other "old-timers" taught her how to make home remedies and recipes that she uses to this very day! In chapter 11 I discuss the importance of merging "American" history with "African American" history and how the two cannot be separated. And finally, in the conclusion, the two of us reflect on why we felt the overarching need to write *If These Stones Could Talk* and how our work dovetails with our mission to ensure that the single Anglo-narrative lens on history ceases to be perpetuated in local and national school systems.

If These Stones Could Talk is our story, a story about the presence and contribution of a voiceless community of people who had a direct role in the development of American society and culture in this neck of the woods. It's our story about remarkable individuals who belong to a collection of folks relegated to the shadows of American history—folks who are dusted off only one month out of the year. We bring you along on our journey.

The epigraph comes from: Edwidge Danticat, *After the Dance: A Walk Through Carnival in Jacmel, Haiti* (New York: Vintage Books, 2004).

[1] Geneviève Fabre and Robert O'Meally, "On the Wrong Side of the Fence: Racial Segregation in American Cemeteries," in Angelia Krüger-Kahloula, *History and Memory in African American Culture* (New York: Oxford University Press, 1994), 133–34.

[2] "New Jersey Burial Act. From the NJ Legislative Session of 1884, Chapter LVI, Approved March 19, 1884, 83" (n.d.)

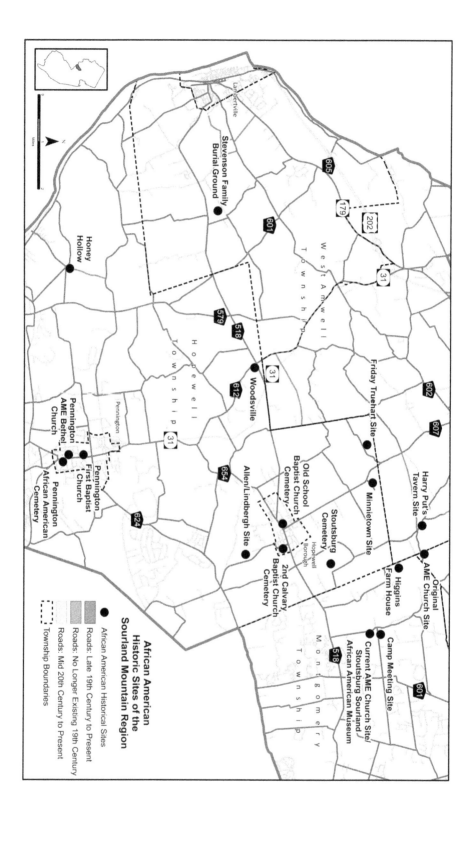

African American Historic Sites of the Sourland Mountain Region

Lambertville

605

179

202

31

Stevenson Family Burial Ground

601

West Amwell Township

Honey Hollow

579

518

31

Hopewell Township

612

Woodsville

602

607

Friday Truehart Site

Harry Put's Tavern Site

Pennington AME Bethel Church

Pennington

Pennington First Baptist Church

Pennington African American Cemetery

31

654

Allen/Lindbergh Site

Old School Baptist Church Cemetery

Stoutsburg Cemetery

Minnietown Site

Original AME Church Site

Higgins Farm House

624

Hopewell Borough

2nd Calvary Baptist Church Cemetery

Camp Meeting Site

Current AME Church Site/ Stoutsburg Sourland African American Museum

518

601

Montgomery Township

African American Historic Sites of the Sourland Mountain Region

● African American Historical Sites

Roads: Late 19th Century to Present

Roads: No Longer Existing 19th Century

Roads: Mid 20th Century to Present

Township Boundaries

CHAPTER 1

HOW THE
JOURNEY BEGAN

by BEVERLY MILLS

There is nothing small or inconsequential about our stories. There is, in fact, nothing bigger. And when we tell the truth about our lives—the broken parts, the secret parts, the beautiful parts —then the gospel comes to life, an actual story of redemption, instead of abstraction and theory and things you learn in Sunday School. If you are a person of faith, it is your responsibility to tell God's story, in every way you can, every form, every medium, every moment. Tell the stories of reconciliation and surprise and new life everywhere you find them.

—Shauna Niequist, *Bittersweet*

In March 2006, Elaine and her husband, John, who is president of the Stoutsburg Cemetery Association, received a panicked call from a man who identified himself as Walter Niemeier. Walter, an elderly White man, reached out to us at the recommendation of an African American friend who knew about the Stoutsburg Cemetery and our roles as trustees.

Thinking that the Stoutsburg Cemetery Association might have some insight on what to do when another local African American cemetery was under threat, his friend recommended that Walter contact us. Walter was frantic for help because he needed more information on what he could do to preserve a slave cemetery located near his house on Rock Road in West Amwell. The site Walter was telling us about, the Elnathan Stevenson Family Burial Ground, is located less than ten miles from the Stoutsburg Cemetery in Mercer County and over the county border in Hunterdon County. Walter was embroiled in an ongoing conflict with local town officials over the Elnathan Stevenson Family Burial Ground, a place that he, as an old-timer, knew was an unmarked slave cemetery less than one mile from his house. In fact, even if the cemetery that once contained numerous wooden markers was now invisible to passersby, Walter, along with others in his community, remembered caring for the site since he was a young boy.

The Elnathan Stevenson Family Burial Ground was now in jeopardy of being plowed up to accommodate a driveway and septic system. Walter maintained that he had personal knowledge about the place and was outraged over the possibility of it being destroyed. As our conversation deepened, Walter stressed that he was raised to respect graveyards and was taught they were always to be preserved and maintained as he had done since he was a child. It was simply inconceivable to him that anyone with a modicum of decency would consider destroying the burial ground of someone's ancestors for the sake of a driveway. He was not about to let it happen and neither were we. This is how our story began.

At Walter's invitation, a week after his initial phone call in March 2006, four of us, Elaine, John, their neighbor Celeste Long, and I, bundled up to make our way to West Amwell on one of the coldest days of the month to trek through a gnarl of brambles and brush. As we piled in the van to make the ten-minute trip to West Amwell to meet Walter, we were reluctant to leave the cozy warmth of the vehicle to step back into the blustery cold. The plan was to meet Walter in the parking lot of a local church located on the corner of Rock Road. Neither Elaine nor I can remember who arrived first, Walter or us, but what I know for sure is this was the first time any of us had laid eyes on Walter Niemeier. Up until this point all communication had been done through the phone so seeing each other, face-to-face, for some reason made us feel like we were old friends meeting up once again.

As introductions were made I recall thinking how energetic Walter was for a man I estimated to be in his early seventies. His step was brisk and his voice strong and hearty as we again took our places in the comfortable van to travel about a half mile down the road. Once we got closer to the spot, Walter directed us to turn right into a driveway close to the area he intended to show us. We got out of the van and followed Walter to the site along an old roadway covered with a tangle of high weeds and dense underbrush showing a faintly visible old roadway underneath. We walked behind Walter to the area where he said the slave cemetery used to be, and we stopped in the center of an area surrounded by pine trees. We stood for a minute to take it all in. When we looked down we could clearly see sunken areas in the ground. My first thought was that I was just looking at sunken areas of dirt—I could not imagine that this area held long-forgotten unmarked graves. Walter started to explain, with a sweeping gesture of his hands, that this was the area he recalled had been a cemetery when he was a child. He told us how for years the area was well maintained by a few people in the community as well as a woman he remembered as Mrs. Douty (or Dowdy), who would faithfully place flowers in the cemetery near a small section that had a white picket fence around it. Walter also told us that when the 1832 cholera epidemic hit the canal area of Lambertville, New Jersey, many stricken canal workers were also buried in unmarked graves along Rock Road and near the Elnathan Stevenson Family Burial Ground. He recalled the slave section of the cemetery was in the middle of an area flanked by trees, and in the ground there had been many wooden markers that surrounded a blue field stone monument that stood in the center. According to Walter, the monument had originally been built by the family of a now ninety-year old local farmer Mr. Hunter to honor the slaves his family had owned, slaves who were buried in the same area near the Elnathan Stevenson cemetery.

As we stood bracing ourselves against the biting wind, we could clearly see the gravestones that identified members of the Elnathan Stevenson family, a White slaveholding family, located along the stone wall at the edge of the property. The wooden markers that Walter recalled were no longer visible; he explained they most likely had disintegrated from years of exposure to the elements. What was still visible, though, were a few red fieldstone rocks that customarily indicated a slave's grave as it was not common to distinguish a slave burial site with a gravestone.[1]

According to Walter's notes from Mr. Hunter, "there were four slave cabins on his farm right alongside of Rock Road West, on the left side of the road heading west and that the cabins stood in a stand of new trees … and there were two more slave cabins on Mt. Airy Road heading north from the corner of Rock Road West."

Although Walter was suffering from fatigue and exhaustion, the entire spring of 2006 Elaine, John, Celeste, and I worked with him to prevent the construction. The facts supporting the existence of the cemetery continued to line up behind our investigative work. For example, Walter quoted an old friend who had been fishing along the Delaware & Raritan Canal: "Walter, you are right about that cemetery on Rock Road West. When I hunted those farms, I saw all of those wooden grave markers, and there were an awful lot of them, and we all knew that it was a cemetery."

When Walter asked his friend why he didn't just come forward and speak out about the cemetery, he never got an answer. Walter was pretty matter-of-fact, saying that it was probably another example of folks being scared and not wanting to get involved or speak up. We could see this troubled Walter, but what proved to be more distressing was when he found out that approval had been granted to proceed with building the driveway through the cemetery. Yet even as things looked grim and the destruction of the cemetery seemed imminent, Walter expressed confidence that God would somehow make things right.

Walter was convinced that this was nothing short of spiritual warfare and firmly believed that no matter what one's religious—or non-religious—persuasion the desecration of a grave was tantamount to the worst sin a human being could commit. One thing was clear: Walter Niemeier never wanted to give up resisting what he thought was a morally reprehensible act.

From the moment we learned about Walter's fight, Elaine, John, and I—as stewards of the Stoutsburg Cemetery Association—knew it was important to support him, but seeing it through wasn't easy. On the first day we visited the site we had been threatened by the landowner, who screamed at us from his car, "Stop trespassing on my property or you will be sued!" Elaine also received a threatening letter from the landowner's lawyer stating that we "would be prosecuted to the fullest extent of the law" if we went back on the property.

In spite of the threats we received from the West Amwell landowner, we received a very warm reception from one of his neighbors on our very first visit to Rock Road. The neighbor, Al Lavery, happened to recognize me as a coworker from twenty years prior when we both worked for the state. Since two decades had elapsed, at first I didn't remember Al, but I soon did once he started talking about the time we had worked together at the Richard J. Hughes Justice Complex in Trenton. While speaking with Al, I noticed that he had a piece of paper in his hand; what it was I had no idea. All I know is that Al made a point of leaving the warmth of his home to come outside in the bitter cold to make sure we had this particular document. What we would soon learn was that Al had a crucial piece of evidence: it was a portion of a will. To this day I can't remember how long it took to dawn on any of us that we were presented with a photocopy of not just any will but the will of Elnathan Stevenson!

The document revealed that Elnathan Stevenson, who purchased eighteen acres from Pearce Matthews in 1796, specified that this ground and the adjoining land were to be preserved as a family cemetery and never to be destroyed or disturbed. As Elaine and I held the document, we found ourselves staring at the spider-web handwriting of a will written in the eighteenth century. In fact, we were so busy reading that we completely forgot to ask Al how he had come to have this portion of Elnathan Stevenson's will.

From there, in our attempt to help Walter, Elaine and I were initially advised to contact the New Jersey State Cemetery Board, which, in turn, recommended that we contact the Office of the Attorney General. After stating our case with a representative in the attorney general's office, we were advised it was not uncommon for developers to encroach upon African American and Native American burial grounds. We were further advised to contact the local police and newspaper for exposure because if a cadaver or bone was dug up the developer could be cited for desecrating a grave site. We opted to contact the local newspaper instead, and they put us in touch with a reporter who was so interested in this story that she began attending some of the West Amwell municipality's town hall meetings. Thus, as news was starting to spread about our campaign to save the West Amwell grave site, a feature story about us appeared in the Sunday *Trenton Times* on April 2.[2] Connections led to more connections. Joe Klett, chief of New Jersey Archives, happened to read the article and contacted Elaine immediately. Joe, a fellow graduate of Hopewell Valley Central High School and friend of Elaine's, wanted her to know he had access to the original will of the Elnathan Stevenson family and that indeed the will stipulated that the land in question was to forever remain a family burial ground for Stevenson's family along with the slaves. Klett also told Elaine that Mr. Stevenson had been a judge in Hunterdon County during the early nineteenth century.

Although we were holding a tangible document in our hands clearly stating the wishes of Elnathan Stevenson, little did we know there would be additional hurdles coming our way. The next weekend, which was the second weekend in April, Elaine was stunned to receive a cease and desist order from the developer's lawyer, which also included a stipulation that an archaeologist would be required to determine whether there were graves on the site. After she received this notification, Elaine was quick to comment that "she didn't know no stupid archaeologist"! Oh, but she did. Only she didn't remember until a neighbor, who read about the West Amwell graveyard situation, reminded her about Ian Burrow, a local resident and an archaeologist.

That was truly a lightbulb moment because Elaine had just worshipped with Ian in a special church service in Hopewell. She contacted Ian and asked if he would accompany her to the property to see if the sunken holes were former graves or percolation test holes, as the landowner claimed. Ian agreed and after surveying the land he determined that the sunken holes were definitely not percolation test holes and most likely sunken graves. That was a pivotal moment in the case. From that point on, the burden of proof now shifted from us to the landowner, who had to prove there was never a burial ground there.

The final outcome came in the fall of 2006. Rather than being faced with the task of proving that the cemetery had never existed, the landowner decided to use the driveway that had been there all along, thus ending his battle to plow through a graveyard.

For Elaine and me, this experience was life-changing; suddenly we were transformed from part-time trustees of a cemetery to historical activists. Almost immediately it became clear that we had a responsibility to be the voice for the voiceless. It was almost as if we had been led to

Walter Niemeier and the Rock Road experience, which turned out to be the catalysts to change the trajectory of our lives. Our role as stewards of the Stoutsburg Cemetery had now taken on additional meaning. The profound support from our community and their willingness to assist, without hesitation, showed us the encounter at Rock Road transcended an "African American problem." Galvanized by this experience and the support of people like Joe Klett, Ian Burrow, Al Lavery, Lisa Coryell, Celeste Long, and others who heard the story, we realized that it was our duty to preserve the memory of individuals who spent their lives living in the shadows of society, all but erased from history.

Hence our mission began. We decided to start by researching who was buried in our beloved Stoutsburg Cemetery, the cemetery we had been involved with for most of our lives; we had been oblivious to the treasures it potentially held. And as we started to scratch the surface, it quickly became apparent that if a story was going to be written it would be up to us to do it. The narrative that Elaine and I would tell, however, would not be a sanitized version of our history written to shield the reader from unpleasant facts.

We soon found out that tracing African American lineage, particularly before the Civil War, isn't easy, even though, in recent decades, there have been many improvements in access to resources such as public, military, church, manumission, and plantation records. We also found that information can also be gleaned from newspaper advertisements, court dockets, post-Civil War Freedmen's Bureau reports, and families' oral tradition. For all of these improvements, the truth is it's still like looking for a needle in a haystack as the institution of slavery so dispersed Black families that finding information about an individual or family is still a monumental challenge. It is common to find records of enslaved individuals who are identified solely by first name and gender, names listed along with household goods and chattel. Sometimes full names and births can be found in family Bibles or wills.

Despite the challenges we faced from the outset of our research, we discovered that Sourland Mountain area slaves and free Black people left surprisingly cohesive paper trails that have enabled us to connect the dots. By starting with a surname and reading manumission records found at the New Jersey Archives, we were able to move forward by grasping at every clue. By beginning with the slaveholding family, we could sometimes find a court record that might provide the date of the manumission and how old the slave was when freed. If we were able to determine a last name it could then lead to a marriage, birth, or death record associated with this individual or family. Thus, inch by inch, we were able to use these two burial grounds—Stoutsburg Cemetery and Elnathan Stevenson Family Burial Ground—positioned slightly less than ten miles from each other, to piece together bits of the lives of early Sourland Mountain area Black Americans—how they lived, where their remains were placed in death, and how their stories intersected with their White owners and neighbors. The next chapter is a story of how local African American residents were able to purchase land that became the Sourland Cemetery, land that for two centuries or more has received people of color to be laid to rest with dignity and respect. I also bring you closer to the world of Black people who lived in the same communities—many possessing identical last names as some of the region's most prominent White families. These Black and White people maintained semblances of relationships all the while living in worlds apart, even in death.

The chapter epigraph comes from: Shauna Niequist, *Bittersweet: Thoughts on Change, Grace, and Learning the Hard Way* (Grand Rapids, MI: Zondervan, 2013).

[1] Sally F. Schwenk, *Cultural Resource Survey, Blue Ridge Boulevard, African American Cemeteries: Prepared for the Concerned Citizens for Highland Cemetery Committee* (Historic Preservation Services, LLC, 2001), accessed March 27, 2018, https://dnr.mo.gov/shpo/survey/JAAS040-R.pdf.

[2] Lisa Coryell, "Cemetery Site Disputed, West Amwell Residents Fear Ancient Unmarked Grave Will Be Paved Over," *Trenton Times*, April 2, 2006

DESCENDANT TRAIL FROM
FRIDAY TRUEHART
TO BEVERLY MILLS

Friday Truehart (1767-1845) – Juda (1773-1855)
↓
Moses True (1818-aft. 1880) – Eliza
↓
Jacob Henry Hoagland (1838-1910) – Sarah Lucinda True (1840 - aft.1910)
↓
Herbert A. Hubbard (1875-1948) – Sarah Matilda Hoagland (1873 - 1923)
↓
Garland Hamner Fields (1897-1974) – Herma Mae Hubbard Fields (1907-1994)
↓
William W. Smith (1923-1993) – Jean Marie Fields Smith (1927-1968)
↓
Beverly Smith Mills (Living)

DESCENDANT TRAIL FROM
WILLIAM STIVES
TO TIMOTHY R. STIVES

William Stives (1760-1839) – Catherine Vanois
↓
Cornelius Stives (1792-1866) – Elizabeth McIntire (1792-1880)
↓
James B. Stives (1818 -) – Hannah Mackintire (1821 -)
↓
Albert H. Stives (1849-1917) – Caroline Garthwaite
↓
Henry R. Stives (1877-1937) – Mary E. Patterson (1890-1965)
↓
George R. Stives (1917-2004) – Shirley L. Stamm (1921-2010)
↓
Timothy R. Stives (Living)

CHAPTER 2

SCHOOL FOR
THE LIVING

by BEVERLY MILLS

The place of the dead must be made a school for the living.

—Gary Wills, *Lincoln at Gettysburg:*
The Words That Remade America

Our story is being told to educate people. It is not an indictment of past sins. We welcome people of all backgrounds to celebrate as well as learn with us as we open the window to our past—indeed to an important aspect of our nation's intermingled and multicultural past—as we share the backstory of the African American contributions to the society and economy of the Sourland Mountain region and surrounding area.

In our own backyard, nestled in the rolling hills dotted with local farms, is the Stoutsburg Cemetery lying at the foot of the Sourland Mountain. People say that on a clear night, prior to 2001, you could see the World Trade Center twinkling in the distance. But did the mountain know how many untold stories the Stoutsburg Cemetery held?

Ancestors of Randolph and Carrie Stout acquired the land that would eventually be owned by Black people, people who would pass the stewardship of this land along to their descendants. To understand their story, we need to begin a couple of centuries ago.

The Stout family hailed from the Netherlands and can trace their genealogy to Penelope VanPrincis, who sailed to America from Amsterdam with her first husband destined for New York (then called New Amsterdam). Penelope and her husband (name unknown) were among a band of unfortunates whose ship became stranded in the Atlantic Ocean off the coast of Sandy Hook, New Jersey. Desperate, the group decided to abandon the ship eventually reaching New York on foot. But Penelope and her husband, who had been hurt during the shipwreck, stayed behind and were soon beset by local Native Americans, who killed Penelope's husband and left Penelope herself badly wounded. With a fractured skull and severe abdominal injuries, Penelope hid for a week in the hollow of a tree. Ironically it was also Native Americans who then found her and cared for her. Eventually making her way to New York, Penelope met and married Richard Stout, with whom she raised ten children. By her eighty-eighth year Penelope and Richard's progeny had reached 502.[1]

Records of the First Baptist Church of Hopewell credit Colonel Joseph Stout, a grandson of Penelope and Richard and the oldest son of Jonathan, with being the founder of Hopewell and of the First Baptist Church of Hopewell. Since worship meetings at that time were held in members' homes, in 1747 Joseph offered to donate land to build a church. In spite of this generous offer, the congregation felt that the proffered land, high in the Sourland hills, would require too difficult a journey for the congregation to attend services. Instead, the Baptist parishioners accepted a gift of land from John Hart, one of the signers of the Declaration of Independence. Feeling rebuffed, Colonel Stout was determined to build a home grander and larger than the Baptist Church. This house, which he finished in 1752, became known as the Hunt House, the name bestowed upon it by George Washington, since it was occupied at the time by Joseph Stout's cousin, John Price Hunt. Hunt's House is where Generals Washington and Lafayette held their great war council to strategize on the Battle of Monmouth, a battle historians regard as the turning point of the Revolutionary War.

Down in the valley from the Hunt House stood another home owned by a Stout descendant, namely David Stout. It was this house that General Lee of the Continental Army supposedly opted to occupy during the Revolutionary War, preferring it to the Hunt House because of its unfettered view of the entire valley. Years later, descendant Randolph Stout came to live in the home with his wife, Carrie, until 1877 when they decided to build in the Borough of Hopewell.

Backtrack to November 7, 1868, nine years before Randolph and Carrie relocated to town. The year 1868 is an important one in our story, as it is when Randolph and Carrie sold 0.34 acres of adjoining land to Stacy Stives, Moses Blew, and Henry Lane, three local African American men, for $30. This transaction took place sixteen years before New Jersey passed the Negro Burial Bill, which was enacted in March 1884 and legislated that refusal to bury an individual based on race would be considered a crime punishable by a fine up to $500.[2]

Previously known as Moore's Farm Burial Ground, the Stoutsburg land had long been unofficially consecrated as a burial place for African Americans before it was legally recorded in Mercer County public records on March 25, 1869. Records also show that in 1858, a decade prior to the official sale, Moses Blew had buried his ninety-four-year-old mother, Judith, a former slave of the "White" Blew family, who had been born in 1763. The Stoutsburg Cemetery adjoined land once owned by Moses Blew, who had sold 100 acres out of his 144-acre farm in 1849. As it turns out, Randolph and Carrie Stout owned land that included the adjoining property previously owned by Blew and sold the men the 0.34 acres adjacent to the "old cemetery." The old cemetery that we so often heard about in oral histories undoubtedly contained the graves of members of some of the earliest African American families, but how many and who they were we'll never know.

In an attempt to glean further evidence, in 2008 the Stoutsburg Cemetery Association hired a company to use ground-penetrating radar in the extant Stoutsburg burial ground to corroborate the existence of graves. How many graves had vanished below the surface? Their findings revealed countless "anomalies" indicating a minimum of eighty to ninety unidentified underground mysteries. Though the investigators could not determine the date of the earliest burial, or the exact number of interments, they estimated that there are far more burials that preceded the time the deed was legally recorded.

Although a few African Americans were buried on the private property of local White residents, traditionally, in the Sourland Mountain region, Black people were not buried with White people. However, the New Jersey Negro Burial Bill, as previously mentioned, was enacted in March 1884 wherein it was declared "officially" against the law to discriminate on the grounds of color or sex in the burial of the dead. Prior to the legislation, the Old School Baptist Church located on the main street in the Borough of Hopewell attempted to dignify their loyal, long-standing African American parishioners with a burial away from their all-White cemetery adjacent to the west side of the church. Their solution, a segregated one, was to lay their Black parishioners to rest in a patch of land on the east side of the church building. The old-timers say these burials were closer to where the outhouses were located, certainly not in the general cemetery. Undoubtedly included among these burials would have been my fourth great-grandfather,

Friday Truehart, as well as William Stives, both dedicated members of Old School Baptist Church for over forty years.

In the beginning of our research the questions we grappled with are these: How did African American people interred in our cemetery come to have last names of French, Dutch, English, and German origin? Who were these people who today have descendants numbering in the hundreds who are scattered throughout the northern continent and beyond? How were we to construct lives purely out of oral histories and in some instances a few scraps of paper and letters in which we would have to decipher a couple names and dates that had been jotted down?

The answer lies in the interwoven history of America's various peoples and cultures. In the late seventeenth and early eighteenth centuries, as New Jersey became a colony of the British Empire, Queen Anne took the necessary steps to ensure that her new province had a constant and sufficient supply of merchantable negroes.[3] Throughout the eighteenth century, as the region continued to thrive, the demand for slave labor was evident in New York, New Jersey, and Pennsylvania, where ads that hawked human flesh were placed in newspapers. The call for male workers as sailors, carpenters, wheelwrights, coopers, tanners, shoemakers, millers, bakers, cooks, and for other household services was unprecedented. Women were needed also, for various kinds of household work: sewing, cooking, nursing, and farming. Black women who had children were sometimes especially prized, as this was regarded as a sign of fertility; a slave owner's labor force thus had the potential to increase without his having to purchase more slaves. Sometimes, though, the opposite happened: mothers were sold away so that the master could avoid the added extra costs and responsibilities of a growing Black family. The contours of this socioeconomic world were reflected in advertisements in New Jersey newspapers, notifying the public of a constant stream of Africans into the region.

May 21, 1761 To be sold by Stocker and Fuller, and to be seen at Mr. Daniel Cooper's Ferry, West New Jersey, opposite the City of Philadelphia, a Parcel of likely Negroes.

August 6, 1761 To Be Sold, On Board the Schooner Hannah, lying in the River Delaware, very near Mr. Daniel Cooper's Ferry, West New Jersey, opposite the City of Philadelphia, a Cargo of likely Negroes, just imported in said Schooner, directly from the Coast of Guinea. For terms of sale apply to Thomas Riche, David Franks, or Daniel Rundle.

May 27, 1762 Just imported from the river Gambia, in the Schooner Sally, Bernard Badger, Master, and to be sold at the Upper Ferry (called Benjamin Cooper's Ferry), opposite to this City, a parcel of likely Men and Women Slaves, with some Boys and Girls of different Ages. [4]

For me, the impact of reading these notices has been powerful. My mind races when I think about how many enslaved Africans were bound to the Sourland region by force, leaving any tangible memory of their former lives continents away. How many future Hoaglands, Truehearts, Grovers, Reasnors, Stives, and Petersons started as seedlings in Africa whose trees would one day yield branches centuries old on another continent? We are the descendants of this invisible population whose story has not yet been fully told, but now must be told.

I thought about the urgency of reframing our nation's historical narrative when I heard Michelle Obama address a crowd in 2016 and highlighted the fact that the White House had been built by slaves. I can't imagine how many were aware of this little-known fact when she said, "That is the story of this country, the story that has brought me to this stage tonight, the story of generations of people who felt the lash of bondage, the shame of servitude, the sting of segregation, but who kept on striving and hoping and doing what needed to be done so that today I wake up every morning in a house that was built by slaves."[5] Mrs. Obama was reminding some—but mostly schooling others—as she recounted the history of the building of the White House. Many questioned the veracity of her statement and chalked it up to an attempt to further divide the country. As difficult as it may be for many to face, when the White House was being constructed in the early 1790s, slavery in the northern states, including New Jersey, already had a significant head start.

From 1726 to 1745, New Jersey practically doubled the number of people it held in bondage from roughly 2,600 slaves to 4,700.[6] So plentiful was the legislation enacted during this time that one can conclude that slavery was much more than a passing stage in New Jersey's development. Slavery had become the economic lifeblood of the colonial Garden State. The Sourland Mountain and the surrounding area in central New Jersey was no exception, as slavery became "the single most important source of labor in the North's most fertile agricultural areas."[7] In the colonial era local farms were referred to as "plantations"—a description that, for many, is more commonly associated with the South. New Jersey, firmly entrenched in the plantation system, has been described as a place where slavery was "no longer an adjunct to an agricultural economy" but a central player, with the male slave population more plentiful than that of landless white male residents. Hunterdon County (which encompassed what is now Mercer County) was a major producer of crops that supplied the Philadelphia market,[8] and the dependency on slave labor led to an increase in demand for African laborers. But New Jersey is a long way from Africa; how were the slaves transported here? Who organized and profited the most from local slave trading? Prior to 1730 the slave trade involved a smaller number of Africans who arrived under a prearrangement with families seeking help in their homes or to local businessmen. This changed around 1730 when merchants not only traveled to the West Indies to purchase slaves but also returned to sell them directly at market. Traders such as the Pennsylvania-based Willing & Morris, the mercantile business that was the predecessor to Willing, Morris & Sandwick, and Garrett and George Meade were all regarded as main players; Thomas Riche, a single trader entering the market in 1760, became one of the wealthiest. During the decade of 1755 to 1765 when Pennsylvania reached its pinnacle in slave trading, ships sailed directly to Africa to import more and more African slaves into the colony. In correspondence to fellow businessman Samuel Tucker, Riche boasted, "This will advise you of my disposing of 24 of the Negroes to be a good advantage. I believe if I had 10 more could have sold them well the profits will be near 400 pounds—& no expense & cash soon."[9]

Our local founding fathers seem to have had a definite plan for Africans, who were to be sold along the Delaware for distribution throughout the region; Samuel Tucker, president and treasurer of the Provincial Congress of New Jersey during the Revolutionary War, owned nineteen slaves. Correspondence between Tucker and Riche through the 1770s also reveals the callousness with which they made plans for their slaves. One document related Tucker's quandary about how to dispose of slaves he was boarding. Riche advised Tucker: "Pray advertise the remainder of them Negros for sale at Vendue if you think they will sell as I am assured they must be in your way."[10]

Pennsylvania was a regular recipient of slaves sold by Thomas Riche. As the agent operating the schooner *Hannah*, Riche told Tucker in 1761 that "I intend sending 15–20 up to you for sale for which we furnish you with advertisements by the Post on Monday."

So successful was Tucker's advertising that two weeks later Riche "furnishe'd [him] with a fresh Parcell." Benjamin Cooper's Ferry, Daniel Cooper's Ferry, Samuel Cooper's Ferry, and Robert's Ferry dotted the edges of the Delaware River, serving double duty as auction sites. Riche, a shrewd businessman who easily adapted to changing conditions, expanded his enterprises to other ports, such as New Bern, North Carolina; he instructed the *Hannah*'s captain to "take care of the slaves and get them shaved and greased before you get up to Newburn lest they discover old age." Nothing was random, and records show not only Riche's successes but also his annoyance when things went awry. One report includes his distress upon reviewing his "cargo" at arrival that some of the slaves had arrived ill and that several had died. While Riche grew to be the largest single trader, his partnership with David Franks also proved nearly as lucrative.[11] Franks, born into one of the leading Jewish families in colonial New York, moved to Philadelphia as a young man.[12] A successful businessman who married into a well-established Christian family, Franks partnered with the College of Philadelphia (now the University of Pennsylvania), to which he provided a hundred men, women, and children directly from Guinea.[13]

Across the state border, New Jersey laws protected slave owners by not allowing manumitted "Blacks and Negros" from other states to relocate to New Jersey. Similarly, freed Black people who traveled beyond their township or county were required to carry an official certificate of freedom, and if they did not do so, they could be punished: "A Negro, if found five miles from home, was taken up and whipped by the party arresting him, for which he received five shillings. If the Negro was from another province, the informer received ten shillings, and the Negro was whipped by the nearest constable."[14]

Slaves passing through New Jersey were governed by equally

strict guidelines: "Any slave from another Province travelling without a license, or not known to be on his master's business, was to be taken up and whipped; and should remain in prison until the costs of apprehending him had been paid by his owner. Persons from a neighboring Colony suspected of being fugitives must produce a pass from a justice, 'signifying that they are free persons,' otherwise to be imprisoned until demanded."[15] The consequences could be dire.[14]

Given such evidence in public records, it's mystifying that some historians have advanced the argument that Northern slave masters were benevolent and paternalistic owners whose slaves were like an extension of the family: "The weight of testimony is that in our county slavery was never anything but nominal, that the owners were kind and indulgent, and the slaves well-fed and clothed, and capital executions were few."[16]

As New Jersey's appetite for free labor increased, slave-owning farmers were able not only to support their families with corn, wheat, rye, oats, barley, flax, vegetables, and fruits but also to sell these goods to the Philadelphia market. It was through cheap slave labor that the land was cleared, cultivated, and readied. Slaves also cared for farm animals, such as hogs, sheep, goats, horses, and poultry. Slaves who had specialized skills worked in tanning and milling; others pressed apples for cider and hard beverages at local distilleries. So large was the peach industry that by the 1890s Hunterdon County boasted over two million peach trees, almost half of those in the entire state. In fact, the peach industry was so productive that several railroad branches were built for the express purpose of hauling peaches to market in Philadelphia and New York. To support this lucrative industry, slaves were transported from Monmouth County to work in the orchards as well as to make peach baskets. The state's largest peach operation was the Obert and Hill factory.[17] Tomato crops were so plentiful the need arose for commercial canneries in the Hopewell, Pennington, and Titusville area; many of the original buildings still stand today. Major landowners included Daniel Cox in the Hopewell tract. By the mid-1800s prominent founding family names in the region included Hart, Hunt, Blackwell, Stout, Moore, and Titus. Each family is recognized as settlers with deep roots reaching back to the inception of the Hopewell region circa 1690–1725. The names of the prominent Dutch and German family names were Hoagland, Van Dyke, Voorhees, Van Zant, Tenycke, Ege, and Weart. Historically there has been little or nothing said about the Black residents whose family roots are planted just as deep in the Sourland region's past—and whose names mirror many of those just mentioned.

When we use the term "plantation," people largely think about the sprawling acreage of a Southern estate replete with cotton fields or of rice paddies. However, the term "plantation" as it pertains to New Jersey correlates to a largish farm plot. For example, the *Pennsylvania Chronicle* of December 5–12, 1768, featured an advertisement for a hundred-acre "plantation" in Hopewell Township, "near good spring and summer fisheries and varieties of water-fowl in their season." The house, "lately repaired with a cellar, … had two rooms per floor, a kitchen and draw well along with the convenience of a blacksmith's shop with two hearths and a coal house and wagon which were newly built of stone."[18] It would be hard to maintain such an enterprise without outside help—almost certainly supplied by slave labor.

It was initially shocking for me to learn of the deep-seated dependence upon slave labor in New Jersey, but it was more disturbing to realize that slavery was fundamental, not incidental. Learning how the practice unapologetically continued to escalate before it began to taper off in the decades following the American Revolution was a particularly ugly revelation. Documents attest to 4700 enslaved individuals in

New Jersey in 1745, with the number topping 12,000 by the time of the 1800 United States Census.[18] Beginning with Pennsylvania and Massachusetts in the 1780s, one by one northern states began to gradually abolish slavery, with New Jersey and New York bringing up the rear in 1804 and 1799, respectively. After 1800, each succeeding census recorded a declining number of slaves in New Jersey.[20]

During our numerous public presentations about the history of the Stoutsburg Cemetery, we've been asked from time to time whether "Northern" slaves were treated better than slaves in the Southern states. As much as many Americans would like to feel more comfortable believing the North was a "better" region in which to be enslaved, the public records do not support this perception. In fact, New Jersey legislators wrote grisly prescriptions outlining how to punish slaves effectively. For instance, the 1790 legislature decreed that "under the provisions of the law [slaves] might be burned or scalded to death, hanged, beheaded or put to any lingering torture their judges might decide upon." The constable in each township, in many instances, served as the public whipper who received five shillings for his services, paid by the slave owner.[21] The whip described by the public "whipper" was made of rawhide thongs pleated with fine wire.

It was startling to me to realize that Hopewell Township, New Jersey, the community where I grew up, where I had been educated and lived most of my life, advertised the sale of human beings. Colonial newspaper advertisements for runaways frequently appeared as masters attempted to retrieve their missing property. With a range of emotions, I read an ad that ran on June 16, 1773, in the *Pennsylvania Journal* for a thirty-dollar reward for anyone who could apprehend three Negro men—Bonturah, Jack, and Frank—who ran away from a Hopewell plantation. It described what they wore, their physical characteristics, their approximate ages, and that they were supposed to have had passes.

One of these men supposedly had a wife in Philadelphia, from whom he had obviously been separated. The notice ended with the offer of ten dollars should they be captured separately.[22]

On March 21, 1765, in the *Pennsylvania Gazette* a to be sold notice appeared for "a likely Negroe man, this country born, about 25 years of Age, understands all sorts of Plantation Work, and is a good Miller; also a Negroe Wench, this Country born, about 15 years of Age, and understands all kinds of House-work, is sold for no fault, but for Want of Employ."[23]

I think about these people and what fate had in store for them. I recall myself as a fifteen-year-old Black female and put myself in the position of this girl-child who was being sold "for want of employ." She understood all kinds of housework and was clearly a marketable piece of property. I think about the man who literally held her life in his hands. Whom would she end up with and what treatment would she be subjected to by her new employer? Was the "owner" separating a child from her mother? Was her mother owned by someone else? Did this girl ever see her mother again? The truth, as difficult as it is to face, is that New Jersey upheld the cruel system of slavery and was as entrenched in it as any Southern state below the Mason-Dixon line. How could we prepare ourselves to truly grasp the connection between the experiences of African Americans—many of whom were my ancestors—with the truth that it was from their free labor that our region blossomed into one of the wealthiest in the Northeast? How do we become the stewards to tell the untold and unvoiced stories, to speak about people who have had such a significant influence on the development of American society and culture? We didn't know, but we knew we had to start. And start we did, by taking it one step at a time.

The chapter epigraph comes from: *Gary Wills, Lincoln at Gettysburg: The Words That Remade America* (New York, New York: Simon and Schuster, 1992).

1 Alice Blackwell Lewis, *Hopewell Valley Heritage* (Hopewell, NJ: Hopewell Museum, 1973), 9.

2 "New Jersey Burial Act," Chapter LVI, New Jersey Legislative Session of 1884 § (1884), 83, accessed June 6, 2018, http://njlaw.rutgers.edu/cgi-bin/diglib. cgi?collect=njleg&file=108&page=0083&zoom=120.

3 Henry Scofield Cooley, *A Study of Slavery in New Jersey* (Baltimore: Johns Hopkins University Press, 1896), 13.

4 Elizabeth Donnan, "1761–1764: Notice of New Jersey Sales," in *Documents Illustrative of the History of the Slave Trade to America*, reprint, vol. 3 (New York: Octagon Books, 1969), 454–55.

5 Obama, Michelle. "Remarks by The First Lady at the Democratic National Convention, Wells Fargo Center, Philadelphia, Pennsylvania." CNN, Turner Broadcasting System, July 25, 2016, accessed May 24, 2018, https://www.cnn.com/2016/07/26/politics/transcript-michelle-obama-speech-democratic-national-convention/index.html

6 Giles R. Wright, "History of Slavery in New Jersey," *Social Science Docket* 1, no. 2 (Summer–Fall 2001), New Jersey Council for the Social Studies, New York Council for the Social Studies (Hempstead, NY, available from Social Science Docket, Department of Curriculum and Teaching, 243 Mason GW, 113 Hofstra University, Hempstead, NY 11549, 2001), 26–29, accessed December 20, 2017, https://eric.ed.gov/?q=social+science+docket&ft=on&id=ED457114.

7 James J. Gigantino II, *The Ragged Road to Abolition Slavery and Freedom in New Jersey, 1775–1865* (Philadelphia: University of Pennsylvania Press, 2016), 15.

8 Ibid., 15.

9 Darold J. Wax, "Africans on the Delaware: The Pennsylvania Slave Trade, 1759–1765," *Pennsylvania History: A Journal of Mid-Atlantic Studies* 50, no. 1 (1983): 41–42, n. 22: Riche to Tucker, August 16 and 25, 1762, Thomas Riche Letter Book I, 1750-1764, HSP, accessed November 27, 2017, http://www.jstor.org/stable/27772875.

10 Gregory E. O'Malley, *Final Passages: The Intercolonial Slave Trade of British America*, 1619–1807 (Chapel Hill: Omohundro Institute of Early American History and Culture, Williamsburg, Virginia, by the University of North Carolina Press, 2014), 58.

11 O'Malley, *Final Passages*.

12 "Guide to the Papers of the Franks Family, 1711–1821 [1965–1968] *P-142 Processed by Rachel Pollack and Deena Schwimmer," American Jewish Historical Society, Center for Jewish History, accessed April 25, 2018, http://digifindingaids.cjh.org/?pID=109177.

13 Craig Steven Wilder, E*bony & Ivy: Race, Slavery and the Troubled History of America's Universities* (New York: Bloomsbury Press, 2013), 73.

14 John W. Lequear, *Traditions of Hunterdon, Early History and Legends of Hunterdon County, New Jersey* (Flemington, NJ: D. H. Moreau, 1957), 154–55.

15 Cooley, *A Study of Slavery in New Jersey*, 33.

16 Lequear, *Traditions of Hunterdon, Early History and Legends of Hunterdon County, New Jersey*, 156.

17 Richard W. Hunter and Richard Porter, *Hopewell: A Historical Geography* (Titusville, NJ: Township of Hopewell, Historic Sites Committee, 1990), 47.

18 William Nelson, ed., "'TO BE SOLD, A Plantation, Acres, Hopewell, Hunterdon County, New Jersey,' Pennsylvania Chronicle, December 5–12, 1768, Archives of the State of New Jersey, First Series, Vol. XXVI," in *Extracts from American Newspapers Relating to New Jersey*, vol. 7 (Patterson, NJ: Call Printing and Publishing, 1904), 333.

19 Wright, "History of Slavery in New Jersey," 26–29.

20 Giles R. Wright, "1790–1870, Second Part," in *Afro-Americans in New Jersey: A Short History* (Trenton: New Jersey Historical Commission, 1989), 36, https://www.njstatelib.org/research_library/new_jersey_resources/highlights/afro-americans/.

21 Lequear, *Traditions of Hunterdon, Early History and Legends of Hunterdon County, New Jersey*, 158.

22 William Nelson, ed., "THIRTY DOLLARS Reward, *The Pennsylvania Journal*, No. 1593, June 16, 1773], as Extracted in William Nelson and A. Van Doren Honeyman, *Extracts from American Newspapers Relating to New Jersey, 1704-1775*," in *Documents Relating to the Colonial History of the State of New Jersey*, vol. 28 (Patterson, NJ: Call Printing and Publishing, 1916), 535–36..

23 "TO BE SOLD A Likely Negroe Man, This Country Born, about 25 Years of Age, Understands All Sorts of Plantation Work, and Is a Good Miller; Also a Negroe Wench, This Country Born, about 15 Years of Age, and Understands All Kinds of House-Work, Is Sold for No Fault, but for Want of Employ. For Further Particulars Enquire of Cornelius Polhamus, Living in Hopewell, West New Jersey. Published at York, Pa., Dec. 20, 1777–June 20, 1778," *Pennsylvania Gazette*, no. 1891 (March 21, 1765).

Virginia Nevius

Dr. Marion T. Lane

CHAPTER 3

TRAPPED IN THE PURGATORY OF HISTORY

A TALE OF TWO MARIONS AND THE DAUGHTERS OF THE AMERICAN REVOLUTION

by BEVERLY MILLS

So many people of color who made major contributions to American history are trapped in the purgatory of history.

—Henry Louis Gates, Professor of History, Harvard University

When I was twelve my grandmother, my mother, and I boarded a Starr bus that took us to Washington, D.C., a place I had only been able to see on my grainy black-and-white TV that sat in an alcove under the stairs. I remembered my grandmother being just as excited as I was as we made a day of sightseeing and dinner before boarding the bus back to New Jersey. I was particularly impressed when we walked up the steps of the Lincoln Memorial. This was because my paternal grandmother had been a dyed-in-the-wool Lincoln Republican and had remained so until her death. Her allegiance to the Grand Old Party was steadfast and unmovable, as it was for most Black people of her generation. I remember staring up at the immense sitting statue of Abraham Lincoln. I knew about his role in freeing the slaves, the Emancipation Proclamation, and Black American loyalty. I looked up at the statue, mesmerized, not wanting to leave. As a child you learn so much about Abraham Lincoln and what he did for African Americans during the Civil War. It seems like Black children have been taught from infancy to hold Lincoln's memory in the highest reverence, evidence of which can be seen framed on the walls in numerous African American homes. If you were to walk into many of these homes, particularly those of older African Americans, invariably you'll find the triumvirate, John F. Kennedy, Martin Luther King, and Abraham Lincoln, adorning the walls above the sofa.

The year we gazed up at the Lincoln Memorial was 1962, a mere thirty years after the famed contralto, Marian Anderson, was banned from performing at the Daughters of the American Revolution (D.A.R.) Constitution Hall, which at that time was segregated. Immediately, petitions gathered names to demand an exception for Anderson, but the D.A.R. was steadfast in its decision that the hall was for Whites only. In direct protest to the treatment of Anderson, First Lady Eleanor Roosevelt resigned her membership from the D.A.R. and invited the singer to perform on the steps of the Lincoln Memorial on Easter Sunday, April 9, 1939, before 75,000 people.[1]

Growing up, the only knowledge I had about the Daughters of the American Revolution was that they did not allow African American members and they banned Marian Anderson from singing in the D.A.R. Constitution Hall. I assumed it was to always remain a strictly White organization because, after all, as far as I knew only White people served as soldiers in the Revolutionary War. As an adult, from time to time

I heard about African Americans who were seeking membership in the D.A.R., but I still couldn't grasp how an African American would be able to qualify for membership in this organization. It wasn't until we started doing the research for this book that the explanation suddenly became clearer.

The stories in this chapter demonstrate the many barriers African Americans faced to entrance in the D.A.R. over the years, which represent a larger omission of Blacks from national history. Although the D.A.R. has taken steps to reverse their historically racist attitude, their existing rules still do not make it easy for African Americans to join even as—in the last couple of decades particularly—the D.A.R. is publicly making efforts to welcome African American applicants. Even though the organization now provides genealogists to help African Americans build their case for why they should be allowed to join, the bar to acceptance is still frustratingly high. In fact, we have recently come to the realization that had our own cherished Hopewell resident Virginia Nevius opted to apply for membership in the D.A.R. as a descendant of a soldier who fought bravely in the Revolutionary War, it's likely that she would have been rejected.

I can't precisely recall when we had our first "aha" moment when we realized that we actually knew someone who might have qualified for D.A.R. membership, namely Virginia Nevius, a woman Elaine and I had known most of our lives. Virginia was Elaine's aunt through marriage, and Beverlee—Virginia's oldest daughter—had been one of my dearest friends. Virginia was a quiet-spoken woman of mixed heritage whom I would see every Sunday at the church I was attending at the time, the Second Calvary Baptist Church in Hopewell, New Jersey. I remember Virginia's wide smile and easy laugh. Back in the day, the neighborhood kids from Hopewell would always joke about how loudly she would clap her hands to signal her children to come home to dinner, a dinner that was served at the same time every single night. Along with running a tight ship at home, Virginia liberally gave back to the community and our church. She would compose beautiful poetry that was read at various church functions, graduations, birthdays, or whatever the occasion happened to be. She always seemed prepared to recognize milestones achieved by people she knew and would present them with a card or gift from a stash she kept in her dining room china cabinet.

The gift Virginia left us, though, was not stashed in her china cabinet. Instead, she left us a roadmap that helped us put together pieces of a puzzle about William Stives, her ancestor. In the early 1990s Virginia, a lifelong resident of Hopewell and the Sourland region, was contacted by Timothy Stives, who had discovered that he, too, was a descendant of William Stives, an African American Revolutionary War veteran. Tim is a White man who had hired a local genealogist, Roxanne Carkhuff, who put him in touch with Virginia and Earl Nevius because of their mutual ancestor. Tim knew that other Stives relatives were buried in Stoutsburg, and he was looking to learn all he could about their family. And despite the fact that it has never been irrefutably proven that William Stives was buried in Stoutsburg (and not in the Old School Baptist Church Cemetery where he worshipped), Tim felt it only fitting that a commemorative marker be placed in Stoutsburg. The marker was placed near the gravestone of William Stives's grandson Jonathan Stives, a Civil War veteran who had fought with the U.S. Colored Troops. So, it is because of Tim's proud recognition of his fourth great-grandfather, William Stives, a free mulatto, that this commemorative marker stands in honor of his service in the 3rd Regiment of the New Jersey Continental Line.

As long-standing trustees of the cemetery, we were proud of the Stives marker, but for Elaine and me the significance at that time still had not brought us to our next "aha" moment. It certainly never occurred to us then that Virginia and her daughters, Beverlee and Carol, could have applied for membership in the Daughters of the American Revolution had they chosen to do so. Unfortunately, Virginia passed away about five years before our research started in earnest. Nevertheless, Virginia's gifts kept giving. Her papers, so meticulously kept, would prove to yield critical clues that helped us tell the story of William Stives.

Elaine and I have thought about what would have happened if Virginia or her daughters, Beverlee or Carol had sought membership in the D.A.R. Clearly they would qualify under the D.A.R.'s criteria for membership: "Any woman 18 years or older who can prove lineal, bloodline descent from an ancestor who aided in achieving American independence is eligible to join the D.A.R. She must provide documentation for each statement of birth, marriage and death, as well as of the Revolutionary War service of her Patriot ancestor."[2] I wonder how many other African Americans, unbeknownst to them, would qualify for membership. My guess is more than I can imagine. One such woman, Dr. Marion T. Lane, entered our lives when we were drawn to her lecture at the David Library of the American Revolution in Yardley, Pennsylvania.

Marion, an African American author and lecturer, was the first female African American historian we had encountered early on in our research, and we were eager to hear what we might learn from her David Library lecture titled "Forgotten Patriots of the American Revolution." As she stepped to the podium and began describing her journey to discover her ancestors and her own application for D.A.R. membership, it seemed as if she was speaking directly to us. Marion's ancestors served in both the Civil and Revolutionary wars.

Impeccably dressed and poised, Marion informed the audience that 5,000 to 20,000 African and Native American soldiers had fought in the Continental Army under George Washington. As Elaine and I stared at each other in utter amazement, she recounted how she had traced her grandfather's service in the Revolutionary War and how this qualified her to become a member of the Daughters of the American Revolution. Armed with her family's documentation, Marion approached the Bucks County Chapter of the D.A.R. to become a member; she was accepted. Further, Marion also served as the Commander in Chief of the Society of Descendants of Washington's Army at Valley Forge from 2010 to 2014.

While our heads were still spinning from hearing that African American and Native American soldiers fought in the Revolutionary War, we knew Marion had to be our speaker for the 2012 Stoutsburg Cemetery Memorial Day Service. We approached her immediately after her presentation.

During the reception after her lecture, Marion was patient as we peppered her with questions as we described the Stoutsburg Cemetery and our roles as trustees. Without hesitation she asked us if we had started conducting our own research. She told us that, based on the age of the cemetery, we might find a few Revolutionary War veterans interred in the Stoutsburg Cemetery. We told her about William Stives and how we had been unable to prove his burial in Stoutsburg. Marion reiterated that we just needed to continue researching and not leave any stone unturned; after all, we were standing in the David Library, which was the perfect place to begin. As our conversation began to wind down she graciously accepted our invitation to be our 2012 Memorial Day speaker and offered to continue helping as much as she could with our research. This meeting at the David Library led to an alliance that did not end after Marion's presentation at our Memorial Day Service. In fact, our relationship has continued throughout the years and has grown from a mentorship into a strong friendship.

In 2017 when we called Marion with more questions and to catch up, we learned that our friend and mentor was in the hospital recovering from injuries she had sustained in a car accident. In spite of her discomfort, Marion was eager to talk to us and get caught up on how we were progressing with our project. How many African Americans to date had been accepted as members of the Daughters of the American Revolution, we inquired, as we thought about the descendants of the Stives family who might have been eligible if they had the desire to apply.

Without hesitation, Marion advised us to check the D.A.R. website and the book they commissioned titled *Forgotten Patriots, African American and American Indian Patriots in the Revolutionary War*, which lists over 6,000 names of African American and American Indian veterans. *Forgotten Patriots*, first written in 2001and expanded in 2008, is a compilation of information published by the National Society Daughters of the American Revolution for the purpose of identifying the names of African and Native American individuals who fought or served in a key capacity in securing American independence.[3]

It was hard to ignore the disillusionment we heard in Marion's voice as she talked about the difficulties African Americans have faced when applying for membership in the D.A.R. And although the D.A.R. has changed considerably, historically it has been much easier for descendants of White patriots to be admitted. To illustrate her point, Marion told us about an article written by Maurice Barboza and Gary Nash regarding the roadblocks and subsequent lawsuit brought on by Lena Santos Ferguson, Barboza's aunt, as a result of her attempt to join a Washington chapter of the D.A.R. In a 2004 *New York Times* article titled "We Need to Learn More About Our Colorful Past," Barboza and Nash outlined how color was used to narrow the field of potential applicants who could be considered for membership.[4] By narrowly classifying the soldiers under three categories, "Black,

Negro or Mulatto," this restriction could potentially omit soldiers who were initially classified as "yellow" or "white" but were born African American.

Lena Ferguson's application to the D.A.R. was accepted in 1983, but it wasn't until the organization was faced with the potential loss of its tax-exempt status that she was permitted to join a chapter and have full membership rights.[5] She also received a settlement agreement from the D.A.R. that barred discrimination and required the D.A.R. to identify every African American soldier who served in the Revolutionary War. As a result of the tenacity of Ferguson[6] and Barboza,[7] an estimated 5,000 African Americans, a figure that is said to be "deceptively low," have been identified as serving in the Revolutionary War. Thanks to Lena Ferguson, significant changes have taken place over the years for people of color seeking membership in the D.A.R. In fact, *Forgotten Patriots* was published as a result of the lawsuit brought by Lena Santos Ferguson.[8] According to her, "I think they are more sincere now … I think they are trying to put a new face on the organization. They do a lot of good work."[9]

Although there had only been a handful of African Americans accepted into the D.A.R. prior to Lena's lawsuit, since then the organization has made some strides in admitting African Americans. However, these gains cannot be easily quantified since the organization does not keep records of applicants' race. A true turning point came in 2012 when a new chapter was formed in Jamaica, Queens, when Dr. Olivia Cousins joined the D.A.R. Along with her two sisters, Cousins is a member of the chapter started by Wilhelmena Rhodes Kelly, an African American woman who also served as its first president. This chapter broke new ground as five out of its thirteen original members were women of African descent.[10]

Regardless of the D.A.R.'s recent accomplishments, the shadow of past discrimination still hangs over the organization. People still remember their refusal to allow Marian Anderson to sing in Constitution Hall in 1939.

And while the struggle to be admitted into the D.A.R. continues for some, Marion maintains that her entry in 2001 was due to the "grace of God" since she was admitted just prior to the requirement that genealogists be hired by the D.A.R. to support Black applications. For further clarification regarding D.A.R. membership requirements, Marion directed us to their website which stipulates criteria for membership under "Researching Your African American Patriot" "Patriotic service is credited to those who took action to further, or demonstrated loyalty to, the cause of American Independence, such as taking the oath of fidelity, paying supply taxes, providing supplies or monetary aid, or serving on a committee made necessary by the war."[11] While Marion understands it was her good fortune to be admitted in the D.A.R., Joyce Mosley, an acquaintance of Marion, has had her application turned down twice. She is a descendant of Cyrus Bustill, who was a bread maker in Burlington, New Jersey, for the Continental Army under the employ of Thomas Ives. Her case has been classified as "half written" and requiring primary documents, some dating back three hundred years.

Upon the advice of Marion, we reached out to Joyce Mosley, who answered our call with a voice so polished and refined she could probably give lessons in elocution. However, we also heard the same fatigue and disillusionment in her voice that we had heard in Marion's. Joyce explained how Cyrus Bustill was the son of Samuel Bustill, his White slave master, and an unnamed African American woman who was his slave. Samuel Bustill had no emotional attachment to his mulatto son and left instructions in his will to sell him upon his death. Cyrus was sold first to the Allen family and second to Thomas Prior who taught him how to bake. Freed, Cyrus was apprenticed to Christopher Ludwig. During the Revolution, Ludwig had been commissioned to bake bread for the Continental Army, but when he retired in 1781 the bread-baking contract then went to Robert Morris, also of Philadelphia. Morris, an extremely powerful man and a signer of the Declaration of Independence, was one of Pennsylvania's original senators and a former slave trader. Morris and his business partner, Thomas Willing, operated as Willing, Morris & Co. As discussed in chapter 2, along with being a mercantile trader, Thomas Willing was also a slave broker as his partner, Robert Morris, had formerly been. Morris contracted with Phelps & Company based in New England to supply bread to the Continental Army. From Phelps & Company a local baker, Thomas Ives, was subcontracted to act as the supervisor of the Burlington, New Jersey, bread-baking operation where Cyrus Bustill was residing. Thinking it would bolster her argument, Joyce was able to uncover a handwritten document located in the Bustill-Bowser-Asbury Collection at Howard University that stated that Cyrus Bustill was commissioned to provide baked goods to the Continental Army. Surprisingly, the D.A.R. did not consider this to be a primary document, which resulted in her application being deemed unacceptable. And although there was a "A Proclamation by the Valley Forge Historical Commission" that commends Cyrus Bustill for his service as a baker to the Continental Army, this was not enough proof for the D.A.R. As of this writing Joyce is gathering still more information before applying a third time.

Similarly, as of this writing, the family of Richard Allen, the founder of the African Methodist Episcopal Church, has never been approved for D.A.R. membership. Allen is credited with undertaking the dangerous mission of driving a salt wagon to supply troops during the Revolutionary War. Yet the D.A.R. insists that there is not enough "documentation" of Allen's contribution.

The challenges that African Americans face in proving their family history is a direct result of the lack of primary documentation—records of accomplishments or achievements in their lives. For centuries African Americans have relied on oral history to preserve stories that are passed down throughout generations, heralding family members' accomplishments. Richly documented narratives for notables such as Frederick Douglass and Harriet Tubman have survived throughout the centuries because of their extraordinary contribution to the African American cause. And though there are probably many other African Americans who have placed themselves in situations of grave danger for patriotic causes worthy of commendation, their stories have been minimized or ignored.

✳

Each time that I drive through the winding roads of the Sourland Mountain, I imagine how hard it must have been for the early Black settlers in our region. How difficult it must have been for them to carve out their lives in the utter remoteness of living on the mountain. How did they farm this less than desirable land with the massive boulders that dot the landscape to this day, land that was practically unworkable? The early Dutch settlers called it "Sauer" land because of the poor quality of the soil and the acrid smell that would sometimes emanate from the woods.

How did people like William Stives, one of the earliest recorded African American settlers on the Sourland Mountain, manage to eke out a living from this unworkable land? More importantly, how did his story begin?

Our fascination with William Stives was likely the turning point in our research. He was the catalyst: his story, along with those of how many others yet to be discovered, would have to be told. At times it felt like the hand of William himself was guiding and urging us to finish a job we knew we had to complete.

We don't know exactly how William Stives came to live on the Sourland Mountain in spite of the extensive research conducted by his fourth great-grandson, Tim Stives. To this day information has been inconclusive as to why Stives chose to settle in this area for the remainder of his years. One theory was that a young William Stives, while serving during the Revolutionary War, was foraging for food for the troops and possibly camping in Hopewell Borough when he first came across the Sourland Mountain he would one day make his home. Tim mentioned that he believed Stives may have come from North Jersey before joining the Continental Army. We can agree that Stives was definitely in the region in 1789 when he married Catherine Vanois, who lived in Somerset County, literally across the street from the Hunterdon County border. The couple had ten children, all of whom were raised on the mountain. They lived on the mountain and worshipped as devoted members of the Old School Baptist Church in Hopewell Borough where William faithfully served for forty years of his life.

Was it the hand of Stives that led us to make one of our many trips to the David Library in Yardley, Pennsylvania, the day we discovered minutes that recorded his Revolutionary War pension application that was originally recorded at the Hunterdon Inferior Court of Common Pleas for the term of August 1820?[12]

We read the papers as if we were viewing a sacred document recorded 197 years ago where it stated, "Be it remembered that on the third day of August eighteen hundred and twenty personally appeared in open court being of record for the said county of Hunterdon, William Stives, aged sixty years who being first duly sworn according to law doth on his oath make the following declaration in order to obtain the provision made by the act of Congress of the eighteenth of March one thousand eight hundred and eighteen and the first of May one thousand eight hundred and twenty."[13]

Before the Court of Common Plea, William laid his military and civilian life out as an open book for all to hear and read. He acknowledged that he was not owed anything from any person in trust any property or securities contracts or debts and that he did not have any income other than what was contained in the schedule described by him.

A lot of twenty two acres of mountain land with a small
improvement
two horses
two cows and a young calf
two hogs
seven sheep
1 old waggon
1 plough
l shed
1 set waggon gears nearly worn out
1 hay fork and dung fork
1 axe
1 shovel
1 pair of tongs
1 trammel
2 iron pot
1 kettle
1 tea kettle
a frying pan and griddle
6 chairs
6 tablespoons
a dresser—
15 old earthen plates a pewter basin
an iron candlestick
2 smoothing irons

a table

an old case of drawers

a small cupboard

6 knives and forks

4 earthen bowls

7 cups and saucers

a teapot

3 earthen pots

2 milk pans

1 wash tub

1 grass scythe

a scythe & cradle

3 pails

1 cider barrel

1 meat tub

1 fish barrel

1 soap barrel

2 meal barrels a looking glass

a chest, a spinning wheel, a bible.

Appraised at $465.03

Amount of Debts $301.13

Balance $163.90.[14]

This William Stives—who at the age of sixty described himself as a "farmer with a lame leg for a number of years and severely afflicted with rheumatism and his wife Catherine at the age of 50 years being in tolerable health but cripple in one hard"—testified before the court his meager plea for a pension that he sorely needed and deserved.

On August 13, 1827, a full seven years after William Stives's court appearance, William Stives was restored to the roll and would begin receiving benefits.

One cannot conclude that the delay had been because William was a Black man. It wasn't until 1826 that Congress was able to provide back pensions to veterans, and the country wasn't able to grant full pay for life for all Revolutionary veterans. So for twelve years William and Catherine's lives were made a little easier as they entered their twilight years together on the mountain.

On October 17, 1839, in commemorating the death of William Stives, the New York abolitionist newspaper, the *Emancipator*, wrote, "If ever there were a country, under heaven, where equal laws and equal privileges should be maintained, and man respected and treated according to his merits, it is this." Described as a faithful and courageous soldier, Stives was heralded as a "true Whig patriot in those days that tried men's souls."[15]

Stives, who joined the Continental Army as a fifer and ended as a private, was honorably recorded in the Books of the Regiment where the signature of his former commanding officer, Richard Cox, appeared. The document memorialized William Stives's receipt of a Badge of Merit, an honor equivalent to today's Purple Heart. As distinguished as this honor was it did not prepare us for the next document we found. After reviewing roll after roll of microfiche, we found the discharge papers of William Stives. As we adjusted the contrast to bring more clarity to the film we were able to finally read:

GEORGE WASHINGTON, Esq. General and Commander in Chief of the Force of the United States of America. These are to CERTIFY that the Bearer hereof William Stives, Private, having faithfully served the United States for five years and two months and being inlisted for the War only, is hereby Discharged from the American Army.[16]

Elaine and I stared in disbelief, not because of the content but because of the signature that was clearly legible before us. The discharge papers of William Stives, a Black man from the Sourland Mountain, were personally signed by none other than General George Washington.

The chapter epigraph comes from: Henry Louis Gates Jr., "Favorite Report," *The Tavis Smiley Show*, March 19, 2018.

1   "DAR Marian Anderson Statement," Daughters of the American Revolution, accessed February 12, 2018, https://www.dar.org/national-society/dar-marian-anderson-statement; National Archives and Records Administration, Still Picture Branch, "View of 75,000 People Gathered to Hear Recital by Marian Anderson at the Steps of the Lincoln Memorial, Easter Sunday, April 9, 1939," NARA, https://www.archives.gov/exhibits/american_originals/eleanor.html.

2   "How to Join," Daughters of the American Revolution, accessed December 4, 2017, https://www.dar.org/national-society/become-member/how-join.

3   Eric G. Grundset et al., *Forgotten Patriots: African American and American Indian Patriots in the Revolutionary War* (Washington, DC: National Society Daughters of the American Revolution, 2008); Daughters of the American Revolution, "Forgotten Patriots Project," Daughters of the American Revolution, accessed February 18, 2018, https://www.dar.org/library/research-guides/forgotten-patriots.

4   Maurice A. Barboza and Gary B. Nash, "We Need to Learn More About Our Colorful Past," *New York Times*, July 31, 2004.

5   Bart Barnes, "Lena Ferguson Dies at 75," *Washington Post*, March 14, 2004.

6   Ibid., 7.

7   Barboza and Nash, "We Need to Learn More About Our Colorful Past."

8   William K. Stevens, "A Detroit Black Woman's Roots Lead to a Welcome in the D.A.R.," *New York Times*, December 28, 1977.

9   Barnes, "Lena Ferguson Dies at 75."

10 Sarah Maslin Nir, "For Daughters of the American Revolution, a New Chapter," *New York Times*, July 3, 2012, sec. Region.

11 Daughters of the American Revolution, *Researching Your African American Patriot*, accessed February 18, 2018, https://www.dar.org/national-society/genealogy/minority-research.

12 "Revolutionary War Pension Application #S33728, Affidavit by William Stives, Dated August 3, 1820. Microfilm Reel 2297. Pensions Are Located in Record Group 15 of NARA" (National Archives and Records Administration, n.d.), accessed February 20, 2018, www.dlar.org.

[13] Ibid.

[14] Ibid.

[15] "William Stives—A Revolutionary Patriot," *Emancipator* 4, no. 25 (October 17, 1839): 100.

[16] "Revolutionary War Pension Application #S33728."

Old Hunterdon County - 1776

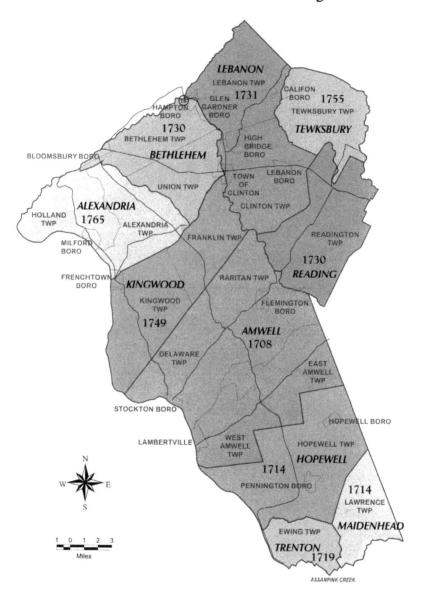

Map of Old Hunterdon County, 1776,
reprinted with permission from the
Hunterdon County Cultural & Heritage Commission

CHAPTER 4

THE AFRICAN AMERICAN FOUNDING FAMILIES OF THE SOURLAND REGION

by BEVERLY MILLS

The Heroism and Desperate Struggle That Many of Our People Had To Endure Under The Terrible Oppression That They Were Under Should Be Kept Green In The Memory of This and Coming Generations.

—William Still, African American Abolitionist

That facing the truth can be a difficult prospect is evidenced by the history of the role of the founding families in the Sourland Mountain and surrounding region. But when confronted with difficult history one must bear in mind that healing cannot begin until the gaping wound is acknowledged and no longer ignored. Our years of research and discoveries have provoked myriad emotions ranging from sheer delight when we stumble upon information relevant to our story to a simmering anger when acknowledging the sheer magnitude of the lie that continues to be perpetrated against the African American to this day. We find that some days are easier than others, but we've come to terms with the fact that when we tell our story we must respect our audience and must reach them where they are. We will share how our historical experience does not validate one truth over another; we'll just tell the story as it happened.

In New Jersey, as in most northern states, we have not been taught much, if anything, about the existence of the slavery and the slave trade in this part of the United States. There's not enough information about how slavery was not considered a crime, and how it seamlessly settled in as an acceptable way of life for the privileged class. Yet the African slave trade was essential to the early development of this region. Of course, the Sourland Mountain region's history is an intertwined story that belongs equally to White and Black residents.

To tell the stories of the earliest African American settlers who came to live in the Sourland Mountain and Hopewell Valley region, we want to breathe life into four individuals who survived the climate of post–Revolutionary War Hunterdon County. Their powerful stories should be told not only because they themselves have been denied the respect they deserve but also because they are representative of many others whose stories have been lost to history.

Who might have taught us that a free Black Sourland Mountain resident and local Revolutionary War veteran named William Stives had his discharge papers personally signed by General George Washington? Or that Stives received the Badge of Merit honoring him for five years of military service in the infancy of this country? Our research shows that Stives came to the mountain as a free Black man after valiantly serving in the Revolutionary War. He made the mountain his home for the next fifty years.

However, less is known about the life of my fourth great-grandfather, Frost Blackwell. We only know that Frost's life began on a farm just outside of Hopewell, but we don't know how he came to be enslaved in the Blackwell family. Our research has revealed that before his manumission via the will of Andrew Blackwell, Frost spent the first thirty-three years of his life enslaved.

The third black local resident we need to honor is Friday Truehart, who arrived in the Sourland region at the age of thirteen as the slave of a local reverend who purchased him in Charleston, South Carolina, in 1767. Friday was purchased at the age of three along with his twenty-year-old mother. He spent the first thirty-five years of his life as a slave, before Oliver Hart's will freed him to carve out a life with his wife and family on the mountain. And then there's Sylvia Dubois, who lived her entire estimated 120 years in the region, part of her life enslaved, and part as a free woman.

There was an advantage for freed African Americans to remain in the communities where they were manumitted. By doing so, they were somewhat protected from kidnappers, who would sell them down south or take them someplace where they were not known and sell them back into slavery. The lives of these African Americans undoubtedly intersected, particularly in the case of Friday Truehart and William Stives, who worshipped together at the Old School Baptist Church in Hopewell. Though their tongues have been silenced for centuries, their unique stories need to be told, because they are the stories of people whose lives and labor molded this area into what it is today. Yet they are stories of people whose lives essentially did not begin until their masters decided when, and how, they could begin.

It may have been a bitterly cold night on November 15, 1789, at 10:00 p.m. when Catherine Vanois of Somerset County gave her hand in marriage to William Stives by the blessing of Rev. William Frazer at St. Andrews Church in Ringoes, New Jersey.[1] Unfortunately, information about Catherine Vanois has proven to be scarce. According to census research by Michael Alfano of the Hunterdon County Historical Society, the Vanois family had farms in Maidenhead (today's Lawrenceville) and Hopewell near Provinceline Road near the Somerset County line. Perhaps Catherine Vanois (or Vannoy, as it was also spelled) was a slave in the Vanois family?

William and Catherine began a union that would endure for a half century. The following year in East Amwell, Hunterdon County, New Jersey, William and Catherine welcomed their first child, Cornelius. At that time the Province of New Jersey had 11,423 slaves.[2] The following year, 1791, the only successful slave uprising took place on the Caribbean island of Saint-Domingue. Slaves left sugar fields and fought their way to freedom, killing slave masters and their families and torching homes and fields. The French-ruled colony was left in utter turmoil as its economic cash cow came to a grinding halt and a new free Black-ruled country, Haiti, was born. The United States, deeply frightened and horrified by the risks involved in having regions where slaves outnumbered White residents, had already started edging toward banning international slave trading. Indeed, the Haitian Revolution played a crucial role in opening the door to what became the Louisiana Purchase. This upheaval, followed by the 1794 invention of the cotton gin (which made it possible to clean cotton at an unprecedented speed), changed many of the dynamics of American slavery and was instrumental in tearing apart enslaved families, particularly those in the upper southern states. The acquisition of 530 million acres from France, which literally doubled the size of the American nation, paved the way for slavery to expand into these new lands, fueling slaveholders' desire to produce more and more cotton. This, in turn, caused the movement of thousands of slaves out of the depleted tobacco farms of Virginia and Maryland into the cotton fields of the Deep South. The so-called Upper South, which previously enjoyed all the wealth and trappings from tobacco production, now took a backseat to the Lower South's "King Cotton." Slave families that had been together all their lives were suddenly ripped apart and, marched in "coffle" lines, scattered to parts unknown.[3] The dictionary definition for coffle is "a line of animals, prisoners, or slaves chained and driven along together." For days or even weeks, manacled men walked; women and children marched behind.

While the nation was expanding, so was William and Catherine's New Jersey family. By February 15, 1804, when William and Catherine welcomed Stacy, their fourth child, legislators were gathering less than twenty miles away in Trenton to enact the Gradual Abolition of Slavery Act, a variation on the abolition policies recently enacted in nearby states such as Pennsylvania, New York, and Massachusetts. The New Jersey Gradual Abolition of Slavery Act stipulated that "every child born of a slave within this state, after the fourth day of July next, shall be free; but shall remain the servant of the owner of his or her mother, and the executors, administrators or assigns of such owner, in the same manner as if such child had been bound to service by the trustees or overseers of the poor, and shall continue in such service, if a male, until the age of twenty five years; and if a female until the age of twenty one years." The law further stipulated that "every person being an inhabitant of this state, who shall be entitled to the service of a child born as aforesaid, after the said fourth day of July next, shall within nine months after the birth of such child, cause to be delivered to the clerk of the county whereof such person shall be an inhabitant, a certificate in writing, containing the name and addition of such person, and the name, age, and sex of the child so born; which certificate, whether the same be delivered before or after the said nine months; shall be by the said clerk recorded in a book to be by him provided for that purpose."

Since the 1804 New Jersey Gradual Abolition of Slavery Act instructed all slave masters to keep records of slave births, there are hundreds of records of children born into enslavement after 1804. Their new title, "slaves for a term," still afforded no protection for these children, who were often subject to mistreatment, to being sold away from their families, or to being kidnapped by bounty hunters who stealthily sold them to southern markets.

The story covers a wide swath of central New Jersey—some forty-four square miles, since, in 1776, Hunterdon County stretched from Lebanon Township all the way down to Trenton. Thus, a review of scores of births recorded by Hunterdon County shows many aspects of the slave experience, since owners were required to record the child's name, the sex, the mother's name, the locality, and the date of certification. The documentation included comments such as the father's name, whether the person was a "mulatto" (mixed race), and the mother's former slave owner. Frequently recurring names include: George, Isaac, Bonaparte, Mary, Ann, Charles, and Nancy, all born to slave mothers in Hunterdon County. And as William and Catherine continued living on the Sourland Mountain, their family eventually blossomed into ten children—ten free children.

In November 1780, while the Stives family thrived on the mountain, the Rev. Oliver Hart arrived in Hopewell from Charleston, South Carolina, to become the new pastor at the Old School Baptist Church. With him was his thirteen-year-old slave, Friday Truehart, who would eventually become my fourth great-grandfather. On December 16, having fled the ravages of the Revolutionary War's "Siege of Charleston," the Reverend Hart met his new flock of 220 members: 89 White males, 124 White females, and seven Black congregants. The moment of learning the circumstances behind Friday Truehart's arrival to Hopewell, has been one of the most exciting discoveries of my life.[5]

Having another piece of the puzzle revealed about one of my ancestors was astounding. The excitement I felt when I found out that Friday originally came from Charleston was literally life altering. Up to that point, all I'd known was gathered from a notation in the *Hopewell Herald* announcing the death of Friday's oldest son, Isaac. The *Herald* noted that "Friday was a native of Africa, and was brought to Charleston, S.C. by the ship's captain, who had stolen him from his native home. He was bought by Oliver Hart of this Captain. Mr. Hart named the African boy after Robinson Crusoe's companion, Friday."[6]

In my research I was able to find information to refute this misinformed narrative—I found a different narrative that surprisingly brought me more comfort. This narrative arose from my reading of Oliver Hart's papers,[7] which encompass Hart's correspondence, diaries, and sermon notes from the colonial and Revolutionary period while he lived in Charleston. Plowing through Hart's writings was, at first, slow and boring work. Most of his records seem almost perfunctory: recounting of sermons and letters describing the conditions in the area, his travels to Virginia and North Carolina, and his patriotic work in South Carolina's low country during the earlier days of the Revolution. There was virtually no mention of his tracts of land or his plantation, which comprised 350 acres near Charleston and an additional 300 acres in St. Mark's Parish. But then I came across his diary.

There is no explanation why, in 1949, Oliver Hart's diary was found transcribed in an old notebook kept by William G. Whilden of South Carolina. But I immediately devoured the document, as

I looked for clues that might tell me anything about Friday Truehart. As with his other documents, Hart's notations were short and to the point. I read two lines about his marriage to Sarah Brees and a brief announcement about the birth of his children, but what I found more interesting was his elaboration regarding his countryside travels and the deadly typhoon of 1761. I continued reading, slightly bored, until I came upon an entry for April 9, 1771. The closest way I can come to explaining how I felt when I read this entry is elation that quickly turned to sorrow. Here before me was a key to a family mystery, but these words also made me face a stark and difficult reality. I wasn't prepared to read, "Dinah and her son Friday were bought April ye 9th 1771. Dinah was then supposed to be about twenty years of age. Friday was born May ye 29th 1767. The two cost 356 pounds." Further down on the page I read another entry, "Dinah was delivered of a daughter August ye 22nd 1772."[8]

My eyes filled with tears when I came to the realization that Dinah, the young slave woman who would be my fifth great-grandmother, was about twenty years old and the mother of an almost three-year-old child when purchased. There was a common custom in the slave trade whereby female slaves were disrobed so that potential buyers could easily assess potential "goods" before purchasing. Strangely, I was comforted to know that mother and son were not separated, that Hart had the decency to purchase the two together, despite the fact that they would remain together only for the first thirteen years of young Friday's life. Nevertheless, I continued to be baffled as to why these entries were the only ones about the purchase of slaves, and I became more confused when I realized that Hart knew Friday's exact birthdate as well as that of Dinah's daughter some sixteen months later. The question begged to be answered: Was it customary for slave owners to be aware of the exact date of a slave child's birth prior to purchase? If so, why have I been unable to find mention of any other slave purchase or reference during his tenure in Charleston? My search for answers led me to review more of Oliver Hart's papers, which are housed in the University of South Carolina Library in Columbia. Yet there were no other entries that mentioned the names or purchases of other slaves.

It's hard to imagine how young Friday Truehart felt when he came to the realization that Hopewell would now be his home; it must have been a shock leaving the sun-kissed warmth of South Carolina to arrive in the frosty chill of the Northeast. How were crops to grow in the cold, unforgiving soil that greeted him upon his December arrival? Was there snow on the ground? Who was there to mother this thirteen-year-old boy? How long did his mother, left behind to serve the family of Hart's daughter-in-law, mourn the loss of her boy? Did she ever forget how her boy looked and smelled? Did she remember things about him that only a mother would know and hold dear? Did Friday ever forget his young mother's face, her voice, and her touch? Was he frightened or awestruck when he first saw the gigantic boulders that dotted the Sourland Mountain landscape? How did he make sense out of any and all of this? The Parsonage Farm, which Oliver Hart was to call his new home, was controlled by the Stout family. Presumably this homestead was located in what was known as the Blackwell/Riley/Drake farmstead. On December 25 Reverend Hart settled in the Parsonage House on Parsonage Farm (as it was referred to in the diary of Oliver Hart) to lead the Old School Baptist congregation. Hart's wife, Anne, who had remained in Charleston, joined him a year later in the sleepy New Jersey hamlet. Along with the parsonage, an additional ninety-five acres had previously been purchased by the Baptist Trustee Board. I imagine Friday's duties revolved around the day-to-day running of the farm. The typical colonial era farm would include the main house, a barn, a shed or sheds, areas for livestock, places to store crops and corn, and a smokehouse and springhouse. From sunup to sundown the Hart Hopewell plantation would have required more than just Friday to keep a farm of that size efficiently running. Unfortunately, our research has not been able to discern the names of other slaves or free Black people who may have worked alongside Friday. Nevertheless, this farm is where Friday would be enslaved until granted his freedom in 1802.

Oliver Hart spent the remaining fifteen years of his life as the spiritual leader of the Old School Baptist Church, which still stands on Broad Street in Hopewell, New Jersey. More austere on the inside than on the outside, the building can be startling for first-time visitors. The creaky floors are slightly sloped and the pulpit is a simple lectern. I wonder how many sermons Hart preached while gazing up at the balcony where slaves were required to sit. How many Sundays did Friday sit in the balcony listening to his master preach on God's goodness and grace? Oliver Hart had been suffering failing health long before his demise in December 1795. In *Hopewell Valley Heritage* author and curator of the Hopewell Museum Alice Blackwell Lewis wrote about the death of Reverend Hart by saying, "Rev. Hart had a faithful and trustworthy slave. Because of his fondness of this man, he called him Friday True. Later this servant wished to have the name of this master added, so he called himself Friday Truehart."[9] This is one of many legends of how Friday's surname came to be and prompted me to conduct further research in the hope of gaining more information about Friday's decision to honor his master by adding "hart" to his last name. Unfortunately, I have not been successful.

I was presented with more answers to my questions after I read the will of Oliver Hart, who started out declaring himself "an unworthy Minister of the glorious Gospel." I read Hart's small, beautifully handwritten script that enumerated each bequeath upon his death. The will also answered the question of the fate of Dinah, Friday's mother, where he apathetically instructed, "My Will is, that Sarah, the widow of my late son, Doctor Oliver Hart, shall keep and have the use of one Negro woman now with her named Dinah, during the widowhood of her life, the said Sarah; but in case she should marry, then the said wench should be sold, and the money arising therefrom be disposed of as follows, that is to say, it shall be put out on interest, and the interest arising therefrom shall go toward the maintenance of the children which my son has left until the youngest of them shall arrive at the age of eighteen years the principal shall be divided between them, share and share alike."[10]

I surmised that the "Dinah" mentioned was Friday's mother, who remained behind within the family. Since the will was probated in 1796 this would mean that Dinah, if sold should Sarah remarry, was still relatively marketable as a slave woman approaching middle age. How much would she have fetched toward the "maintenance of the children"? While Hart was providing a financial legacy for his grandchildren with the potential sale of Dinah, it occurred to me that Friday, when freed, would not have seen his mother in twenty-nine years and most likely never laid eyes upon her again. Yet another item literally took my breath away when I read, "I give and bequeath into my son John Hart, one Negro man, named Friday; also my watch with the chain and seal, likewise a silver soup spoon and a silver pepper box, together with a seal set in gold on which our family coat of arms is engraved; to him and to his heirs forever."[11]

I read and reread this entry, all the while trying to wrap my mind around such a stunning example of how the fate of a human being was controlled by the stroke of a pen. I continued reading until I came to the end of the will, which contained a surprising codicil written in January 1793: "Whereas by the above will I have given and bequeathed my Negro man Friday to my son John Hart, I do hereby revoke that bequest, and my will now is that the said Negro Man Friday shall be fully and absolutely free, at the expiration of seven years after my decease. During which term of seven years, said Friday shall be under the care and control of my dear wife, Anne Hart, to dispose of his time or labor, or any profits arising there-from, as she may think proper." After seven years under the "care and control" of Anne Hart, Friday would finally be freed at the age of thirty-five.

I have no information as to the circumstances under which Friday and Judah (or Juda) Shue of Somerset County met and married, but it was definitely before 1802 when he was still under the "care and control" of Hart's widow. Friday and Judah welcomed sons Isaac in 1792, Aaron in 1805, and Moses in 1816. Life for the Truehart family began in the Sourland Mountain in a log cabin that still stands today.

While the Trueharts were raising their three sons on the mountain, Frost Blackwell, my paternal fourth great-grandfather, continued to be enslaved by Andrew Blackwell in the Hopewell Township area known as Mount Rose. Andrew Blackwell, a descendant of one of the region's founding families, was a man of very considerable means and amassed a 166-acre plantation. In 1990, historians Richard Hunter and Richard Porter described "the initial impetus for the growth of Mount Rose" as "the breakup of Andrew Blackwell's 166-acre plantation at the end of the second decade of the nineteenth century."[12] After Blackwell's death in 1818, his executors subdivided his property and sold parcels of land, which provided for the growth of the small village. It seems likely that the sale of these parcels also added to the considerable inheritance bequeathed in Blackwell's will. Since Andrew never married and had no children, some of the beneficiaries included his nieces and nephews, who benefited handsomely from his generosity. "Signed, sealed, published and declared to be his testament and last will in the presence of us," Samuel Titus, Richard Stout, and Jonathan Blackwell attested to the soundness of Andrew Blackwell's last wishes. Andrew's brother Benjamin along with his brother-in-law Isaac Dunn were both listed as executors, responsible for distributing one hundred pounds bequeathed to Andrew's siblings (or their descendants in the event of their death). Once again, I found myself stunned by how the fate of one man could rest in the stroke of another's pen, in this case Frost. I then read the seventh point of the will, which read, "I give to Frost my servant Blackman his freedom and one hundred dollars."[13] An unbelievable sum of money gifted to a servant man of color.

Frost started a life with Nancy Vanvactor, an enslaved woman, who most likely came from Somerset County. They married on December 8, 1816, two years prior to Andrew's death in 1818. One can surmise that Andrew's gift made it possible for Frost to purchase his wife's freedom, because on April 9, 1827, Frost Blackwell appeared before David Stout of the Hunterdon County Court to buy the freedom of his wife, Nancy. Eight years had elapsed since Frost had obtained his own freedom and $100. The document also listed other souls who were being manumitted that April day. Nancy was joined by Julian, aged 23, and Marian, aged 37: both received manumission from Hopewell slaveholders as the 1804 Gradual Abolition laws began to take hold.[14]

In 1830, about 13.7 percent (319,599 people) of the Black population in the United States were free. Out of this number, 3,776 free Blacks owned 12,907 slaves out of the total of 2,009,043 slaves throughout United States. These numbers clearly show, however, that the number of slaves owned by Black people was still quite small in comparison to the number owned by White people. Most free Black people who owned slaves were most likely purchasing a family member as a means to protect them. There were some Blacks, as unbelievable as it is, who owned slaves to exploit their labor in the same way their White brethren did.[15]

That same year in Hopewell Township there may have been somewhere in the vicinity of three dozen free Black households, seventy-five households where free Blacks were residents, and twelve slave owners still on record.[16] Among the free Black households listed were the Blackwell family, which included Frost, his wife, Nancy, their sons, Samuel, Noah, and Benjamin, and their two daughters (names are unknown).

Although the Blackwells resided in Hopewell Township as free Blacks, the internal slave trade and kidnapping of Jersey slaves was still an important reality. According to Robert Fogel and Stanley Engerman, the decline in the Black population in states with emancipation laws was not due to the International Slave Trade ban of 1807 but likely due to the underreporting of free Black people and the fact that ex-slaves moved to other states. Could this mean that many slaves did not gain their freedom but instead were sold internally to the Deep South? According to Fogel and Engerman, some records "did not survive or more likely never existed because slaveholders removed their slaves without official license."[17]

Meanwhile, in the eyes of the law, the Stives, Truehart, and Blackwell families could all be regarded as free Black people. Sylvia Dubois, the final of our four protagonists in this chapter, gained her freedom in a way that made headlines. You'll have to read more to learn Sylvia's complex and dramatic tale.

Born into slavery on March 5, 1768, to Dorcas Compton and Cuffy Baird, Sylvia (also Salvia or Silvia) entered this world in an old tavern formerly owned by her grandfather Harry Putnam. Sylvia's father, Cuffy, was a fifer in the Battle of Princeton and was owned by John Baird. Her mother, Dorcas Compton, was a slave to Richard Compton, the proprietor of the hotel at Rock Mills. Her grandfather had been a slave to General Rufus Putnam and then to Richard Compton. From Richard Compton, Harry was able to bide his time and become free. Taking the last name of his former master, Harry Putnam became known as Harry Put, for short. Harry eventually became the proprietor of the tavern formerly owned by Richard Compton, and the tavern came to be known as Put's Tavern, where homemade whiskey and other types of drinks were served. Legend has it that Put's was known to have the best peach brandy you could ever find. People would come from all over—Trenton, Princeton, New Brunswick, and as far away as New York and Philadelphia—to Put's for cockfighting, gambling, prizefights, race mixing, and alcohol. When Sylvia was in her prime, her strength and size were renowned. At the tavern "some of her most noteworthy feats were accomplished when suppressing a row of parting combatants; indeed, her presence often prevented a fight. For if a fight began contrary to her will, often she, to make them more obedient in the future, and to terrify others of a quarrelsome or pugilistic nature, would severely whip both the combatants."[18]

In 1883 Dr. Cornelius Wilson Larison, a West Amwell resident, historian, and collector of oral histories, started a series of interviews with Sylvia Dubois, who at that time was believed to be 115 years old. Sylvia lived in a cabin deep in the Sourland Mountain, which she shared with her daughter, Elizabeth. Over the course of numerous visits, Sylvia told her story to Dr. Larison. I could not help but wonder what it must have been like for Sylvia to recall the painful memories of her enslaved life. How did Sylvia feel when she told the story about how her mother was nearly beaten to death with an ox goad, three days after giving birth, because she failed to adequately hold fast to a hog while her master tried to yoke it? How hard was it to recount how, as a young child, she was frequently on the receiving end of severe beatings from a displeased mistress? Or to talk about receiving a beating with a shovel so severe that it left a permanent dent in Sylvia's skull, proof of the cruelty she was subjected to that she would carry to her grave. How did she really feel to once again describe witnessing the mass flogging of slaves in Flemington, beatings so severe she recalled how their backs were reduced to bloody slits?

Why did Sylvia not know the answer when Dr. Larison asked, "Do you know how old you are?" Sylvia was quoted as saying, "Not exactly—can't tell exactly. They didn't used to keep a record of the birth of niggers; they hardly kept a record of the birth of white children; none but the grand folks kept a record of the birth of their children—they didn't no more keep the date of a young nigger than they did of a calf or a colt; the young niggers were born in the Fall or in the Spring, in the Summer or in the Winter, in cabbage time or when cherries were ripe, when they were planting corn or when they were husking corn, and that's all the way they talked about a nigger's age."[19]

Sylvia's mother, Dorcas Compton, was a slave of Richard Compton, who owned the hotel at Rock Mills. Dorcas wanted to be "free" so she made an arrangement with Minical Dubois to give her a loan to "buy her time" from Compton. But Dorcas failed to make payment to Dubois, so she, along with two-year-old Sylvia, became Dubois's property. According to Sylvia, Dubois resented taking on the burden of a slave woman and her child and was therefore cruel to both. Eventually Dorcas started looking for a new master and made an arrangement with William Baird to buy her time from Dubois and become her new master. Seeking her freedom once again, Dorcas was able to buy her time from William Baird, but, as in the past, she missed payments and once again became his slave. Subsequently, Baird sold Dorcas to Miles Smith, who proved to be a more benevolent master. However, in spite of his benevolence, Dorcas still longed to be free. Once again Dorcas entered into an arrangement to purchase her freedom and, once again, failed to make her payment. Dorcas thus reverted to being owned by Miles Smith and remained so for the rest of her life. But Sylvia had remained with Minical Dubois and his wife and had moved with their family to a new home near Flagtown.

The accuracy of Sylvia Dubois's story has sometimes been questioned by other writers who have read the account of Sylvia's life. Her recollections, for example, included seeing her master return from the Battle of Monmouth when she was ten years old. She also remembered when her father and others had returned from the Battles of Trenton and Princeton. In my estimation, however, there was too much detail for these stories to be totally fabricated.

Larison's book, *Silvia Dubois, A Biografy of the Slav Who Whipt Her Mistres and Gand Her Fredom*, was so titled owing to the circumstances of how she actually gained her freedom. It was Sylvia's fourteenth year when she moved with the Dubois family to Great Bend across the Susquehanna River. It is not clear how long Sylvia was with the Dubois family in Great Bend, but it was long enough for Minical to become a very accomplished businessman and tavern owner. It was in the barroom of this establishment when the unthinkable happened: Sylvia raised her hand against her mistress. Perhaps, in Sylvia's mind, this was absolutely the last straw: when she punched her mistress she practically knocked her out. Sylvia knew she was in trouble and had to leave, so she went north to find work. Several days later Sylvia was summoned by her master to return. Sylvia feared returning to face her master and the consequences of her actions. But, to her amazement, Minical told her if she returned to New Jersey he would grant Sylvia her freedom. So Sylvia struck out with her year-and-a-half-old baby through the Beech Woods to make her way back to Flagtown to find her mother. She reminisced about how she had to carry her child the entire time through the woods, how she heard wild animals howling around her through the night, until she made it to Flagtown, only to find that her mother was then living fifteen miles away in New Brunswick. Sylvia remained in New Brunswick for several years before coming to Princeton to work for the Tulane family. She came back to the mountain after visiting her grandfather, who by that time was over one hundred years old. Upon his death, Sylvia inherited his property and lived there until "them damned Democrats set fire to my house." Sylvia lost everything she had in the fire and from that time on lived with her daughter Elizabeth at the cabin where the interviews took place.

Sylvia was the mother of six children, Moses, Judith, Charlotte, Dorcas, Rachel, and Elizabeth. Sylvia and Elizabeth lived simply on the mountain and would be periodically seen in the area where neighbors would give them food and supplies. Famous for her longevity, Sylvia was reported to be dead two times during her life, once by the *Hunterdon Democrat* on April 1, 1888: "that old Silvia Dubois had died during the blizzard week at her home on Sourland Mountain is denied by the old woman herself. When such testimony as this is offered, it must be accepted. We don't know who started the false report. May Silvia live on until she dies."[20]

The second notification of her death, however, was accurate when in May 1888 it was reported by the *Hopewell Herald*:

A Famous Negress: The severe weather in America has killed Sylvia Dubois, the famous negress of Sour Land Mountain, New Jersey. She is said to have been 122 years old, "beyond doubt." She was for years the slave of a man named Dubois. Then she was sold to a man who kept an hotel, where she became famed for her feats of strength and for the prize fights in which she engaged. She boasted that she was never beaten and had knocked out scores of the strongest men. One day she got angry at her mistress and nearly killed her. She picked up her child and fled across the Susquehanna and tramped all the way to the Sour Land Mountain, where she lived the rest of her life. Her fondness for fighting, liquor, and her profanity soon made her notorious. All her children died but the youngest; who remained with her mother; and is eighty years old. It is said that she inherits all her mother's pugilistic prowess and has maimed many men.[21]

Sylvia's funeral was held at the "Black church" on the mountain where Reverend Pitman eulogized her life. We surmise that the reference to the Black church on the mountain was the Mt. Zion AME on Hollow Road. There was no mention of where Sylvia Dubois was buried. This remains an unanswered question to this day and one more reason to make sure that her story is told and that Sylvia is properly remembered.

The chapter epigraph comes from: Larry Gara, "William Still and the Underground Railroad," *Pennsylvania History: A Journal of Mid-Atlantic Studies* 28, no. 1 (1961): 39, accessed April 25, 2018, http://www.jstor.org/stable/27770004.

1 Henry Race and William Frazer, "Rev. William Frazer's Three Parishes, St. Thomas's, St. Andrew's, and Musconetcong, N.J., 1768–70," *Pennsylvania Magazine of History & Biography* 12, no. 2 (July 1888): 212–32, accessed November 28, 2017, http://www.jstor.org/stable/20083262.

2 Cooley, *A Study of Slavery in New Jersey*, 31.

3 Ibid.

4 "An Act for the Gradual Abolition of Slavery Act of 1804. Passed at Trenton, February 15, 1804," accessed December 15, 2017, http://njlegallib.rutgers.edu/slavery/acts/A78.html.

5 "Diary of Oliver Hart. The Oliver Hart Papers, 1741–1795," South Caroliniana Library, University of South Carolina, accessed November 25, 2017, http://library.sc.edu/p/Collections/Digital/Browse/OHart.

6 Ibid.

7 Ibid.

8 Ibid.

9 Lewis, *Hopewell Valley Heritage*.

10 "Hart, Oliver. Will and Codicil of Oliver Hart. Hopewell, Hunterdon County, New Jersey. NJ Secretary of State Wills, Hunterdon County, #1753. 16 December 1791. Codicil Dated 15 January 1793" (Trenton: New Jersey State Archives, n.d.).

11 Ibid.

12 Richard W. Hunter and Richard Porter, *Hopewell: A Historical Geography* (Titusville, NJ: Township of Hopewell, Historic Sites Committee, 1990).

13 "Blackwell, Andrew. Will and Codicil of Andrew Blackwell. Hopewell, Hunterdon County, New Jersey. 23 September 1815. NJ Secretary of State Wills, Hunterdon County, #2928" (Trenton, NJ: New Jersey State Archives, n.d.).

14 Hunterdon County Court of Common Pleas, "Minutes of the Court of Common Pleas. Volume II, Page 247 [Manumission of Nancy]" (1827).

15 Henry Louis Gates Jr., "Did Black People Own Slaves?" *American Renaissance*, March 8, 2013, accessed February 17, 2018, https://www.amren.com/news/2013/03/did-black-people-own-slaves/.

16 Phyllis B. D'Autrechy, *Some Records of Old Hunterdon County*, 1701–1838 ([Pennington, NJ]: D'Autrechy, 1979).

17 Robert William Fogel and Stanley L. Engerman, "Philanthropy at Bargain Prices: Notes on the Economics of Gradual Emancipation," *Journal of Legal Studies* 3, no. 2 (June 1974): 392–93, accessed November 28, 2017, http://www.jstor.org/stable/724019.

[18] "Sylvia Dubois, Slave of the Sourlands, Related Life Story to Larison," *Princeton Recollector, a Monthly Journal of Local History, Princeton History Project* 5, no. 4 (Winter 1980): 11.

[19] Cornelius Wilson Larison, M.D., Silvia Dubois, and Jared Lobdell, *Silvia Dubois: A Biografy of the Slav Who Whipt Her Mistres and Gand Her Fredom,* Schomburg Library of Nineteenth-Century Black Women Writers (New York: Oxford University Press, 1988).

[20] "That Old Silvia Dubois Had Died During the Blizzard Week at Her Home on Sourland Mountain Is Denied by the Old Woman Herself," *Hunterdon Democrat,* April 1, 1888.

[21] "Sylvia Dubois Is at Last Really Dead, So, at Least the Hopewell Herald Announces," *Princeton Press,* May 5, 1888.

Old Billy Truehart Loved Home, Defied Lindbergh

HOPEWELL, N.J.

The one man who defied Col. Charles A. Lindbergh and all his wealth was William H. (Billy) Truehart who died here May 4, 1932, at the age of 86 after scorning the flier's cash offer to buy Truehart's 40 wooded acres adjoining the famous Lindbergh mansion.

Held Home 105 Years

Truehart never married, but he and his father before him lived in a frame structure on the property for the last 105 years. Lindbergh had the 40 acres surveyed and then visited Truehart. This was while the great white mansion from which the Lindbergh baby was kidnaped was in the finishing stages of construction.

Truehart was abrupt. "To some people their native home means everything—more than all the money in the world," he told the flier. With that Truehart dismissed Lindbergh, locked his door, and went to stay with his niece, a Mrs. Brodkaw, 41 Model Avenue here.

"I'll never sell as long as I live," he told his niece.

The property was leased to a white couple named Miller after Truehart's death. They occupied it up until the past week when they moved away to New Brunswick.

In Swampy Section

The Truehart land is a wild, swampy, section with a frame house located in the midst of a clearing. However, even today there is a contest on foot by other neighbors to purchase the property. Mounting taxes may force a public sale of the place and a local bang holds a mortgage on it.

Mrs. Brokaw, Truehart's nearest known relative, recently has been seriously ill and in a Trenton hospital. She has three children, but none is in Hopewell.

There are other branches of the Truehart family, one of them living somewhere in the nearby Sourland mountain range and directly descended from an Indian chief of the same name.

It could not be definitely learned Friday whether Carey Truehart, late Elk leader of Atlantic City, was related to the Hopewell families.

Truehart left no will.

Only about a hundred colored people live here. The total population is 1700. Hopewell regards its colored population without the slightest prejudice. In fact local residents are probably totally unaware of the color line.

On Friday the Truehart place and surrounding land was almost verdant with an early spring. The Lindbergh estate was deserted save for two white caretakers. The Lindberghs abandoned the Tudor style home in 1932 after the baby was found.

In 1933 the property was deeded to a welfare organization of which the Lindberghs are trustees. Named Highfields, the property was to be a center for education, training and hospitalization of children. No children ever came, however.

No move was made to develop the project. Taxes are paid regularly and signs reading "no trespassing" are posted.

"Old Billy Truehart Loved Home, Defied Lindbergh," reprinted with permission from the *Baltimore Afro-American*, March 2, 1932

CHAPTER 5

PROPERTY AND LAND: RELATIONSHIPS TRUMPED THE LAW

by BEVERLY MILLS

We hold these truths to be self-evident: that all men are created equal; that they are endowed by their Creator with certain unalienable rights; that among these are life, liberty, and the pursuit of happiness.

—U.S. Declaration of Independence

Every time I drive through the winding roads of the Sourland Mountain, I think about the struggles of the early African American settlers. In particular, I imagine how hard it must have been for them to carve out their lives in the remoteness of the mountain. How did they farm this less-than-desirable land, with the huge boulders that dot the landscape to this day?

New Jersey, or New Cesarea as originally named, is 7,417 square miles of fertile land. Flanked by the Atlantic Ocean and crisscrossed by rivers and lakes, the area was the ideal location for the early proprietors to settle, to lay claim to, and to sell land. The soil would yield endless possibilities. And although it wasn't until 1875 that New Jersey officially received its nickname, the Garden State, by Abraham Browning of Camden during a speech he was giving at the Philadelphia Centennial Exhibition, New Jersey had long been living up to its name.[1] New immigrants setting foot in this new colony could only imagine what would come from this fruitful land, possibilities that—in the state's early years—could bring material gain only to people of European descent.

In this chapter I will talk about the realities of landownership at the inception of the colony and how legislation eventually was enacted to ensure that land and Black ownership went hand in hand. There was, at first, legislation that prevented even freed Black people from taking part in the American dream as landowners. But there are also stories about how a few African American families, some of whom were my ancestors, were able to seize the opportunity to become land*holders*, and then lay claim as equal landowners, in the Sourland Mountain. I will also tell you about how the power of land opened the door for Black communities to take shape and for churches to be built through relationships that trumped the "law."

Property ownership offers concrete security and status, which translate into real power and sovereignty over one's life, in any historical period. In New Jersey's early days, the privilege of voting or holding public office was restricted to male landowners of European heritage who were more than twenty-one years of age.

"SIXTY ACRES FOR EVERY SLAVE"

You might not know that property ownership and ownership of slaves were connected in colonial New Jersey. The leadership of colonial New Jersey and Queen Anne of England rewarded colonial proprietors by promising them a constant supply of slaves at moderate rates. The queen and her colonial proprietors viewed these incentives as the means to ensure the new colony's success: "the Lords Proprietors granted every colonist that should go out with the first governor seventy-five acres of land for every slave, to every settler before January 1, 1665, sixty acres for every slave, to every settler in the third year thirty acres for every slave."[2]

By 1713, An Act for Regulating Slaves essentially prohibited free Black people and Indians from holding real property, which meant they could not possess any house or land in New Jersey.[3] Recognizing the importance of landownership, the founding fathers restricted this privilege to people of European descent. In 2014, Joe Grabas, an expert in historical land title research, described just how important landownership was to the development of the state: "long before paper money was backed by gold and silver in New Jersey, it was supported by land bank mortgages. Land ownership was the pathway to wealth, power and influence in New Jersey."[4]

In our research there were times I would come across a description of a local slave that was for sale. I was initially surprised when I first realized that farms in the North were described as "plantations." I was struck by a typical advertisement that appeared in the *Pennsylvania Gazette* in which the public was notified about

> a valuable plantation situated in Hopewell Township and county of Hunterdon containing by estimation 296 acres of good land, 200 or more of which are cleared, the rest well-timbered, and watered with a number of good springs, has a quality of good mowing ground, and more may be made with little expense. On the said premises are a large stone dwelling house, two stories high, with nine rooms well finished, six fire-places and a large entry through the center; a cellar and cellar kitchen, a well of

excellent water at the door, a stone barn and other out-houses, an orchard of grafted fruit, peaches, pears and cherries of the best kind, and a variety of other fruit. The situation is very healthy and pleasant, and would suit a gentleman or farmer.[5]

I thought about what it must have been like working for free in this bucolic land, a lifestyle that seemed light years out of reach. It shouldn't be hard to understand freed Blacks' desire to own land that would bring them one step closer to living the American dream. But African Americans residing in New Jersey, those fortunate enough to be free, would have to wait until 1798 for the repeal of the law prohibiting them from owning land. Once the law was repealed, Black New Jerseyans seized the opportunity to purchase land—some by way of existing personal relationships with White landowners. So began Black-owned hamlets that included what was deemed the least desirable land in the Sourland Mountain region.

If Albert Witcher, an African American man who lived on the Sourland Mountain for most of his life, were alive today, he would most likely be able to supply the answers to some of these questions; he could at least tell us what he was told by the old-timers. Albert used to talk about how the old folks told him how the name "Sourland" came about. He said it came about because of the "sour" nature of the land. Jim Luce wrote in 2001 that the early Dutch settlers called the region the "sauer" land because of the poor quality of the soil and the acrid smell that sometimes would come from the woods. Thus, describes Luce, "early cultivators recognized acid soils when they encountered them and that liming, to neutralize the acidity of the soil, was carried on in the eighteenth century."[6]

In spite of the poor quality of the land, Luce concluded, the Sourland Mountain area had—and has—its own natural mystique.

As a former member of the Sourland Planning Council (the precursor to today's Sourland Conservancy), Jim was particularly inspired to write about the region after becoming active in the historic and environmental preservation of the Sourland Mountain. Jim took great care to ensure that readers were aware of the exact location of the mountain, and he made sure to mention the indescribable aura of the region: "The Sourland Mountain in west-central New Jersey is roughly seventeen miles long and four miles wide, running northwest from the Delaware River to a point just beyond the village of Neshanic. It is fifty miles equidistant from Philadelphia and New York and parallels a section of the metropolitan corridor stretching from Boston to Washington, D.C. The silence and the remoteness create a strange and mysterious atmosphere, which at times seems alien—even a bit sinister. You have entered an altogether different world from the one you left moments before."[7]

The mystical impressions of the region ran alongside a more practical commentary. Richard Hunter and Richard Porter, authors of *Hopewell: A Historical Geography*, take pains to describe the farms of the colonial era. Agreeing with the assessment of the poor quality of soil, the writers also described other less-than-desirable qualities of stretches of land where farming would be more than a challenge: "depending on their properties, the soils in the Hopewell area have had a varying effect on man's use of the land."[8]

So how did African Americans become landowners in this notoriously "sour" land? Was it because of the harsh condition of the soil that opportunities for landownership in the Sourland Mountain region were given to African Americans so they could finally realize the American dream? Were these families, some who were my ancestors, so pleased to have a deed of ownership in their hands that they were willing to take on any challenge no matter how punishing the land might be?

One of the earliest African American landowners in the Sourland region was the same Moses Blew who was instrumental in purchasing the land that became the Stoutsburg Cemetery. How did the transaction materialize? The most likely story appears to stem from a mortgage arrangement with the Stout family, White neighbors with whom the Blew family had a personal relationship.

The Dutch Blew (or Blau) family migrated to the Sourland Mountain region from New York in the mid-eighteenth century. Among the "possessions" of patriarch Michael Blew was a Negro man named Tom, a woman "Jonah" (Judith), and a child believed to be Moses, her son. After Blew's death in 1788, his estate paid ten pounds for the liberation of "Negro Tom" with the likely arrangement that Tom would be responsible for farming 201 acres out of the 360-acre estate. As it was illegal for freed Blacks to own land prior to 1798, this arrangement could be considered extremely bold. Regardless, "Tom Negro Blew" appeared in the Montgomery tax lists as a landowner in 1789, 1790, and 1792. The lease arrangement is murky, but it seems to have involved splitting profits from a leased portion of the land that Tom farmed, a system similar to the sharecropping that is now mostly associated with the post–Civil War South. This shared arrangement of land and crops may explain how Tom appeared on the tax records as a Black man. However, when the deceased Blew's oldest son became of legal age to own the 201 acres in question, Tom mysteriously disappeared from the tax records on the same date.[9]

In 1802, Tom Blew resurfaced in the tax records, but he was not listed as a farm owner. However, three years later, when Tom passed away, Susannah Lane, a widowed White woman, sold a half acre of land to Tom's widow, Judith, and her son Moses. In 1811 Judith apparently bought an additional six acres of farmland, and three years later, in 1814, Moses sold the farm and left his mother in the Stoutsburg region, first to make his fortune in Montgomery Township and then in Middlesex County. Apparently his quest was successful. Fifteen years later he returned to Stoutsburg, bringing resources to purchase a 144-acre homestead in Hopewell and an additional 29 acres in Amwell for an impressive price of almost $4,000. A quarter acre of Blew's Hopewell property formed the nucleus of the present day Stoutsburg Cemetery. This was some of the same land that had once belonged to David Stout, which Stout's daughter Mary Sexton sold outright to Moses Blew. This was a strong example of how a personal relationship could triumph over law when it came to this generations-old, tight connection between these Black and White neighbors.[10]

Black and White family connections seemed to also be a factor in the manner in which the Truehart family came to own their property. Once again, we have not discovered exactly how the Truehart family came to own this land, but it most likely came from a man named Gabriel Hoff with whom the family may have had some semblance of friendship or acquaintance. Though Friday, the Truehart patriarch, could legally own land outright when he became free in 1802, it appears that it was not until 1828 that the land was legally recorded in his name. After that, the land was distributed among Truehart family members throughout the years for well over a century. During that time a total of three deeds were drawn up between Truehart family members, the first one in 1844, a year after Friday's death, when Friday's son Aaron and his wife, Eunice, along with his brother, Moses, and his wife, Eliza, sold 20 acres to their brother Isaac for $150.[11]

To think that Friday, once a slave boy of thirteen brought to the intimidating landscape of the Sourland Mountain region, was one day able to become a landowner after receiving his freedom from Anne Hart, the widow of his former master, greatly touches me. I marvel at the kind of tenacity it took for a man who, at that time, was obviously in his senior years to purchase land that would remain in the Truehart family for over a century. However, what was more surprising for me while researching these deeds in the Hunterdon County Records is when I noticed they were all recorded on the exact same day, April 27, 1899. How did it happen that deeds dating back over a half century had never been recorded? I needed to seek the advice of someone who would be able to offer an explanation of how this could have happened and whether this was a common occurrence for the time period, when it came to interfamily legal transactions.

I sought the advice of Joe Grabas, the land-title expert cited earlier in the chapter. Joe explained it was common practice among African Americans, particularly during that time in history, to keep important documents in a Bible or some other place of safekeeping locked away in their home, rather than to trust their precious documents to untrustworthy public authorities. He went on to point out several other impediments to recording a deed in a place of public record. First, getting to the county seat involved traveling some distance from home, and even for free African Americans it was considered risky to travel far beyond familiar surroundings, particularly in 1844, when the sale took place. In New Jersey, during this time period, African Americans were still subject to random stops by White people who could legally demand their accountability and could kidnap them and sell them into the South. One would think this threat would not be prevalent since the 1798 revision of the New Jersey slave code "that required that free blacks traveling outside their home County carry a certificate of freedom signed by two justices of the peace" (*Thomas Gibbons v. Isaac Morse*, NJL 1821).[12] But well into the 1850s such a risk remained all too real. Joe further explained that traveling to record a deed would possibly require having to find lodging to stay overnight or longer until the documents were recorded by hand. None of this was an easy prospect for early nineteenth-century African Americans traveling. Also—and perhaps more important—the Black landowner would have to trust White officials to keep their most valued document safe until it was recorded.

The Truehart land, which stayed within the family for well over a century, would later become the center of Charles Lindbergh's desperate attempt to add acreage to his famous estate. This is the unfortunate way in which Friday Truehart's grandson William one day came face-to-face with Charles Lindbergh.[13]

Charles Lindbergh, the aviator who made his fame flying nonstop across the Atlantic, quickly became America's fair-haired hero. When he married Anne Morrow in 1929 he became one of the wealthiest and most well-regarded individuals in America—let alone New Jersey. Supposedly it barely required a second thought when Charles and Anne happened across the isolated region Sourland Mountain range: they almost immediately knew this area would be the perfect place to construct their new home, a secluded spot that would guarantee the young family a place out of the prying eyes of the public. By 1931 their spectacular estate, which they named Highfields, was built. It wasn't long, though, before Lindbergh sought to increase the acreage that surrounded his newly constructed enclave. It was because of this quest that Lindbergh decided to knock on the door of William Truehart.

When the March 28, 1938, article in the *Baltimore Afro American* newspaper memorialized the 1932 death of William, or "Old Billy," Truehart, it could not do so without recounting the story of how one fateful day Old Billy, a Black man from the Sourland Mountain, came face-to-face America's icon, Charles Lindbergh.[14]

I can only imagine that when the knock came on the door, an

elderly Billy Truehart was not prepared to deal with the command of Lindbergh, who appeared before him holding a fistful of money and all but demanded that he be allowed to purchase Truehart's forty-three acres of land that abutted the Lindbergh estate. Interestingly, according to the description in the article, this land was not a desirable-looking parcel: the article went on to describe the Truehart land as a "wild, swampy section with a frame house located in the midst of a clearing." However, for Old Billy, there wasn't enough money in the world to entice him to sell the family homestead. The *Afro American* article further reported that Truehart was abrupt and told Lindbergh, "To some people their native home means everything—more than all the money in the world." With that, Truehart dismissed Lindbergh, locked his door, and went to stay with his niece Martha, telling her he would never sell as long as he lived.

It was reported that Old Billy was true to his word. Though he never returned to the family homestead, he refused to part with it. He ended up leasing the property to a couple who lived there up to 1938, when the article appeared in the *Afro American*. When Old Billy died at the age of eighty-seven, he had never married, back taxes had mounted on the property, and a public sale was imminent. The Trueharts had managed to keep the property within the family for over 105 years.

Another African American family who were significant land-owners were the Hagamans. The same family also spelled the name Hageman and Hagerman. I recalled the name because I remembered hearing it as a child so many years ago when my grandmother Herma would tell me stories about life on the Sourland Mountain on those steamy summer nights. Her father, Herbert Hubbard, was a relative of the Hagaman family. As a result I had to put my research hat on once again, to take another look at a story I grew up hearing about, one that would resurface again long after my grandmother's death. Why were my grandmother and her siblings named heirs in a tax sale notice concerning land once owned by the Hagaman family? Was this why my grandmother always held legal documents in a strongbox on the shelf in her bedroom closet? The mystery was soon to be solved.

Nestled in the corner of East Amwell is 44.8 acres of land once owned by the Hagamans, an African American family whose land bordered the western side of the future estate of Charles Lindbergh. It is unfortunate that documents do not reveal the exact year the Hageman family became landowners or how they came to purchase the land. What can be ascertained, though, is that the Hagaman family had been landowners prior to the death of patriarch John Hagaman in 1839, leaving his son Abraham executor of his will.[15]

In the Hagaman family, fathers continued to pass the land down to their sons; John to Abraham, Abraham to George, and George to David by 1866.[16] However, in 1927 when David died, leaving no children, the 44.8 acres was left to his niece Laura Belle Bergen and two nephews, David Bergen and my great-grandfather Herbert Hubbard.[17]

As answers to long-ago questions began to be revealed, it became clearer that this was the land my grandmother used to tell me about. It still did not explain, though, what happened to the land. A major clue was uncovered in my research when I read an article that appeared in the *Trenton Evening Times* on January 23, 1957, where it was reported that Richard Weber had outbid all interested parties by paying $3,200 for nearly 50 acres of land in two tax certificates that had been held since 1938 by Hopewell Township.[18] By July 5, 1957, a notice appeared once again in the *Trenton Times* summoning Hagaman heirs to satisfy the complaint or be considered in default with the intent to foreclose. Then, three months later on October 22, 1957, thirty years after the death of David Hagaman, a Notice of Defendants of Redemption appeared that listed the heirs associated with the Hagaman property, offering the opportunity for "foreclosing the equity of redemption of two tax sale certificates" for approximately 50 acres of land originally valued at $1,543.08.[19]

The story my grandmother told me on those summer evenings so long ago turned out to be true. Her father's relatives had been landowners in the Sourland Mountain region. How unfortunate it was that this story was attached to such a sad ending, that the heirs were unable to pool together enough money to settle the lien that appeared in a notice in the *Trenton Times* on October 22, 1957. The heirs would have been required to settle thirty years of tax arrears, not to mention being outbid from the outset. Raising $1,543.08 in 1957 was just not feasible; in today's dollars that would total $13,782.00.[20]

The examples I bring concerning past Black landownership have tragically all resulted in the loss of land. It makes me sad as I wonder how the lives of the Blew, Truehart, and Hagaman descendants might have been impacted if the circumstances had been different. If these properties had remained in the families, how would it have changed the trajectory of their lives? This question, I'm afraid, will continue to haunt me.

In spite of the extremely disappointing ending for the landowners discussed above, a different outcome emerged for the African American community as they sought land to establish houses of worship. These purchases, including the First Baptist Church of Pennington, the Second Calvary Baptist Church of Hopewell, the Bethel African Methodist Episcopal Church of Pennington (Bethel AME), and the Mount Zion African Methodist Episcopal Church of Skillman, were all made with the money of Black congregants. These transactions were also made possible in some cases through an arrangement or relationship with White supportive neighbors (as in the case of Bethel AME in Pennington).[21]

As we bring you our next chapter, Elaine opens the doors of the church to the world of our Black houses of worship and shows how the stewardship of these churches and land has endured. She will tell you how Second Calvary Baptist, First Baptist, and Mount Zion were formed over a century ago while Pennington's Bethel AME recently celebrated over two centuries of Black ownership. Elaine will further enlighten you on the traditions of the Black church and how each one served a particular portion of the African American community, as spiritual anchors in the Sourland Mountain region and surrounding area. We invite you to learn about how the church has always galvanized local African Americans to be of service in their respective communities and how the church provided solace to a population who tried to navigate through a world that regarded them as incidental beings in a world of Whiteness.

---

[1] New Jersey Office of Information Technology, "Nickname," Official Web Site of the State of New Jersey, accessed February 20, 2018, http://www.nj.gov/nj/about/facts/nickname/.

[2] Cooley, *A Study of Slavery in New Jersey.*

[3] "An Act for Regulating Slaves. Mar. 11, 1713/14, 2 Bush 136–140," March 11, 1713/14, accessed April 18, 2018, http://njlegallib.rutgers.edu/slavery/acts/A13.html.

[4] Joe Grabas, *Owning New Jersey: Historic Tales of War, Property Disputes & the Pursuit of Happiness* (Charleston, SC: The History Press, 2014), 13.

5   "TO BE SOLD A Likely Negroe Man, This Country Born, about 25 Years of Age, Understands All Sorts of Plantation Work, and Is a Good Miller; Also a Negroe Wench, This Country Born, about 15 Years of Age, and Understands All Kinds of House-Work, Is Sold for No Fault, but for Want of Employ. For Further Particulars Enquire of Cornelius Polhamus, Living in Hopewell, West New Jersey," *Pennsylvania Gazette*, no. 1891 (March 21, 1765).

6   T. James Luce, *New Jersey's Sourland Mountain* (Neshanic Station, NJ: Sourland Planning Council, 2001), 13.

7   Ibid., 1.

8   Richard W. Hunter and Richard Porter, *Hopewell: A Historical Geography* (Titusville, NJ: Township of Hopewell, Historic Sites Committee, 1990), 16.

9   Jack Davis, "From Slavery to Freedom," *Hopewell Valley Historical Society Newsletter* (Late Winter/Spring 2017): 835–36.

10 Ibid.

11 "Hageman, George. Will and Codicil of George Hageman. Hopewell Township, New Jersey, 18 September 1865. New Jersey Secretary of State Wills, Mercer County, #1722K. Recorded in Book D of Wills of Mercer County, New Jersey, Folio 450" (Trenton, NJ, n.d.).

12 Grabas, *Owning New Jersey*.

13 "Old Billy Truehart Loved Home, Defied Lindbergh," *Baltimore Afro American*, March 28, 1938, 4.

14 Ibid.A

15 "Last Will and Testament of Abraham H. Hageman. Recorded in Book D of Wills of Mercer County, New Jersey, Folio 450. Sworn and Subscribed September 13, 1839, but Recorded September 5, 1866" (Mercer County, NJ, 1866).

16 Last Will and Testament of George Hagaman—Recorded in Book D of Wills of Mercer County, New Jersey, Folio 460, September 11, 1866, n.d.

17 "Hageman, David S. Will and Codicil of David S. Hageman. Princeton, New Jersey, 10 April 1922. New Jersey Secretary of State Wills, Mercer County, #K6592" (Trenton: New Jersey State Archives, n.d.); 2016 Property Location Map, Feather Bed Lane, Hopewell Township, Current Block and Lots of David Hagaman Land, (David Hagaman Property) (Office of Planning: Mercer County Administration Building, 640 South Broad Street, Trenton, NJ, n.d.).

18 "Bids on Land Run Up Price: Hart's Corner (Laura Bergen Hicks)," *Trenton Times*, January 23, 1957, accessed April 18, 2108, GenealogyBank.com.

19 "Notice of Defendants of Redemption [Listed Heirs Associated with the Hagaman Property Offering the Opportunity for 'Foreclosing the Equity of Redemption of Two Tax Sale Certificates,'" *Trenton Evening Times*, October 22, 1957.

20 "Deed of March 8, 1850 between Joshua Bunn & Wife to Samuel Blackwell, Thomas Ten Eyke and George Stout—Trustees of Bethel AME Church. Recorded Volume S of Deeds, Page 114, Office of the Clerk of Mercer County, New Jersey" (Mercer County, NJ, 1850).

21 Ibid.

Bethel AME Church of Pennington, New Jersey, and
Mt. Zion AME Church of Skillman, New Jersey

CHAPTER 6

THE IMPORTANCE OF THE AFRICAN AMERICAN CHURCH

by ELAINE BUCK

O! Jesus, hope of glory, come, And make my heart thy humble home; For the sort remnant of my days, I want to sing and shout thy praise.

—Richard Allen, hymn, 1801

In the last chapter Beverly, my friend of over thirty years and writing partner, explored the significance of landownership as one of the only—and very limited—sources of empowerment for African Americans in our little corner of the woods in central New Jersey. We made some surprising discoveries about land records that demonstrated that our ancestors sustained a too often overlooked presence in the community. A natural extension of that historical exploration brings us to the centrality of the church and all of the many contributions of church leaders in our ancestors' lives.

My given name is Sharon Elaine Buck, but I've always been called Elaine. I was a young girl full of innocence in the early 1960s, when I first visited the Bethel African Methodist Episcopal (AME) Church of Pennington, New Jersey, founded by Richard Allen. I remember the musty smell when I walked in the door, the flecks of dust waltzing in the sun's rays. I thought to myself, man this place must really be old. As the founder of Mother Bethel in Philadelphia (the first AME Church) Richard Allen has been so important to the development of countless African American communities, not to mention a central figure in my own church history. His visionary genius paved the way for Blacks to not only worship freely but to enact social change, contributions I will be discussing at great length in the chapter.

When I walked into the beautiful AME church, as a child, my thoughts weren't yet with Richard Allen. Not yet knowing about Allen or his legacy in my own community, I was content to gaze upon the colorful portrait of Jesus that hung over the pulpit. Painted by Earl Hubbard, a much-loved local violinist and artist in the 1950s (and Beverly's great-uncle) the portrait made me feel as though I'd stepped centuries back in time. I suppose I was literally a "baby Christian" then, where the high-backed wooden benches, wide-planked floors, and antique hues all added to the spiritual ambiance. In this place surrounded by beauty, I felt safe and empowered.

LOCAL CHURCHES IN THE HOPEWELL VALLEY REGION & DIFFERENT STYLES OF WORSHIP

In the Hopewell Valley and Sourland Mountain region there were four main African American churches that served as our houses of worship. That Sunday in the early 1960s the Second Calvary Baptist Church of Hopewell, which was my home church, was visiting

Pennington, New Jersey's Bethel AME, Beverly's church at the time, as we had often done. We joined with Pennington's First Baptist Church and the Mt. Zion AME Church of Skillman congregations to promote a fundraiser, one of many common occasions where the churches would work together to benefit the host church. Church members often got together not only to worship but to share a meal, socialize, and support each other, Baptist or Methodist. Indeed, for the African American community often the church represented an important symbol of property ownership and a seat of community life where Black people could gather together like this and support each other freely, and without reprisal.

Spiritual anchoring has been a tradition of many early Black American communities and was part of the fabric of my own family. Going to church on Sunday was not an option. It was an understanding. Even the teenagers and young adults of the church community knew if we stayed out late on Saturday night there would be no chance to sleep in on Sunday because it was Sunday School, and it was Church, and it was not open for discussion! I didn't mind, however, because the music always drew me in. The church music became an extension of my Saturday night dance music, because it was so good, and the beat was so uplifting. At my own church, Second Calvary Baptist, the music bordered on rhythm and blues, jazz, and a little bit of everything else. It made me want to stand up and dance in the name of the Lord. My family was so involved in the church and its music that in the 1970s I played the piano, while my Uncle Ronnie played the drums. Even at home, my family sang gospel music with as much fervor as we did at church.

In Beverly's family, church attendance was not particularly at the top of their list, as her parents were not churchgoers themselves. Both her mother and father came from mothers who were serious about church, and her grandparents were convinced it was up to them to "right the ship" when it came to be setting an example on her behalf. Every once in a while, one of Beverly's grandmothers, or sometimes a cousin who stopped by for a Sunday visit—usually after service in the afternoon— would ask why they did not go to church. Her folks' response were variations of, "I just can't stand all that 'hoopin' and hollerin' that some of these preachers do!" and "That's not preaching to us." In Beverly's household, the message was clear: praising the Lord with too much vim and vigor was not how some Blacks were to conduct themselves in church. It seemed the more you could imitate the "White way" of worshipping, with quiet unreadable reverence, the more acceptable.

The style of worship at Bethel AME Church in Pennington, New Jersey, neatly fits into the category of a restrained "joyful noise unto the Lord" whereas the First Baptist Church, around the corner, did not have a problem with parishioners "feeling the spirit," or as it was also commonly known, "getting happy." Oh yes, they got happy at the Baptist churches, First Baptist in Pennington and Second Calvary in Hopewell, but not in a Pentecostal way! That was a whole other level of "bein' slain in the spirit," because most times in the Baptist church they would rarely speak in tongues or roll on the floor! Though Beverly's family tried to convince her parents that their Minister did not preach that way and they should come and see for themselves, that never happened, except for the obligatory Christmas and Easter visitations. Since both of Beverly's grandmothers encouraged her to go to church and she valued their opinions, Beverly took it upon herself to go to Sunday School at Bethel AME.

At the time I sat in the Bethel AME church, I was too young to realize just how much was changing in the 1950s and 1960s and what was at stake. I wasn't aware of the policy changes that were playing out in America at that time, of how many had to fight, repeatedly, for those changes, or of how integral the church was during not just the civil rights movement but even further back than I could have imagined. The desegregation of schools and voting rights came to the forefront of the news, progress that was unheard of in earlier generations. I remember my grandmother, who'd been illiterate most of her life, and the gleeful smile that beamed from her face when she first wrote her name on a ballot. She'd learned to read and write from a teacher at my school, finally allowing her access to a basic American right—voting. How had we gone from slavery to this?—I wondered. But more importantly, why had it taken so long? The central role of the churches in the pursuit of social justice was something I'd learn much later in life.

The influence of Black churches began way ahead of the civil rights movement, perhaps most significantly with Richard Allen's opening of Bethel Church in Philadelphia and the founding of the African Methodist Episcopal denomination, to which I've devoted most of this chapter. These milestones would soon leave their mark in our hometown and our own lives.

RICHARD ALLEN: FOUNDER OF THE BETHEL AME CHURCH

I first came across Richard Allen's name when I was about thirteen. Our pastor, Rev. John A. Gaines, was speaking as the guest preacher at Bethel AME that steamy summer Sunday afternoon. I remember the elderly church mothers sitting in the front pews. Dressed all in white, their heads covered with white lace doilies gave the collective the appearance of a field of lilies of the valley. Because of the uncompromising heat, the windows were opened to catch whatever breeze we secretly prayed would bless us with its circling. The paper fans the ushers passed out had images of finely dressed Black couples and families on the backs of them, and the music was so loud that I'm certain the neighbors, especially Ms. Leona Stewart next door, could hear not just every note but every breath in between. I can still recall the choir and Mrs. Helen Driver cheerfully singing "I Surrender All" in her high soprano voice, Mr. Donald Jennings accompanying her on the organ in a metrical beat that I had never heard before. The congregation kept time by clapping and clicking their heels on the wooden floors.

As I glanced through the *AME Church Hymnal*, I noticed a song that began, "O God my heart with love enflame."[1] I was not familiar with this song nor its author: Bishop Richard Allen (Tribute to Our Founder), the Hymnal read. As I continued to read the words of the song, I began to realize that this Bishop Richard Allen was someone that should be revered. I wanted to know who he was, because I already had a hunger for more information about Black historical figures. At the time, I didn't have any idea what a central figure Richard Allen was in American history or where I could learn more about him. I would only later learn how Bethel AME and Mount Zion AME played such a pivotal role in anchoring the Black community.

In 1794, Richard Allen founded the first national Black church in the United States, which was officially established in 1816. The African Methodist Episcopal Church of Philadelphia, called Mother Bethel, became a safe haven for African Americans to worship. As I mentioned above, it also provided safety for people to gather and freely discuss how to continue the fight for social justice. In its earliest years, the church housed escaping slaves, financially supported the Underground Railroad, and assisted newly freed people to re-establish themselves. The control center for community worship, Mother Bethel quickly became the place where organization for social change began. Its activism didn't end with slavery, however, but continued well after the civil rights movement. The website of Mother Bethel, as well as many scholars, have documented Mother Bethel's leadership. A number of distinguished leaders, including Frederick Douglass and Martin Luther King, Jr, have spoken at Mother

Bethel, and it continues to be a beacon today.[2]

Richard Allen, born in 1760, spent the first years of his life as the slave of Benjamin Chew, a Quaker lawyer. Chew, though born a Quaker, left the faith in the early 1750's for the Church of England, which had fewer scruples with slave-ownership. An influential member of Pennsylvania society, Chew became the Penn family's attorney, and then Chief Justice. Nevertheless, despite close friendships with George Washington and John Adams, Chew's loyalty to the crown led to his arrest and imprisonment in New Jersey during the American Revolution, and to the temporary loss of his home Cliveden, which was commandeered by the British and damaged in the Battle of Germantown.[3]

The Quaker faith has often been described as synonymous with the abolitionist movement, so it surprised me to learn that there were Quakers who owned slaves. Quakers, (also known as members of the Religious Society of Friends) like other English settlers, owned slaves, before morality won out for some. Among the strongest opponents of the slave trade, many Quakers had decided that they could not reconcile their faith with the practice of owning humans as property. The epistle or directive from the 1758 Annual Meeting in London, dispatched to Quakers in the colonies such as Pennsylvania, Virginia, and New Jersey, asked their colonial Friends to avoid "the unrighteous profits arising from that iniquitous practice of dealing in negroes and other slaves; whereby in the original purchase one man selleth [sic] another as he doth the beast," which is a "direct violation of the Gospel rule," regarding how one treats others. The London Religious Society of Friends continued its rejection of slave-ownership, urging its members to "keep their hands clear of this unrighteous gain of oppression." At Pennsylvania's regional gathering of Friends, that same year, some members decided to visit the homes of slave-owners to ensure slaves were treated humanely, and to convince their owners to free their slaves. Over succeeding years, this peer pressure led to the barring of slave-owners from being leaders and, finally, to the outright disowning of slaveholders as Quaker members. This adjustment of ideals even led some Friends to become active in the Underground Railroad, working alongside black organizers, as some of the station masters and abolitionist fighters that fill our history books and general consciousness today.[4]

In 1768 Chew sold Richard Allen, along with his parents and siblings, to Stokely Sturgis of Delaware. It was under Sturgis's ownership that Richard Allen attended the Methodist church, where he felt such a deep spiritual connection that soon he was preaching himself. Meanwhile, upon hearing the sermon of Freeborn Garretson, an ex-slave owner turned minister, Sturgis was deeply moved and found himself "wanting" in the eyes of the Lord.[5] As a result, Sturgis felt compelled to free his slaves, but financially he couldn't make the commitment due to his mounting debts. Historian Gary Nash suggests that Allen's conversion, devotion to the Methodist faith, and subsequent preaching was the catalyst for Sturgis's change of heart and desire to free Allen. Allen, eager to seize the opportunity, worked out an agreement with Sturgis to pay off the astronomical amount of two thousand Continental dollars, the U.S.'s first currency minted during the Revolutionary War, to purchase his freedom in five years.[6]

The possibility of freedom drove Allen, who said in his autobiography, "I had it often impressed upon my mind that I should one day enjoy my freedom; for slavery is a bitter pill, notwithstanding we had a good master. But when we think that our day's work was never done, we often thought that after our master's death we were liable to be sold to the highest bidder, as he was much in debt; and thus my troubles were increased, and I was often brought to weep between the porch and the altar. But I have had reason to bless my dear Lord that a door was opened unexpectedly for me to buy my time, and enjoy my liberty."[7]

In his quest to earn money and obtain his freedom, Allen worked several jobs and placed himself in a perilous situation, driving a salt wagon when he must have been around sixteen years old for the Continental Army during the Revolutionary War. Salt wagons were often ambushed by British troops, but Allen was able to elude capture. At the same time, Allen was able to develop his reputation as a preacher throughout the communities where he traveled. By 1783 he was able to buy his freedom from Sturgis, roughly two years ahead of schedule. He soon began preaching to congregations both Black and White, including at St. George's Methodist Episcopal Church in Philadelphia.[8]

THE BLACK CODES & FREEDOM OF ASSEMBLY

It is important to imagine the environment Allen faced when he took to the pulpit as a free Black man in the late eighteenth and early nineteenth century. While White congregants found themselves enraptured by this new Black preacher, Allen's speaking went against the current of White public opinion and the sweeping collection of laws commonly referred to as the Black Codes. These laws were explicitly designed to control the activity of free Blacks and slaves. Also called the Slave Codes, these types of laws were based on King Louis XIV's 1685 *Code Noir* for the French colonies.[9] The first U.S. colony to adopt the codes was Virginia in 1705.[10] Many colonies soon followed using Virginia's model, altering it like a hand-me-down dress to suit each colony's unique style of oppression.

Slave codes were designed to do far more than inhibit movement of free people of color. Though the individual characteristics and penalties varied by state, the laws generally focused on prohibiting people of color from owning property, preventing intermarriage with Whites or testifying against Whites, and, in New Jersey for example, forcing their free-born children into servitude until age twenty-one or twenty-four for women and men, respectively. After different states mandated abolition, such laws became a brutally clever way of legally owning people who were allegedly free, by codifying subordination to prevent their ability to advance.[11] Such restrictive laws, for instance, would certainly deter Blacks from freedom of assembly and the ability to form churches.

Thus, Allen began his preaching career just as Northern states limped toward abolition, but repressive laws remained on the books. The state in which Allen preached, the Commonwealth of Pennsylvania, as well as the neighboring colony of New Jersey, had its own laws designed to differentiate the treatment of free Blacks and slaves. In 1706 in Pennsylvania, crimes considered to be a capital offense carried different penalties according to whether the offender was Black or White. That same year the Pennsylvania Assembly passed a law that prohibited Blacks from meeting together in great companies, but this statute was not widely known because a similar ban was petitioned in 1723.[12] In 1726 when the Quakers controlled the Pennsylvania Assembly, a law was enacted to restrict free Black people based on skin color. Although this law was considered to be less restrictive than those in other colonies, slaves were still required to carry a pass if they traveled from their masters. If a master planned to manumit his slaves, he would be required to post a bond worth thirty pounds. This amount was substantially lower than the requirement of two hundred pounds in New York and New Jersey.[13] No matter the amount charged or how much lawmakers tried to rationalize that the funds were necessary, the intent was the same—to make slave manumissions as financially onerous as possible.

Slaves could *not* freely assemble in groups or stray five miles from their master's property without a pass. The 1704 Act for Regulating

Negro, Indian and Mallatto Slaves specified: "No one to buy anything from or sell anything to a slave; slaves found over ten miles from master's home to be apprehended and whipped and returned; slaves from other provinces without written license from masters to be whipped and jailed; provisions for trial and punishment of slaves for various crimes."[14] In Pennsylvania, these restrictive laws were largely nullified with the state's 1780 decision to emancipate its slaves. A gradual emancipation took place, resulting in some African Americans in the state still being slaves as late as 1840. In New Jersey, the original Act of Gradual Abolishment was passed in 1804,[15] but slavery was not officially abolished until 1846.[16]

Ironically, though the Pennsylvania emancipation law of 1780 did precious little to change the current lives of the state's slaves, it made a near instantaneous difference on the population of African Americans already free. No longer subject to the restrictive laws that marked the previous time, free Blacks were suddenly bestowed with something akin to citizenship, finally able to exercise their inalienable rights and have control over their personal and financial affairs and that of their offspring. In some Western Pennsylvania counties, those rights apparently even extended to voting.

What does all of this legal history have to do with the church besides demonstrating that gathering to worship was a hard-won battle? Well, during the early-mid 1800s, newly independent free Blacks and the newly emancipated slaves sought the church for guidance both spiritual and social, and Reverend Richard Allen's star turned out to be ascending at the right time.

As free African Americans, such as Richard Allen, rejected the idea of being relegated to second-class citizenship, they began to make efforts to found their own churches. Segregation and discriminatory policies of most White churches made integration nearly impossible and was the catalyst for the founding of Black denominational churches. The need to develop independent Black churches was the overarching goal, as parishioners longed for a place of worship where they would not be segregated to the balconies of the White churches or required to follow restricted laws. Richard Allen led by example.[17]

THE ST. GEORGE'S EXODUS AND THE BIRTH OF THE AME CHURCH

One historic morning in 1787 Rev. Allen was preaching at St. George Methodist Episcopal Church in Philadelphia, where he was joined by Absalom Jones. Jones, also a former slave, would later found the African Episcopal Church of St. Thomas. The White and Black parishioners of St. George's Church had recently been segregated in no small part due to Allen's preaching attracting more Black congregants and the chagrin of some of the White parishioners. When Jones and Allen defied White church elders by sitting in the downstairs of the church instead of the balcony, it was perceived as an insult to White congregants. The church owed a fair portion of its current prosperity to its Black preacher and Black parishioners, yet they were treated like second-class citizens. Moreover, the elders refused Allen's requests to create a church of their own. Some White people firmly held the belief that the supposedly inferior minds of Black people made them incapable to correctly run the business of a church.[18]

When Allen and Jones knelt down to pray at the altar that morning in 1787, White elders attempted to physically remove the two men. Allen wasn't having that. This caused a considerable disruption, and Allen described the violent scene as the White men tried to drag them off their knees, even after Jones' repeated that they would move only after their prayer. Later, furious and disheartened, Allen recalled, "we were treated like heathens" rather than brothers in Christ. Therefore, after Allen and Jones finished their prayers, they left the building with the other Black parishioners, promising never to trouble the White congregation again.[19] It was a promise the pair would keep even though their religious beliefs led them to part ways, at least spiritually, and form different churches.[20]

Their famous 1787 exodus from St. George's was not the last time that Allen and Jones would work side by side, nor was it the last time they would witness impossible barriers in achieving recognition for their contributions to the White community. For instance, during the Philadelphia Yellow Fever epidemic of 1793, just before the birth of the AME church, Allen and Jones received a letter from Dr. Benjamin Rush, one of the signers of the Declaration of Independence and former Surgeon General for the Continental Troops. He needed help. Since Rush believed that African Americans were immune to Yellow Fever, a viral infection transmitted through a mosquito bite, Blacks were thought to be in a unique position to help the sick. Allen, Jones, and Black abolitionist, William Gray, among many others, were recruited to help. Black people served as nurses and grave-diggers as the death toll climbed to epic proportions. Unfortunately, Dr. Rush was to learn that he was wrong in his assumption about African Americans' apparent immunity to Yellow fever. Many African Americans died during this epidemic. Richard Allen, also stricken with the dreadful illness, was blessed to have survived.[21]

After the epidemic subsided, I would have expected that Allen, Jones, and the others who risked their lives nursing the sick and handling dead bodies to have been hailed as heroes. They were not. Conversely, they were accused of being money hungry opportunists. Matthew Carey, a resident and publisher from Philadelphia, distributed a pamphlet in 1793, on the heels of the epidemic's end. In it, the African Americans who assisted Allen and Jones during the Yellow Fever crisis were made out to be villains. Carey hailed the White community and successful Philadelphia businessman, Stephen Girard, as heroes for their efforts in constructing a hospital outside the city limits.[22]

In Allen's efforts to change the single-story narrative, a phenomenon many minorities still face today, Richard Allen counteracted by distributing a pamphlet of his own defending the actions of African Americans. Though Allen's pamphlet came just one year after the outbreak, by 1794 Carey's pamphlet was in its fourth edition. Allen was not deterred however, as the AME church was conceived from protesting injustice.[23]

The Blacks parishioners who left St. George's in 1787 first turned to the Free African Society (FAS), formed by Allen and Jones. According to Paul Lawrence Dunbar, societies like the FAS and Prince Hall Masons, the African American masonic lodge incorporated in 1775, served as a place where members could provide "mutual aid" and tackle the "social, political, and economic problems" that plagued African Americans.[24] Allen helped to minister to the spiritual needs of those in the group as well. Over time, the FAS began to take on some of the trappings of Quaker culture, since many Quakers were admired for their abolitionist views, philanthropy, and moral rectitude. In fact, the FAS charter mandated that all treasurers of the society were to be Quakers. This would also help facilitate the Society's dealings with White financial institutions. While the aid the FAS provided was important to him, it was not enough. Allen needed to answer his spiritual calling.[25]

By 1794 Allen formally founded the Bethel Church in Philadelphia, after he and other "exiles" raised money on their own. Beginning in an abandoned blacksmith shop, Mother Bethel was born from just over one hundred parishioners. By 1805, the church matured to nearly five hundred.[26] Notables like Benjamin Rush and, according to records in

Mother Bethel church history, even George Washington contributed to the effort. In fact, George Washington donated to the building of the African Church in Philadelphia.[27] Allen would deliver a eulogy for George Washington at his church in 1799. To Allen, Washington was a leader who failed to see the evils of slavery early on, but eventually saw the light. According to Allen, Washington managed to "wipe off the only stain with which man could ever reproach him" by not only immediately freeing and providing an annuity for his personal "manservant William Lee" in his will but also by stipulating that all the slaves in his possession would be freed upon his wife's death.

Despite Allen's stellar reputation and the church's growth in membership, the fight for autonomy was not over yet, and the General Assembly from White Methodists tried to take control of Allen's Church.[28] Trouble came during incorporation in 1796 when a trustee from St. George's tricked Richard Allen into signing over Mother Bethel's land to the Methodist Conference, essentially transferring ownership to St. George's and the Methodist Church. In turn, they were repeatedly outmaneuvered by Allen, who blocked their attempts to preach at the church by ensuring a preacher was already on the pulpit when they arrived, inhibiting their ability to wade through the impenetrable congregation, and leveraging the support of "respectable White citizens who knew the colored people had been ill-used."[29]

This dispute lasted over a decade, and the case eventually went to the Pennsylvania Supreme court in 1807. The courts ruled that the Black Methodist parishioners owned the property, and they could determine who preached there. Joining with a Black church in Baltimore, which suffered similar injustices, in 1816 the African Methodist Episcopal was officially formed and recognized by the Methodist Church with Allen named as its first Bishop.[30]

Mother Bethel went well beyond attending to the community's

spiritual needs. Pastors were free to preach about abolishing slavery, and the church basement served as an Underground Railroad stop where Allen and his second wife, Sarah, hid runaway slaves. Allen felt passionately about the importance of education, so the church was also used as a day school for children and a night school for adults. The church was more than just a place of worship. It was also a place of advocacy and protection.

One struggle for Allen and his followers came in the form of the American Colonization Society (ACS), which surfaced just as the AME Church was officially recognized in 1816. Some Whites, especially Robert Finley, a Presbyterian minister from Basking Ridge, New Jersey, championed plans that called for a forced migration of Blacks to Africa. Finley was trying to appease two groups on the subject of what to do with freed African Americans. One group was the slave owners who were afraid that free people of color threatened their livelihood. The second group included some abolitionists and clergy who wanted to free American slaves, and provide them with transportation back to Africa, where they would form a new colony. Both groups agreed that they didn't want free blacks living in America. At the time several million Black people lived on American soil; 200,000 of them were free. On December 21, 1816, at the Davis Hotel in Washington, DC, southern congressman Henry Clay met with an exclusive group of powerful White males including James Monroe, Francis Scott Key, Daniel Webster and Bushrod Washington (President Washington's nephew). Clay is quoted as saying that because of "unconquerable prejudice resulting from their color, they [Blacks] never could amalgamate with the free Whites of this country."[31]

By 1819, Congress awarded the ACS $100,000 and provided a ship to transport these free people. When James Madison signed an ACS membership certificate, in 1833, memberships throughout the

United States grew rapidly. More than 13,000 African Americans had emigrated from the United States to the colony of Liberia by 1867. Though Richard S. Newman and other scholars suggest that Allen may not have opposed Black migration in theory, he vehemently opposed what many of these plans lacked in practice: African American autonomy and the rights of people of color to enjoy the benefits of American citizenship.

Allen wrote about this, saying: "Africans have made fortunes for thousands, who are yet unwilling to part with their services; but the free must be sent away, and those who remain, must be slaves. I have no doubt that there are many good men who do not see as I do, and who are sending us to Liberia; but they have not duly considered the subject—they are not men of colour.—This land which we have watered with our tears and our blood, is now our mother country, and we are well satisfied to stay where wisdom abounds and the gospel is free.[32]

Allen took on the challenge of helping freed slaves avoid this deportation. He called a mass meeting on January 15, 1817, to discuss the problem of free Blacks not receiving United States citizenship and being sent back to Africa. The AME church helped many newly freed people find homes and work. The church also fought against unjust policies and organizations with questionable motives.

RICHARD ALLEN IN PENNINGTON, NEW JERSEY

Allen's teachings took hold and blossomed right in my backyard. In fact, Allen traveled here to Pennington, New Jersey in 1784 and resided with a local White family, Jonathan and Mary Bunn, for at least six months. Cutting wood by day to serve his earthly needs and preaching by night to serve those of heaven, he likely interacted with many area residents, sowing seeds which would grow to create his early AME congregation. When I learned about Allen's connection to Hopewell Valley, it's hard to explain how humbled I felt thinking about this great man actually living in our region, to read his words describing his stay in the area and his fondness and admiration for the Bunn family, a Methodist couple whom he describes as a "father and mother of Israel."[33] The significance of Allen's historical footprint in our community has been passed down and taught by the African Methodist Episcopal Church.

One of the oldest churches in the state of New Jersey, the Bethel African Methodist Episcopal Church of Pennington was founded as a sister church to Allen's Philadelphia Mother Bethel. This began the founding of many other AME churches throughout New Jersey. For the Bethel AME Church in Pennington, New Jersey, their humble beginnings in some ways echoed the original group that met in its little blacksmith shop in Philadelphia. Pennington Methodists met in each other's homes until their church was formally built. It was his old friends, the Bunn family, eager to spread the Methodist gospel to their Black neighbors, who formed the very first Methodist Church in Pennington in 1816. For the sum of seventy-five dollars church trustees Samuel Blackwell, Thomas Ten Eyke, and George Stout purchased land from Joshua Bunn and his wife, Fanny, to build a house of worship.

Over six decades after the initial relationship had been established by Richard Allen and Jonathan Bunn (1744-1815), Joshua Bunn's father, the church was built in 1847. The foundation of the relationship between Allen and Jonathan and Mary Bunn must have been strong indeed, if more than half a century later Bunn's son, Joshua, provided the very land where the Bethel AME Church would be built.

As Joshua Bunn was born in 1783, he was just an infant when Allen resided with his family in 1784. It is inspiring to see the unbreakable bond that must have existed between Allen and the Bunns at a time where inequality between Black and White was the world order. It gives me hope; for though we still have a ways to go, it doesn't mean we can't get there. It also shows the power of the church in bringing people together.

Though Allen died in 1831, his contributions to African American religion and equality created a legacy that is still felt today, particularly in my own community. Richard Allen's abolitionist teachings, writing and sermons as well as his political activism organizations have had a longstanding legacy in national and local churches that bear his name.

EMANCIPATION AND THE TRADITION OF WATCH NIGHT

Another powerful example, showing the Black church's role for building community and support, beyond a place of worship, is the tradition of "Watch Night," a service that originated in the Methodist Church in celebration of the Emancipation Proclamation. As the new law was to be enacted on January 1, 1863, all across the country free Blacks gathered in churches, like Mother Bethel, on New Year's Eve 1862 waiting to hear if their brothers and sisters in bondage were free. Families waited for news via anything from telegraph to word of mouth. Would it actually happen? Sure enough, they learned that at the stroke of midnight Lincoln signed the document stating that slaves in the Confederate states were legally free.[34]

I imagine the feelings on that New Year's Eve must have been cooked with a recipe of particular excitement, perhaps a generous dash of fear, mixed with a sprinkle of disbelief. There must have been shouts of joy and true jubilation that first free dawn. This tradition has passed down from generation to generation, every New Year's Eve. It is still celebrated in many churches to this day. In our church, the Second Calvary Baptist

Church, our Watch Night Service begins at 10 p.m. It is an evening celebrated with songs, prayers, and testimonies about how far the Lord has brought us. We start our service with foot-stomping praise and worship songs that make you want to clap your hands and do a dance. The congregation is invited to give a personal testimony of how the Lord has blessed them throughout the year, and we partake in the sacrament of holy communion as a sign of remembrance that Jesus Christ died for our sins and is coming back again for His believers. A service of prayers and a rousing sermon is given by the Pastor until the stroke of midnight. Cheers of jubilee, tears of joy, and shouts of hallelujah fill the air in the sanctuary as we welcome a new year.

Immediately following the service, a southern soul food meal is served. For as far back as I can remember, my ancestors have held fast to the superstitious legend that eating black-eyed peas on New Year's Day brought you good luck. Legend has it that eating black-eyed peas represented prosperity, and the golden color of cornbread is believed to represent gold or coin money. Whatever the case may be, this meal served with rice and along with pigs-feet, has been passed down through the years and is enjoyed as we share our first meal of the New Year together. This tradition most likely dates back to the celebration meal eaten during the Emancipation celebration in 1863. Black-eyed peas were traditionally known to be eaten by slaves, especially during the winter months. Not many crops grew that time of the year, but black-eyed peas held up well. It was a cheap meal to prepare by using smoked pork to season the dirty tasting peas and collard greens.

Of course, for freed slaves in the Methodist church during the very first Watch Night in 1863, their temporary joy marked the beginning of a new trail of struggles and more sorrows. With freedom arose a multitude of complexities and challenges that were linked to the institution that had finally crumbled ... at least in name. When

I asked my great-grandmother Ada Hightower if her parents who were slaves left as soon as they found out they were free, her answer was surprising to me. She said they didn't leave because they had nowhere to go. The laws had changed, but circumstances, financial and practical, had not.

Freedom in both the North and the South did not come with land or homes or jobs and, being sent as refugees to another country wasn't the solution either. Freed slaves were not truly free. They were, however, considered quite expensive. Though the Confederate slave-owners who signed allegiance to the Union would soon receive compensation for the lost "property" freed by Lincoln's proclamation, the slaves who had spent years and generations forced to labor for another's wealth received nothing. Soon they were being arrested for "vagrancy" after being made homeless, put back to work at plantations to pay for their alleged crimes, or coerced into sharecropping which with its exorbitant rent, in some ways, left the newly freed people feeling worse off than when they were slaves.[35]

After the Civil War in our neck of the woods, the Bethel AME served as a cornerstone in our region, a day school for African American children under the direction of school superintendent and Civil War veteran William Boyer. As I noted earlier about the power of our local church community, Bethel AME in Pennington was joined by other African American churches that were formed after Emancipation such as Mt. Zion AME of Skillman, Mt. Zion AME of Rocky Hill, Second Calvary Baptist Church of Hopewell, and First Baptist Church of Pennington. Right from the start, these churches supported each other financially and socially as many friends and relatives connected one congregation to another.

AME AND BEYOND: OUR AFRICAN AMERICAN CHURCH COMMUNITY

According to information gleaned from local church and oral history, new Black Baptist churches were formed by the late 1800s and early 1900s, strengthening the connective tissue of the already established AME congregants in the region. The establishment of local Black churches during this period seemed to coincide with Black people who relocated to the region, many from Virginia and North Carolina, shortly before the Great Migration. The same as their predecessors who formed the AME church by meeting in private homes a century earlier in the region, the First Baptist Church of Pennington began in 1902 with a small band of Baptists who gathered with one another in their houses. By 1904, two years later, the First Baptist Church body was able to locate a building, which formerly served as the Borough's public school.

Similarly, the Second Calvary Baptist Church of Hopewell, first known as the First Colored Calvary Church of Hopewell, was formed between 1894 and 1895 from the humble beginning of people meeting to worship in their homes. The first pastor to shepherd Second Calvary was Thomas Johnson who migrated from the South, as did Virginia-born Thomas Crawley, who was the first pastor at the First Baptist Church in Pennington. The common thread among these migrants and the Black people already here was their need for a place to gather and worship in peace.

Of course, before Black churches began to form, whenever they were able to, Blacks by and large attended White churches. Throughout the years of research, Beverly and I have had interest in one White Church in particular, the Old School Baptist Church. Beverly's ancestor, Friday Trueheart attended The Old School Baptist Church 1780-1843. She and I both have often wondered what Friday must have experienced as a free Black man in a predominately White church. When the Old School Baptist Church was first formed in the early to mid 1700s, how were Black members treated? Were they afforded the respect and dignity of the White members of the congregation? Clues to this question became clearer when we read entries in the *Town Records of Hopewell, New Jersey*, that listed the names of early Black parishioners at the Old School Baptist Church.[36] These Black colonials were generally only listed by their first names. I have bolded our relatives.

September 14, 1799	James, a Black, **Friday, a Black**
September 21, 1799	William Stiver (Stives) a Black
December 15, 1799	Judy a Black
December 25, 1803	**Jude**, a slave of Jacob Blackwell
April 18, 1807	Samuel, a Black (dismissed)
September 23, 1809	Catherine, a Black woman
November 26, 1809	**Juda Shue, wife of Friday**
March 1812	Off, a Black belonging to Hezekiah Stout
During Spring 1813	Dinah, Hezekiah Stout's Black girl

OSBC Persons Dismissed, Deceased, Etc.

1832	Amy, a colored woman, deceased
August 24, 1839	**William Stives "An aged colored member"**
August 26, 1843	Friday Truehart deceased, an aged colored member

Excommunications

September 16, 1769	Nelly, a Black, for bearing a bastard child

See full list at end of this chapter.

As we researched the familiar names listed in these church records, we wondered if William Stives and Friday Trueheart would have been able to give voice on behalf of their still enslaved Black brethren listed right next to their names? Could they dare? Or, was the inferred message from their fellow White congregants that they were welcomed at the church only so long as their voices and concerns remained silent? If they had been members of Black churches, might Stives and Trueheart have played more significant leadership roles such as stewards, trustees, or deacons?

It must have taken considerable determination to establish Black places of worship and support. While Bethel AME served a dual role by seeing to the community's spiritual and educational needs, according to oral histories recorded in the *Princeton Recollector*, the Mt. Zion Church focused on spreading the word of the Gospel through revivals and Camp Meetings, which started at the end of the nineteenth century.

COMMUNITY REVIVALS AND CAMP MEETINGS

Back then, there was no social event more important to the community than the Camp Meeting. Originally Camp Meetings ran the last two Sundays in July through the first two Sundays in August. Camp meetings were held to financially benefit the Skillman Mt. Zion AME Church which, sadly, closed its doors as a place of worship in 2005. Everyone, Black and White, young and old, looked forward to this event. Beverly remembers her aunts and uncles and, in particular, her grandmother, Herma, talking about the Camp Meetings. In October 1975, the *Princeton Recollector*, a now defunct local newspaper published by the Princeton History project, ran an article memorializing oral histories of some of the elders who had years of history in our local churches and in the African American community.[37] It was over forty years ago when Mae True, Howard and Sally Hoagland, Earl Hubbard (Grandma Herma's brother and local artist), Sara Blackwell Harris, and Leona Hubbard Stewart gathered to reminisce about what the Camp Meetings meant to them.

Their stories and simple drawings painted such a vivid picture that I could shut my eyes and envision life in the early 1900s along with the excitement around the annual church event. People came by horse and buggy and by train. Crowds were so thick coming in from Trenton it was said extra train cars had to be added to accommodate the number of people. I could picture the festivities. Everyone would be elaborately dressed and coiffed, in one joyous celebration to worship and sing and feast together. The ladies brought chicken and dumplings, corn on the cob, succotash, potatoes, chopped cabbage, pickled beets and all sorts of cakes and pies and homemade ice cream. The men set up wooden planks and tomato crates for seats and a pulpit. They were not concerned with the fact that it was all very rustic, and even considered crude by some, because the point of the Camp Meeting was to raise money, and not to spend money on any type of fanciness or fanfare. But, you didn't need anything fancy to sing at the top of your lungs. If the Camp Meetings had nothing else, always, there was the music.

There were many prominent people at the early Camp Meetings too, preachers and singers that would "set the place on fire." Two such folks were Archibald Campbell Seruby, more popularly known as "Spader the famous Peanut Man" and George Blackwell, who is Beverly's third-great uncle. Seruby got his nickname from selling peanuts at area sporting events, and he and Uncle George sang powerful duets together at meetings. Seruby could engage the audience with his heavy bass voice, and people used to pay Uncle George a dollar to sing, "They Stole My Mother Away." When Uncle George would go on and sing the song again substituting with "my sister" and "my brother," "my poppa" and "my mother," he stole them away … and the crowd would ask him to sing it again. No doubt the song evoked emotions and touched on a reality with which many in attendance were all too familiar. Uncle George Blackwell, a short man of about five-foot-one, was very religious and always had a joke. He had a team of horses, which he used to cart stones for a living. When not entertaining the crowd with song, he told stories about his grandfather, Frost Blackwell, who was a former slave and Beverly's fourth great-grandfather. The Blackwell family lived on the Still House Farm (now called the Mt. Rose Distillery Property) owned by Andrew Blackwell.

At the turn of the twentieth century in the early days of the Camp Meeting, John Robinson, a former slave who lived in Stoutsburg, New Jersey, was a faithful member of Mt. Zion AME. John was the "boss" of the Camp Meetings. He would go up to Hopewell to meet the trolley with his horse and wagon to bring the preacher along with goodies back to the Camp Meeting. Mr. Robinson knew how to read the bible, a little, and would make little prayers. He often told stories about his experiences and one story in particular stuck in Beverly and my minds. That story was retold in a 1975 *Princeton Recollector* article. Earl Hubbard, as a young man, recalled John's story, "One day they were going to sell him. So he ran in the house to get his pair of red boots. He said if they took him, they'd have to take his boots too. He said he cried, but they didn't sell him". Even now, I'm certain it is one of the saddest things Beverly and I have ever read. To think that one's life could be so out of one's control, it is necessary to cling to the smallest semblance of control, the tiniest semblance of ownership. Those red boots were the only thing that belonged to him, since even his very body legally belonged to someone else. Whether told then or generations later, I imagine stories like these made the free Blacks in attendance reflect on the state of the country, their brothers and sisters in bondage, or praise God for the little freedoms they had themselves.

By the 1930, times began to change, and an idea was presented to charge for parking at the Camp Meetings. The farmers who donated their pastures also wanted to be paid for their services. A decision could not be reached, so the free Camp Meetings that brought happiness and joy to so many came to an end. The event reminds me of the resilience of the Black community and how this tradition may have started out as a revival or fundraiser but seemed to transcend its original purpose. The Camp Meeting was instrumental in bringing New Jerseyans of African and European descent together for a couple weekends each summer to enjoy a feeling of cohesiveness. Largely segregated in everyday life, the Camp Meetings brought them together in fellowship and song. Beverly and I have worked hard with the Sourland Conservancy and Stoutsburg Sourland African American Museum (SSAAM) to help recreate the sense of community celebration and music in the air that the Camp Meetings cultivated in our region and we are thrilled to once again draw a crowd every year.

When I was a young I didn't even know enough to question any of this. I simply sang, as I sat on my grandmother Hester Coleman's lap at Second Calvary Baptist Church. Even at that young age I felt the holy spirit coursing through my veins while she belted out testimony songs like, "Every Time I Feel The Spirit," "Stood on the Banks of Jordan," "The Old Ship of Zion," "Heaven Is My Goal," and "This May Be Your Last Time." For so many years I would listen to and sing these songs, never giving a thought to the origin of gospel music or spirituals, or whether there was difference between the two. Songs like "Sometime I Feel Like a Motherless Child" and "Nobody Knows the Trouble I've Seen" were sung to express their faith and to help slaves endure the constant oppression and severe persecution in hopes that they would one day be free after all. Later I'd discover that spirituals were influenced not only by the conditions under which slaves lived, but also held clandestine messages to slaves about ways and times to strike out for freedom.

The song "Steal Away," for example, was reportedly used as a secret code to help lead the slaves to freedom on the Underground Railroad. The lyrics to "Steal Away," apparently composed in the pre–Civil War years by Wallace Willis, who was a Choctaw "freedman" in the old Indian Territory, tells the escaping slaves the day, the time and the place to flee. The lyrics imply moving at night, during thunderstorms: "Green trees are bending. ... He calls me by lightening." Some versions of the song urge runaways to cover the scent of their tracks from pursuing bloodhounds. Although the swamps and woods were undoubtedly infested by deadly animals from alligators to snakes, the roads held a much deadlier creature, man. As we sang these songs at Church, even the adults were likely unaware of the depth of meaning beneath them; we were singing songs that meant life or death for people, our ancestors, as they escaped to freedom.

When Beverly and I give our "Proud Heritage" presentation, we always open with a Negro spiritual song. Our intent is to not only to infuse the presentation with reverence, urgency and feeling of the songs that still fill our churches, but also to educate our audience on the greatest source of strength for African Americans who suffered enforced labor. These songs represent the voice of souls who survived unspeakable, unconscionable physical and mental torture. These songs mean more to us now, because we have learned more about African American church history and slave history. We have gained a deeper understanding of the scope of how inhumane slavery was and the mark it has left on African Americans, even to the present day. We were never taught these things as children, but because of those who have gone before us, because of people like Richard Allen and Absalom Jones, we now have a wealth of resources that inform our work and enrich our lives.

Recently my husband, John, and I participated in ecumenical worship services at the Old School Baptist Church. During the service, we talked about how life has come full circle especially when recognizing how some of the early Black members were John's and Beverly's ancestors. Sitting in the front pew, I recalled how as a Girl Scout I went on a tour of the Old School Baptist Church. When I stepped inside the door and was guided upstairs to the balcony, for an inexplicable reason I had the feeling I had been there before. I did not know at that time that this was the area the slaves sat among those who couldn't pay their seat tax. Further still, I remembered a story I have never been able to forget, that was told to me as a teenager by John's aunt, Virginia Nevius. Aunt Virginia told the story about a young girl from the Cray family who died and was to be buried at the Old School Baptist Church. When the church officials arrived to collect the girl for burial, it was discovered that she was actually a Black child, so she was not allowed to be buried in the intended plot, which was for Whites only. Instead her young body was put on a horse sled overnight to wait for a new grave to be prepared on the westerly edge of the cemetery. She was to be buried near where the outhouse was located at that time along with other Black people and paupers. That outhouse is adjacent to the present-day Hopewell House. It saddens Beverly to think about her ancestors, Friday and Juda Truehart, who were marginalized even in death, and that Friday's life and service to the most celebrated Pastor of this church meant nothing as skin color trumped relationship and dedication. Moreover, William Stives risked his life during the Revolutionary War to fight for the birth of a new country only to be buried … where?

Is it ironic that my husband, John, now leads ecumenical services as a worship leader in front of many guests who are descendants of these former local slave owners? Putting aside my feelings of pride, I can't help but wonder if Richard Allen could have known that one day his spiritual legacy and social justice movements would lead to the formation of different denominations. I think about how we survived America's darkest days of slavery, how we were able to shed shackles once imposed by plantation traditions that caused Black people to hide in the woods to worship. I also cannot help but think about the joy expressed on my grandmother's face when she learned to read and write at almost fifty years of age, a direct example of the Jim Crow law she was forced to endure while growing up in Virginia.

For me, I feel honored to be a part such an evolving history. When I walk through the doors of Second Calvary Baptist, I have peace of mind, because I am grateful to have a place to worship. My appreciation and reverence for those who preceded me has grown immeasurably.

FULL LIST OF THE EARLY BLACK PARISHIONERS OF OLD SCHOOL BAPTIST CHURCH[38]

November 27, 1768	Jack a mulatto
November 20, 1756	Black *James and Naomi* dismissed to Middletown Church (p. 133)
May 18, 1765	*Dina*, a Black (p.135)
September 14, 1765	*Tonty & Cate*, Blacks (p.135)
August. 5, 1797	*Dinah*, a Black *Kate* a Black *Bontura* a Black *Weld* a Black *Frank* a Black (p.150)
May 20, 1798	*Hannah*, a Black page 151
July 15, 1798	*Thomas*, a Black (p. 152)
July 28, 1799	Oaff, *(Off)* A Black (p. 153)
September 14, 1799	*James*, a Black, **Friday**, a Black (p. 153)
September21, 1799	**William Stiver (Stives)** a Black Richard, a Black;
Dec. 15, 1799	*Judy* a Black (p. 153)
August 17, 1800	*John* a Black (p. 154)
December 25, 1803	**Jude**, a slave of Jacob Blackwell (p. 157)
April 18, 1807	*Samuel*, a Black (dismissed) (p. 159)
September 23, 1809	*Catherine*, a Black woman
November 26, 1809	**Juda Shue**, wife of Friday
February 1810	*Margaret*, a Black (p. 160)
April 14, 1810	*Dinah* died (p. 160)
August 5, 1810	*Jude*, a Black woman, living at Jacob Blackwell's dismissed to the Church at Lamberton, Trenton (p. 161)

December 28, 1811	*Thomas*, a Black belonging to Wm Fisher, deceased (p. 161)
March 1812	*Off*, a Black belonging to Hezekiah Stout (p. 161)
During Spring 1813	*Dinah*, Hezekiah Stout's Black girl (p. 162)

OSBC Persons dismissed, deceased, etc.

1832	*Amy*, a colored woman, deceased (p. 168)
August 24, 1839	**William Stives** An aged colored member (p. 169)
August 26, 1843	**Friday Truehart** deceased, an aged colored member (p. 170)

Excommunications

| September 16, 1769 | *Nelly*, a Black, for bearing a bastard child (p. 176) |

The chapter epigraph comes from: Richard Allen, "'O God My Heart with Love Enflame,'" in *In A Collection of Spiritual Songs and Hymns*, 2nd ed. (Philadelphia: John Ormrod, 1801), accessed March 30, 2018, https://hymnary.org/text/o_god_my_heart_with_love_inflame.

1   Robert O. Hoffelt and African Episcopal Methodist Church, *African Methodist Episcopal Church Hymnal AME Bicentennial Hymnal*, AME Bicentennial Hymnal (Nashville: African Methodist Episcopal Church, 1984).

2   "Church History," *Mother Bethel: African Methodist Episcopal Church*, 2018, accessed June 18, 2018, https://www.motherbethel.org/content.php?cid=112.

3   "The Chew Family," Nonprofit, Cliveden, accessed December 2, 2017, http://www.cliveden.org/the-chew-family/ ; "Penn Biographies: Benjamin Chew (1722–1810)," University of Pennsylvania Archives and Records Center, accessed December 2, 2017, http://www.archives.upenn.edu/people/1700s/chew_ben.html.

4   Gilbert Thompson, "Epistle, 1758," in *Epistles from the Yearly Meeting of Friends Held in London to the Quarterly and Monthly Meetings in Great Britain, Ireland, and Elsewhere, from 1681 to 1817* (London: W. & S. Graves, 1818), 305–9, accessed November 18, 2017, https://archive.org/details/epistlesfromyea00meetgoog.

5   Allen, *The Life, Experience, and Gospel Labours of the Rt. Rev. Richard Allen, 1760–1831 … To Which Is Annexed the Rise and Progress of the African Methodist Church in the United States of America. Containing a Narrative of the Yellow Fever in the Year of Our Lord 1793: With an Address to the People of Colour in the United States. Written By Himself* (Philadelphia: Martin & Boden Printers, 1833), 6, accessed November 11, 2017, http://docsouth.unc.edu/neh/allen/allen.html.

6   Gary B. Nash, "New Light on Richard Allen: The Early Years of Freedom," *William and Mary Quarterly* 46, no. 2 (April 1989): 335–36, http://www.jstor.org/stable/1920258; Allen, *The Life, Experience, and Gospel Labours of the Rt. Rev. Richard Allen.*; Carol V. R. George, *Segregated Sabbaths: Richard Allen and the Emergence of the Independent Black Churches, 1760–1840* (New York: Oxford University Press, 1973), 28.

7   Allen, *The Life, Experience, and Gospel Labours of the Rt. Rev. Richard Allen*, 8.

8   Nash, "New Light on Richard Allen," 336–37.

9   Nicole Atwill, "Slavery in the French Colonies: Le Code Noir (the Black Code) of 1685," in *Custodia Legis, Law Librarians of Congress*, January 13, 2011, accessed February 20, 2018, https://blogs.loc.gov/law/2011/01/slavery-in-the-french-colonies/.

10 "6f. Slave Codes. U.S. History Pre-Columbian to the New Millennium," US History.org, accessed February 20, 2018, http://www.ushistory.org/us/6f.asp; "Virginia's Slave Codes. 1705. The Terrible Transformation. Part 1: 1450–1750," *Africans in America*. PBS. WGBH, accessed February 20, 2018, http://www.pbs.org/wgbh/aia/part1/1p268.html.

11 "An Act for Regulating Negro, Indian and Mallatto Slaves within This Province of New Jersey. December 12, 1704, 2 Bush 28–30. Repealed by an Order of Council, October 24, 1709," New Jersey Digital Legal Library, June 5, 2012, accessed April 18, 2018, http://njlegallib.rutgers.edu/slavery/acts/A11.html.

12 Joe William Trotter and Eric Ledell Smith, eds., *African Americans in Pennsylvania: Shifting Historical Perspectives* (University Park: Pennsylvania State University Press, 1997), 78.

13 Gary B. Nash and Jean R. Soderlund, *Freedom by Degrees: Emancipation in Pennsylvania and Its Aftermath* (New York: Oxford University Press, 1991), 13.

14 "An Act for Regulating Negro, Indian and Mallatto Slaves within This Province of New Jersey. December 12, 1704, 2 Bush 28–30. Repealed by an Order of Council, October 24, 1709," New Jersey Digital Legal Library, June 5, 2012, accessed April 18, 2018, http://njlegallib.rutgers.edu/slavery/acts/A11.html.

15 An Act for the Gradual Abolition of Slavery Act of 1804. Passed at Trenton, February 15, 1804.

16 "Slavery in New Jersey," Slavery in the North, n.d., accessed February 20, 2018, http://slavenorth.com/newjersey.htm.

17 George, *Segregated Sabbaths*, 7–8.

18 Leroy Fitts, *A History of Black Baptists* (Nashville: Broadman Press, 1985), 25.

19 Allen, *The Life, Experience, and Gospel Labours of the Rt. Rev. Richard Allen*, 13–14.

20 Richard S. Newman, *Freedom's Prophet: Bishop Richard Allen, the AME Church, and the Black Founding Fathers* (New York: New York University Press, 2008), 68–72.

21 "The Yellow Fever Epidemic," Historical Society of Pennsylvania, accessed April 26, 2018, https://hsp.org/history-online/exhibits/richard-allen-apostle-of-freedom/the-yellow-fever-epidemic.

22 Mathew Carey, *A Short Account of the Malignant Fever, Lately Prevalent in Philadelphia: With a Statement of the Proceedings That Took Place on the Subject in Different Parts of the United States*, 2nd ed. (Philadelphia: Printed by the author, 1793), accessed November 27, 2017, https://catalog.hathitrust.org/Record/100072995.

23 Howard Anton, "Stephen Girard and the Yellow Fever Epidemic of 1793," *Stephen Girard Forgotten Patriot*, accessed February 18, 2018, http://forgottenpatriot.com.

24 Paul Lawrence Dunbar, "Hidden in Plain Sight: African American Secret Societies and Black Freemasonry," *Journal of African American Studies* 16, no. 4 (December 2012): 623, accessed November 10, 2017, http://www.jstor.org/stable/43525440.

25 "Preamble of the Free African Society 1787," PBS, WGBH, *Africans in America. Brotherly Love Part 3: 1791–1831*, n.d., accessed April 19, 2108, http://www.pbs.org/wgbh/aia/part3/3h465.html; "The Free African Society," Historical Society of Pennsylvania, accessed April 25, 2018, http://hsp.org/history-online/exhibits/richard-allen-apostle-of-freedom/the-free-african-society.

26 "Church History: A Brief History of Mother Bethel African Methodist Episcopal Church," *Mother Bethel: African Methodist Episcopal Church*, 2018, accessed June 18, 2018, https://www.motherbethel.org/content.php?cid=112.

27 Richard S. Newman, "'We Participate in Common': Richard Allen's Eulogy of George Washington and the Challenge of Interracial Appeals," *William and Mary Quarterly* 64, no. 1 (Jan. 2007): 118, accessed November 10, 2017, http://www.jstor.org/stable/4491601.

28 Craig Bruce Smith, "Status of Slaves in Washington's Will," Mount Vernon, n.d., accessed April 19, 2018, http://www.mountvernon.org/digital-encyclopedia/article/status-of-slaves-in-washingtons-will/; Mary V. Thompson, "Washington and Slavery," Digital Encyclopedia, Mount Vernon, n.d., accessed April 19, 2018, http://www.mountvernon.org/digital-encyclopedia/article/george-washington-and-slavery/.

29 George, *Segregated Sabbaths*, 23.

30 Ibid., 89.

31 "Historical Perspective: American Colonization Society," New Dawn Liberia, October 6, 2010, accessed April 27, 2018, http://www.thenewdawnliberia.com/feature-op-ed/special-feature/8689-historical-perspective-american-colonization-society%20American%20Colonization%20Society.

32 Richard Allen, "Letter from Bishop Allen," *Freedom's Journal*, November 27, 1827.

33 Allen, *The Life, Experience, and Gospel Labours of the Rt. Rev. Richard Allen*, 9.

34 "The First Black Watch Night Service Occurs in America, African American Registry."

35 Richard Allen, "Eulogy for Washington." *Lift Every Voice: African American Oratory from 1787–1900*, ed. Phillip S. Foner and Robert James Branham (Tuscaloosa: University of Alabama Press, 1998), 56–58.

36 Lisa Cokefair Gedney, "Town Records of Hopewell, New Jersey," in *The New Jersey Society of the Colonial Dames of America. Old School Baptist Church, by Authority of the Board of Managers of the New Jersey Society of the Colonial Dames of America* (Hopewell, New Jersey: Little & Ives, 1931).

37 "Camp Meetings," *Princeton Recollector, a Monthly Journal of Local History*, October 1975.

38 Gedney, "Town Records of Hopewell, New Jersey," 133–76.

127th Regiment United States Colored Troops
"We Will Prove Ourselves Men"
"Let Soldiers in War be Citizens in Peace"

CHAPTER 7

PIONEERS OF LIBERTY: LOCAL AFRICAN AMERICAN MILITARY HISTORY

by ELAINE BUCK

You are pioneers of liberty. ... With the United States cap on your head, the United States eagle on your belt, the United States musket on your shoulder, not all the powers of darkness can prevent you from becoming American citizens. ... If you rise and flourish, we shall rise and flourish. If you win freedom and citizenship, we shall share your freedom and citizenship.

—Frederick Douglass, social reformer and abolitionist (1818–1895)

Every year since the late 1960s, on the grounds of the Stoutsburg Cemetery, with the flag raised high in early summer, while peonies are often blooming, we host a Memorial Day Service. The event, which draws community members near and far, not only honors but also gives voice to the accomplishments of local unsung heroes, our African American veterans. Stoutsburg Cemetery has been situated at the foot of the Sourland Mountain, in Hopewell Township across the border from Montgomery Township, for close to three hundred years. Flags waving in the gentle breeze adorn the graves of American Revolution, Civil War, World War I, World War II, and Vietnam veterans as well as others who served our country in times of peace. This cemetery is a final resting place of African American trailblazers.

Through the years, our Memorial Day services have also united descendants, Black and White, of the region's families—and have acted as glue to bond people together. In our role in arranging these Memorial Day services, Beverly and I have repeatedly felt gratified to act as catalysts for bringing together descendants from local families like the Hoaglands, Trueharts, and Crays, to name a few. In a moving ceremony in 2017, we watched the African American side of the Stives family meet some of the White family members for the first time, on the most appropriate occasion of Memorial Day.

Each new connection, each shared memory is proof of how interrelated we are. Only together can we begin to break the cycle of America's historical omissions, such as the story of African American military service. Memorial Day is our day to reflect and uphold the most honorable of those who have gone before us.

In the early 1960s, my husband, John Buck, now president of the Stoutsburg Cemetery Association, first stumbled on our mountaintop grounds. He was about eight or nine years old. While camped in the woods with local Boy Scout Troop 71, John was playing a game of hide-and-seek, the boys raiding each other's campsites and throwing stink bombs into each other's campfires. After running out of the woods into a field full of weeds and brush, he suddenly found himself flat on the ground. He had tripped over something, but he didn't know what. Knowing the boys from the "enemy" campsites must be somewhere behind him, he scrambled to get back on his feet and upon doing so noticed one, then two, then many upright stones spread all across the weathered field. The night was silent and still, but the stones seemed to whisper around him. It was late and too dark for him to investigate the writing on the stones, and he had been gone from his campsite for too long. Slowly, he walked through the field, stepping around the stones with an unexplained sense of reverence, and rejoined his troop. Later in life, John realized that he had literally stumbled upon the Stoutsburg Cemetery. Unbeknownst to him at the time, those stones and their cemetery had enduring ties to both his past and his future.

If young John Buck had been able to make out some of the names chiseled on the headstones that night with the Boy Scouts, he might have read close to a dozen names associated with the United States Colored Troops (USCT), formed during the Civil War. At that young age, it is not likely he would have recognized many of the names that appeared on the headstones, but as an adult, he would definitely be aware of their connection to the region. Some of these men were among more than 10,500 Black soldiers trained under the command of Louis Wagner at Camp William Penn in Pennsylvania, the first U.S. recruiting and training center for African American men. The camp was built on thirteen acres of land owned by Edward M. Davis, the son-in-law of famed abolitionist Lucretia Mott, who hosted former slaves and abolitionist notables such as Frederick Douglass, Sojourner Truth, and Harriet Tubman.

*

Stoutsburg Cemetery has always been a family affair. John's grandfather Elmer (Pop) Nevius, became a caretaker of the cemetery sometime after returning from World War II, and, in the late 1950s, his son Earle Nevius took over the job. Uncle Earle trained two generations of his family, with both his nephews Glen Nevius and my husband, John, and his grandson Baron Holland and great-nephew (my oldest) Joseph Buck. In the late 1960s and early 1970s the president of the cemetery was Robert "Bobby" Grover, whose father, Wilmer Grover, had been the caretaker in the 1940s and 1950s. It was Bobby who recruited John as vice president. John had been there on and off with Uncle Earle since he was a teenager, and the VP position was vacant after his uncle Robert True passed away. Little did John know that Bobby would take sick and pass away too, leaving him to fill the position as president of the historic Stoutsburg Cemetery. Now, John carries the torch of those vigilant men who came before him to oversee the valiant men who died before them and the stones that mark their resting place.

Our Memorial Day Service is the perfect place to begin this chapter, because as you'll read throughout, these annual celebrations, devoted to our local Black veterans, will take you from the present—as we salute the soldiers buried here—deep into the past, into lives of service, achievements, and local stories. The soldiers in our cemetery served in the 24th, 41st, 45th, and 127th United States Colored Troops. The 41st and 127th regiments were instrumental in capturing Petersburg and joined the charge after the retreating army of General Robert E. Lee. It remains important to Beverly and me that these names be documented and remembered.

We are going to introduce you to some of our Memorial Day speakers who have changed the course of our research and lives over the years: the pages that follow move you consecutively through the wars in order to showcase the extent to which African Americans—men and women—have participated in every single conflict in U.S. history. Finally, at the very end of this chapter, you'll find a list of names that is likely to move you as much as it did us, as we discovered, for instance, the names and regiments of Black soldiers in the Revolutionary War as well as the Hopewell Borough World War II Honor Roll and soldiers buried in the Stoutsburg Cemetery.

Every year, during our service, we highlight a guest speaker to present to our Stoutsburg community. Speakers have ranged from historians to genealogists to soldiers. The most important of our most recent guest speakers in terms of our chapter on military history brings us to the Civil War reenactor of USCT 6th Regiment Sergeant Major Frederick Lewis Minus. Minus is not just an active member and docent in the Camp Olden War Roundtable based in Hamilton Township, New Jersey. He travels around the country visiting African American cemeteries to highlight the role of Black soldiers throughout American history. Minus currently serves as a member of the staff at the Old Barracks in Trenton, New Jersey, giving tours and recounting the story of the role of Black soldiers during the Civil War. Minus's presentation reminded us that Black Americans have fought for their country in every American war, including defending a nascent United States in wars like the French and Indian War, the War of 1812, the Mexican-American War, and the Spanish-American War.

THE AMERICAN REVOLUTION

Hearing stories about the local presence of Black Revolutionary War soldiers fighting in our own backyard was beyond exciting. It piqued our interest to learn more, especially about veterans who actually lived in our backyard, such as Revolutionary War veteran William Stives, one of the Sourland Mountain's earliest Black settlers. Anecdotally, we first learned about Stives's patriotic actions through a *New York Times* article from January 1880, based on oral history of the "barbarians" who lived on the Sourland Mountain.[1] Apparently, the writer felt compelled to write the article because he was so outraged that Black and White people were cohabiting in the Sourland Mountain.

But back to what we learned from the historic *New York Times* article. In interviews with some of the locals about Sourland Mountain residents, William Stives was mentioned as not only having been under the command of General George Washington but also to have "crossed the Delaware with him on that eventful winter night." We mentioned William Stives earlier in the book, as one of the oldest and most traceable community members and Black soldiers in the Hopewell Valley region. Stives served as a fifer with the 3rd New Jersey Regiment called the Jersey Blues and wintered with George Washington at Valley Forge. According to oral history, when the campaign was being waged in the area between Trenton and Hopewell, Stives was sent out to forage for food. While on this mission, he beheld the uninhabited Sourland Mountain range, and he vowed to make this area his home.

To learn that African American men fought during the American Revolution was mind-boggling to us. Why was this not taught in our school? —we wondered. Why was this not in students' history books? It emboldened our desire to make this information better known. For example, many Americans know the story of General Washington winning the Battle of Trenton, and most know about him crossing the Delaware River on the Christmas night that preceded it. What few people seem to know is that the crossing and, consequently, the victory were made possible by a unique mixture of Black and White men called the Marbleheaders, sailors from Marblehead, Massachusetts, a fishermen's town across the bay from Salem, a Puritan town that frowned upon drinking.[2]

In order to consume alcohol without puritanical restrictions, the sailors crossed the bay and started the town of Marblehead in the early seventeenth century. Part of George Washington's foot contingent, the Marbleheaders, started out with Colonel John Glover in the 14th Continental Line, fought during the first Battle of Trenton, and captured several Hessian soldiers. At the time Washington was not interested in enlisting soldiers of color. Colonel Glover, a Marblehead native and shipowner, however, was likely familiar enough with working with Black sailors such that he respected both their physical and mental abilities. When asked by Washington if his men would be able to manage this treacherous crossing of the Delaware, Glover immediately answered in the affirmative. The Marbleheaders not only were responsible for transporting soldiers, artillery, and frightened horses across the river on the forty Durham boats but they had to do so on the bitterly cold and moonless nights through a half-frozen river. After landing on the other side of the river, the men still had the task of trekking nine miles to reach Trenton, where they immediately engaged in battle. It was a feat that showed the Continental Army that ability and determination know no race.

"On the ship, you don't care what color the guy is who's holding the rope," says a White Marblehead regiment, Revolutionary War reenactor. "That is why the Yankees, who were more nautical," he continues, "had a more open mind to the possibility of a more egalitarian society. Glover's Marblehead regiment reflected that."[3] The Marbleheaders were considered by many as the first integrated regiment in the United States. Many Marbleheaders joined the newly formed navy after the Battle of Trenton. One of the men, "Black" Joe Brown, later returned to Marblehead, opened Joe Brown's Tavern, and became a very wealthy man and politician. I cannot help but think that the Marbleheaders' performance directly influenced Washington's opinion on enlisting African Americans, for on December 30 he issued this statement: "As the General is informed that numbers of free negroes are desirous of enlisting, he gives leave to the recruiting officers to entertain them, and promises to lay the matter before the Congress, who, he doubts not, will approve of it."[4]

The contribution of Black soldiers like those from Marblehead was instrumental to winning America's battle for independence. General Knox stated the following without Glover's regiment, the expedition would no doubt have failed: "Had not Colonel John Glover's splendid regiment of seafaring men from Marble head, Massachusetts, lent a willing and skillful hand, as he had promised they would, the expedition would no doubt have failed."[5]

During the Revolutionary War period, some White people questioned the Black man's intellect and competence to serve in battle. That a Black man could be as good a soldier as his White counterpart was, for many, unfathomable.[6]

During the Revolutionary War, some White colonists, including George Washington, also feared the possible repercussions of a Black man having a gun. White colonists had a, perhaps justified, fear of uprisings among the enslaved. It was ironic, to some, to arm a Black man to fight a war against oppression, one espousing the ideals of liberty, when he or his brethren were enslaved.[7] One Massachusetts committee advised that having slaves fight was "inconsistent with the principles that are to be supported."[8] However, taking advantage of this hypocrisy, in November 1775 Lord Dunmore, royal governor of Virginia, issued a declaration inviting indentured servants and "Negroes" to join the British army.[9] Undoubtedly, the British promise of freedom became the overwhelming reason why African Americans joined the British armies. For some, it made sense to fight for whichever side offered them freedom.

We know that Revolutionary War soldiers owned slaves. However, this did not preclude Black men in all thirteen colonies from fighting on behalf of the Patriot cause. Even before the official decree allowing Blacks to fight in the Continental Army, several regiments consisted of free Blacks. There are many accounts suggesting the participation of Blacks in the Revolutionary War, such as in a letter written by Baroness von Riedesel. A Loyalist prisoner of the colonists at the time, she was being escorted through Massachusetts and allegedly commented, "You do not see a regiment in which there is not a large number of Blacks." This is one of several comments on the racial diversity of the colonial soldiers. On the side of the Continental Army, there were between 5,000 and 20,000 patriots of African and Native American descent who fought under the command of General George Washington and performed as fifers, drummers, wagoners, cooks, waiters, or laborers. In spite of their refusal to recruit Blacks to the army, some southern states made exceptions to use free and enslaved Black men as pilots and seamen; some even served as sailors in the navy.[10]

We have pulled together the names of those Black soldiers who fought in the Revolutionary War from our region and listed them in full at the end of the chapter. A sampling of this list can be found below. As you can see when you observe the listings, Black soldiers were often marginalized in the way their names were omitted from formal records. Instead some Black soldiers were listed with only the word "Negro" as their title or part of their first name. However sadly, these identifiers helped Beverly and me find evidence of the Black military presence in our region as we pursued our research.

Some soldiers were listed with the word "Negro" as their title or part of their name:[11]

Negro Cuff fifer	3rd New Jersey
Dick Negro	1st New Jersey
Negro Sambo	4th New Jersey

Other soldiers were listed, showing they served as a proxy for their masters:

Cudjo (for his master Benjamin Coe) possibly named Cudjo Clark, 5th Regiment Massachusetts[12]

Samuel Sutphin, New Jersey line (sub for Casper Berger)[13]

Samuel Sutphin's war-time record, resurrected in 1914, was recounted in the *Somerset County Historical Quarterly*.[14]

Fortunately, others were listed by their full names, which makes it much easier to verify who they were and their achievements:[15]

Pompey Black, 2nd New Jersey (Col. Shreve's Regiment)

Oliver Cromwell, 2nd New Jersey (Capt. Lowery)

Robert Walling lists the potential soldiers at Trenton in his Prince Whipple article.[16]

POTENTIAL SOLDIERS AT TRENTON

This list was created based on the Whipple list. See full list with additional information about these soldiers in the table at the end of this chapter.[17]

Cesar Cipeo	Durkee's 20th Continental
Primus Coffin	New Hampshire
Dick Fortune	Durkee's 20th Continental
Hanobel	Baldwin's 26th Continental
Luther Jotham	Baldwin's 23rd Continental
Abraham Pharoah	Connecticut
Samuel Pompey	Connecticut
John Pompey	Connecticut
Thomas Semor	Bailey's 23rd Continental
Cudgo Shephard	Connecticut
Sipeo	Baldwin's 26th Continental
Nathaniel Small	Baldwin's 26th Continental

One soldier with strong ties to our region was:

Name: William Stives

Regiment: 3rd Regiment New Jersey

Rank: Private

Enrolled: February 1778

Mustered in: 1778 at Valley Forge, Pennsylvania

Length of Service: 5 years

Mustered out: June 5, 1783, in Newburgh, New York

Comments: William Stives was a fifer. He wintered with George Washington at Valley Forge. (See chapter 8 for an extended profile.)

After the war William Stives traveled back to the Hopewell Valley to make his home on land near present-day Lindbergh Road. Recognized for his patriotism, Private Stives received the highest military achievement, the Badge of Merit, awarded by George Washington for service in the Continental Army. Stives's illustrious five-year service culminated in discharge papers that were personally signed by General George Washington.

William Stives was a member of the Old School Baptist Church in Hopewell Borough for forty years and is believed to be buried in their cemetery. Unfortunately, the Old School Baptist Church has no record of William Stives in their list of graveyard burials, but, based on historical norms, we assume that he was not laid to rest with White Revolutionary War veterans who were interred on this site and honored with military markers. If indeed he is buried in this cemetery, it is our sincere hope he is not buried in the segregated area near the outhouse, like the other Black congregants. It saddens us to think that after helping ensure this country could establish itself as an independent nation, a nation of equals, Stives's Revolutionary actions could be so easily disregarded because of his difference in race. Timothy Stives, his fourth great-grandson, placed a commemorative marker in the Stoutsburg Cemetery to honor William Stives and his loyalty to the patriotic cause.

AMERICAN CIVIL WAR

It was at a 2012 Memorial Day celebration that we first learned about the United States Colored Troops (USCT) as well. Our guest speakers were Eric and Jeanette Schwartz, a couple who researched the Civil War veterans who are buried at Stoutsburg Cemetery. On that warm spring afternoon, we listened to Eric describe how the USCT were part of the 175 regiments and constituted 10 percent of the Union Army. Eric particularly focused on the soldiers from the 127th and 45th regiments because of their presence at some of the most historic events in Civil War history, such as being on duty during President Abraham Lincoln's second inauguration and the only Colored Troops in the procession. The 127th accompanied General Grant at the Appomattox Courthouse on April 9, 1865. The Battle of Appomattox Court House in Virginia was one of the last battles of the war. According to Eric, local men Jonathan Stives, Louis Fisher, Tracey Peterson, Aaron Truehart, Ira Bergen, and James Schenck became eyewitnesses to history because of their presence at this event. The 127th regiment was instrumental in cutting off Confederate general Robert E. Lee's supply line and forcing his surrender, thus ending the war and preserving the Union. These local soldiers were buried in Stoutsburg Cemetery or Pennington African Cemetery although their markers no longer exist. See their listing in the Civil War table at the end of the chapter.

Even after hearing the Schwartz's presentation, the magnitude of soldiers' accomplishments did not fully register. It wasn't until a few years later that we began to understand the significance of the men from this region who were soldiers in the Civil War. We were also surprised to learn about another local connection. The flags for the USCT were especially designed by David Bustill Bowser, the grandfather of Princeton resident and notable figure Paul Robeson. Bowser created a specific design for each individual regiment united by the common theme, "We

Just Want to Be Men." For instance, the 127th USCT flag motto under which Aaron Truehart soldiered was, "We Will Prove Ourselves Men." The determination of African American men to join the Civil War effort showed what this war meant to them: an opportunity to prove themselves as equals to their White countrymen.

At the beginning of the Civil War, the Union did not recognize or train any colored soldiers. In fact, it took over a year of fighting before the United States allowed Black men to enlist, and this was mostly due to high death tolls in the Union army. These heavy losses discouraged many Whites from enlisting and swayed President Lincoln to start recruiting African Americans. The passage of the Second Confiscation Act in 1862 proved to be the turning point in terms of racial composition of the Union Army. Newly freed slaves soon became a major asset and some of the first soldiers of African descent officially admitted into the Union Army. Their contribution was something President Lincoln could no longer ignore. At the end of the war Lincoln admitted that "without the military help of the Black freedmen, the war against the South could not have been won."[18]

Black participation in the Civil War formally began in 1862. Under pressure from African Americans who wished to fight but were denied the opportunity, the War Department announced that states could form regiments "consisting entirely of colored citizens." The United States Colored Troops was born. Eventually, more than 179,000 African Americans would serve in the army, with some 19,000 more in the navy. According to the State of New Jersey website, of the 88,000 New Jerseyans who participated in the Civil War, Blacks numbered upwards of 2,900, and represented almost 500 of New Jersey's more than 6,000 fatalities, though these numbers are contested by other Union statistics.[19] Even after the recruitment of Black soldiers was sanctioned by the Union, New Jersey refused to organize a troop of their own and pay a bounty to Black soldiers, a fact that may contribute to the discrepancy in the numbers of Black soldiers credited to the state. Despite New Jersey's reluctance to support its Black residents' desire to fight for the Union, an impressive number of Black men from the Sourland Mountain area rose to the cause. Some Black soldiers even went to other states to enlist, and then were credited to New Jersey. There were several nearby recruitment places for colored troops, including Tanyard Alley in Trenton, so locals with the patriotic zeal did not have far to go.[20]

Heeding the call were local residents like John Naz, William Reasnor, George Dillam, Jonathan Ridley, and Asher Hagerman. These men and many more made the trek to Camp William Penn in Pennsylvania to prepare for duty. Similarly, less than ten miles away, Pennington residents Charles Jennings and William H. Boyer traveled to Rhode Island and Connecticut, respectively, to enlist. William Boyer joined Company E 29th Connecticut Volunteer Infantry. After serving in the 29th Connecticut, Mr. Boyer also served as headmaster and teacher for the school for Black children housed at Pennington Bethel AME Church.

Charles Jennings joined the 14th Rhode Island Regiment. An all–African American volunteer regiment—the 14th Rhode Island Heavy Artillery, later renamed the 11th United States Colored Artillery (Heavy)—served honorably during the Civil War. His great-grandson James Charles Jennings, or Charlie, proudly showed us the dress sword and two guns owned by his namesake. Jennings's story is among those featured in our oral history in chapter 8. The historic weapons were last displayed on a Memorial Day parade in Pennington in 1927 where Charles Jennings was the oldest living Civil War veteran who marched. Charlie also shared his great-grandfather's story about his service in the 14th Rhode Island Regiment, as the regiment was traveling by train in Louisiana. Unbeknownst to them, a plantation owner had armed his slaves and told them the train was coming to take them all away to other parts of the South. As the train went by a field, the deceived slaves opened fire and many soldiers were killed right before his eyes. Charlie said his grandfather never got over it, because it was only by a miracle that he was spared.

Undoubtedly, though, one of the most heart-wrenching stories we learned from Kellee Green Blake, Civil War historian and retired National Archives Regional director, was about the local African American men who survived one of the Civil War's bloodiest battles, one that many have never heard about: the Battle of Olustee or Ocean Pond. Olustee, Florida, made believers out of many White Americans who had harbored doubts about the Black soldier's honor in battle. The 8th United States Colored Troops was placed under the command of Charles Wesley Fribley, a White man who swiftly answered the call to duty shortly after the attack on Fort Sumter. Fribley passed the board to become "Colonel of first class" on September 19, 1863, and took command of the 8th USCT, which included local residents James Schenck, George Boldin, George Williamson, and Sam Montgomery. The regiment traveled south, arriving in Jacksonville, Florida, in February 1864. A large number of battles occurred involving the 7th Connecticut regiment, which required the 8th Regiment to assist. Under the command of General Seymour, who apparently forced them to use unfamiliar and largely inoperative muskets, confusion and disorder ensued. The 8th was left to take the lead in battle though they were new to battle, outmanned, and out-trained by their opponent.

In 2012, historian Jennifer Thompson described how the 8th USCT "maintained their position "before a terrible fire … fire in front, on their flank, and in the rear, without flinching or breaking."[21] At the Battle of Olustee, the Confederates killed and wounded as many Black soldiers as they possibly could, perhaps similar to the more famous Fort Pillow massacre, where the Confederates vengefully killed rather than captured Black soldiers, even after they had surrendered. The losses at Olustee were extreme with dozens killed, several hundred wounded, and more than a dozen listed as missing, including Fribley, who was shot in the chest and died shortly thereafter. The 8th USCT suffered "the heaviest regimental loss in the Battle of Olustee in the Civil War." Even after their commander's early death in battle, the soldiers of the 8th remained in control for longer than expected. According to Captain John Hamilton of the 3rd U.S. Artillery, the sergeant carrying the regimental flag "was hit in his right hand by a ball which nearly tore off the hand." Rather than let the flag fall, the sergeant calmly seized the staff with his left hand and retained possession of the flag until he found a corporal to give the flag to for safekeeping. These kinds of stories remind us of the bravery and sacrifice of our African American veterans.

Moreover, in addition to the African American soldiers, the formation of USCT was the official entrance to the war for other non-White Americans; its troops also comprised Native and Asian Americans, Pacific Islanders, Hawaiians, Chinese, Filipinos, South Asians, Mexicans, and Puerto Ricans.[22]

While we were excited to learn about the remarkable contribution the United States Colored Troops made in the War Between the States, unfortunately, the role of Black women has not received the same amount of acclaim or study as that of their Black brethren. As more information becomes available about Black men who served in the United States Colored Troops, what information will come forth about these nameless, faceless women who volunteered to serve their country? Black women served in the military in various capacities.

While the majority of women served as nurses on both sides of the war, there are stories of women who dressed as men to serve in battle and those who risked their lives as spies for the Union. One of these women was Lucinda Rosser, who lived in Pennington next door to Beverly's oldest living cousin, Oliver Smith. Mrs. Rosser—called Bam by her grandchildren—originally hailed from Alabama. Oliver never knew how old she was, because when he was a little boy she was already an old lady. As a small boy, anytime he was in the Rosser house, Bam would be chewing her snuff and spitting—with the accuracy of a sharpshooter—into one of the many spittoons she had dotted around the house. She was the kind of woman you did not mess with. One day, he mustered up enough courage to ask Bam why she always dipped snuff. She looked down at him and said, "Well, honey, it's because it settles my stomach." She added that it had worked for her during the war. "What war?" he remembered asking. "Boy, I'm talking about the Civil War!" Without hesitation Bam answered, before taking another sharp shot at one of her spittoons, the brass pot crying out as if it felt the pain of the blow. "I was a nurse during the Civil War!" she finished. Oliver said he never forgot that conversation. He couldn't believe that he actually knew someone who lived during the Civil War.

Like Bam, my Aunt Jenny was born sometime in the 1800s, and no one ever really knew how old she was. Not knowing your age was not uncommon for Black folks back then, because often there was no formal record keeping of births. If someone in the family was able to read and write and had a Bible, births would be recorded; otherwise there was no record. Aunt Jenny, who must have been a child during the Civil War, remembered taking care of the wounded soldiers. She described going down to the creek to collect leeches to place on the pus-and-maggot-filled wounds of the soldiers. She also washed bandages, made from white cotton bedsheets, on the washboard. When I was a little girl, she would always tell me, in her deep southern drawl, "Baby, don't ever get rid of these cotton bedsheets—they might come in handy one day … you never know when you might need 'em." I would look at her confused, wondering why she would say these things to me, but she would just stare back at me with a snuff-filled smile and a faraway gaze in her eyes. The recollections of Bam and Aunt Jenny are just some of the untold stories of female patriots during the Civil War.

If African American men have been unsung heroes of U.S. wars, these heroines have barely had their songs written. Notable women like Harriet Tubman and Sojourner Truth joined in the Civil War effort, but there are hundreds more who served without recognition. As medical treatment for African Americans was cursory at best and often nonexistent, Black women were often "practiced folk healers" who learned these caretaking skills from previous generations, some traditions stretching as far back as the African continent. They used their other domestic skills, including those garnered from forced servitude, to voluntarily serve in the war effort as "seamstresses, quilters, gardeners, cooks," and laundresses.[23]

Literate former slaves and more educated women from the North also served as teachers of freed slaves and soldiers alike. Like their White counterparts several Black women patriots traveled with their husbands' units, providing mess service when the army refused to provide for these troops. In her memoirs of her time as a nurse during the Civil War, Susie King Taylor wrote about the eighteen months when "colored" troops did not receive their pay from the Union. As a result, "their wives were obliged to support themselves and children by washing for the officers and making cakes and pies which they sold to the boys in the camp." No doubt the sales were to the White boys who were being paid for their wartime service.[24]

Additionally, the Ladies Sanitary Commission of the St. Thomas African Episcopal Church in nearby Philadelphia, Pennsylvania, joined similar groups that provided food, cloth for bandages, medical supplies, and clothing for the Black soldiers. They held fairs and bazaars in order to purchase supplies needed to nurse the sick and injured soldiers, since

African American women were not allowed to participate in the fundraising activities of the United States Sanitary Commission and Ladies Aid societies run by Whites. Additionally, Ann Bradford Stokes was among five African American nurses who served on the first U.S. Navy hospital ship, the USS *Red Rover*. While some African American army wives like King applied for and were granted widows' pensions, Stokes was the first African American woman in the United States to receive a pension from the navy—and perhaps any branch of the military—in recompense for her *own* service. African American women contributed their patriotic service to the Civil War, just like their brothers and husbands did in the USCT.[25]

THE SPANISH-AMERICAN WAR

The United States Colored Troops terminated in 1869, after several years of occupying Southern cities during Reconstruction. They were then incorporated into the regular army units, which ironically were soon sent off to fight against Native Americans— another badly treated minority—in the American West. I imagine the USTC hoped that this was a sign of integration and respect. Unfortunately, it was not. Though Black Americans were admitted, the army was both segregated and restricted. The volunteer regiments were disbanded, and the army kept only six regiments as part of the regular service, all with White officers. What this meant was that for conflicts, such as the Spanish-American War, there was a quota, a maximum number of Black men who were allowed to soldier for their country.[26] Pennington resident Archibald Seruby ("Spader," the Peanut Man) served during this time.

During the Spanish-American War African American women were used again in a nursing capacity. This time, similar to what had happened during the 1793 yellow fever epidemic in Philadelphia,

African Americans were presumed to be immune to tropical diseases like typhoid fever. Eight regiments of male "Immunes" were mustered to fight as volunteers in Cuba, and Black women were recruited to nurse the sick and tend to the soldiers. The 8th Regiment, under Colonel Eli Huggins—recruited from as far as Louisville, Kentucky, and as nearby as Newark, New Jersey—became Company A. And Huggins's staff included groundbreaking African American officers, such as a Black assistant surgeon, First Lieutenant William W. Purnell, a Howard University Medical School graduate, and First Lieutenant Benjamin O. Davis, who, in 1940, would become the U.S. Army's first African American general.[27] Perhaps because of the quota, none of the local Sourland-area soldiers fought in the Spanish-American War.

The war was short and victory was swift. And, as in the Civil War, the African American units were disbanded after the war's end and our patriotic brothers had to wait until the next military conflict to prove their mettle.[28]

WORLD WAR I

Originally called the Great War, World War I was the largest coordinated war effort thus far, spanning not just several countries but several continents. As in previous wars, African Americans stepped forward to prove themselves as patriots. When the United States joined the war in April 1917, the army turned away some Black American volunteers, since the four African American regular army units were filled in less than a week of President Wilson's declaration of war against Germany. Ironically—and likely as a result of this decision to limit Black participation—the United States had to create the Selective Service Act in May 1917 in order to obtain the required manpower. The draft conscripted Black men into service anyway, and because of the need for troops, the racial quota system did not last long. Soon, more regiments had to be created to accommodate the African American soldiers. The draft, however, seemed to work to the African American man's detriment, as the entirely White draft boards called up a disproportionate number of African American names. Moreover, some postal workers apparently secreted Black men's registration cards so they would appear to be dodging the draft and consequently be arrested.[29]

Additionally, Black men who had families—or who owned land— were often drafted before single White men. Though it was obvious that some of their White countrymen resented that Black men were ostensibly being treated as equals, some things did work in the Black soldier's favor. In May, the army decided it would also begin training African American officers to command its African American units. In a reversal of their earlier opinion, the army now seemed to believe that African American soldiers would respond better to commanders of their own race. Of the approximately 1,250 men who trained in Fort Des Moines in Des Moines, Iowa, roughly half graduated in its only class of officers in October 1917. Subsequent Black officers were trained in Caribbean outposts, in the Philippines, or in other camps around the country. While some programs were integrated and largely equitable, many officers still trained in segregated camps and suffered extreme indignities at the hands of White superiors and subordinates alike.[30]

My (Elaine's) great-uncle Jesse Barksdale served in the 807th Pioneer Infantry in World War I. Several Black regiments served in glorified labor camps, stateside, but the 807th was deployed to France. I'm not sure if Uncle Jesse was part of the 807th band that was so highly acclaimed by W. E. B. DuBois in his letter about the return of the troops to Camp Dix, New Jersey. However, it was very likely Uncle Jesse saw his share of combat, considering several members of his regiment received French honor the Croix de Guerre.[31]

Black troops were often noncombat regiments, working as stevedores or as diggers of trenches, graves, and latrines. They built hospitals, roads, and railroad lines and bridges. However, dissatisfied with the menial army jobs in the states and abroad, many Black men longed for their chance to engage in combat and show their ability to fight and earn the respect of their White brethren. Emmett Scott, who was an assistant to Booker T. Washington, pressed for more options. As a result, 92nd and 93rd combat units were formed. Unfortunately, sabotage by racist officers, inadequate training, and lack of cohesion with their White counterparts sometimes resulted in questionable performances in battle.[32]

Though Uncle Jesse's 807th was praised for their musical and military prowess, their return to native shores did not bring with it equality and comradery. Like many African American units, after being treated like equals in Europe, they felt the sting of being treated like lesser humans by their own compatriots for whom they had just risked their lives. It was a disappointment that brought their unasked question to the surface: What sacrifice would be enough to prove themselves worthy of respect by their White countrymen? For women, their fate was similar. Though they were urged to join the American Red Cross, and many did—with the hopes of helping our soldiers during this time of war—it was not until just before the war's end that the army finally admitted Black women to nurse Black soldiers and German prisoners of war. One such nurse, Aileen Cole Stewart, described her participation in the war as "anticlimactic."[33]

Though race relations in the United States seemed to stand still, and in some cases to regress, that did not stop African Americans from doing what they saw as their patriotic duty. Black men still continued to enlist in the armed forces, and their biggest test of fighting for equality was on its way: World War II.

WORLD WAR II

As it had during World War I, the United States tried to remain disengaged during World War II, considering it a problem on "the other side of the pond," but the Japanese, as we know, had other ideas. The bombing of Pearl Harbor thrust the United States into the fighting fray, and her African American sons and daughters were soon in line to defend its shores. Young Black patriots from Hopewell, New Jersey, and every town across America headed to foreign countries to serve in the U.S. military. As in previous wars, African American draftees and volunteers continued to fight for freedom, including freedom from the harsh treatment of the segregated troops, segregated housing, and segregated mess halls.

Though locating information on World War II veterans is easier than it is for those from the Revolutionary or Civil War—largely due to better record keeping and the ability to actually speak with the living veterans themselves—Dean Ashton's book *Be It Ever So Humble*[34] has been an invaluable resource in understanding the contributions of local African Americans in the military. The African Americans from Hopewell and surrounding areas had their names displayed on an honor roll in their communities along with the names of their comrades during World War II. Hopewell Borough provided more than two hundred men and women to the armed forces, and the Hopewell Borough Honor Roll is an object of pride, displaying the names of the borough's servicemen and women. It was displayed in the center of town for years.

Many other volunteers came from nearby Stoutsburg, Mount Rose, Rosedale, Marshall's Corner, and Wertsville. The prospect of losing a loved one to the war was hitting close to home for many local residents. The Daniels family, however, was placed in particular jeopardy when their seven sons volunteered to go in the service—all at once. James, Floyd, Milford, Charles, Richard, David, and Wilmer Daniels served their country throughout Europe, Casablanca, Africa, Burma, and Sicily, Italy, until they returned safely to the states. One can only imagine their parents' relief after what must have been years of worry and countless sleepless nights. I can imagine Mrs. Daniels holding onto her sons with very little desire to ever let go.

Our local veterans were on the beachheads at Normandy, Omaha Beach, Okinawa, and Iwo Jima. Some worked as aviation engineers, some in army signal construction battalions and the medical corps. Blacks played a very important role in supplying the front-line troops with ammunition, food, and equipment, and African Americans were often used in such areas as quartermaster truck companies, vehicle repair, food service, and medical units.

Listed in the Hopewell Borough Honor Roll are Earl C. Bartlett, Samuel Hightower, Virdia D. Hoagland, Paige Hoagland Jr., Oscar Hodnett, Samuel Hodnett, Verna L. Nevius, Emmanuel "Manny" Staton, and Thomas R. Waldron.

Corporal Thomas R. Waldron, Elaine's uncle, for instance, entered the service on August 29, 1942, where he was an army cook. His favorite phrase was, "They didn't die from eating in the army!" Uncle Thomas served with 99th Railhead Company, Quartermaster Corps, and—after training at Fort DuPont, Delaware—he was deployed to North Africa and Italy from March 1943 to November 1945.

Another Hopewell resident was Sergeant Earl "Ace" Bartlett, who worked with the "Red Ball Express" in France and Belgium. Ace, who had been a truck driver for the 3137th Quartermaster Truck Company, now took on the dangerous job of transporting ammunition and nitroglycerin.

John's uncle Private Elmer Earle Nevius joined the army on June 22, 1943, where he was assigned to the Engineers. Private Nevius went to Fort Belvoir, Virginia, where he learned how to operate a power shovel.

After two years of service, Uncle Earle became ill, spent six weeks in the hospital, and received a medical discharge on December 22, 1945.

More notable is another of my (Elaine's) husband John's relatives, Verna L. Nevius (Witcher). She served as a member of the Women's Army Auxiliary Corps (WAAC), the organization that preceded the Women's Army Corps, better known as WAC. Private First-Class Verna Lee Nevius was the first Black woman to be enrolled in the WAAC from the Southern New Jersey & Delaware District and the only WAAC from the Hopewell area during this time. She was assigned to Fort Clark, Texas, where she joined the 1885th Service Unit of WAAC and worked as a dispatcher in the motor pool. This was the first time that women were allowed in the military in a capacity other than nursing. These women served in roles such as switchboard operators, mechanics, and stenographers, to name a few. The idea was to use women to fill noncombat jobs and thus to allow more men to be sent to the front lines. WAC unit 6888th was one of the few to actually serve overseas, sorting through a backlog of soldiers' letters that apparently "reached the ceiling" at warehouses first in Birmingham, England, and then in Rouen, France. While serving in uniform, Verna likely faced not only discrimination as an African American, during a time of racial segregation, but also as a woman. The idea of women in the military was met with great opposition by the many who believed that a woman's only place was in the home. The WAAC was often greatly slandered and accused of sexual promiscuity by both men and women alike. Many male soldiers apparently saw them as a threat to their masculinity. Some considered their role as male companions, an expectation that has doubly plagued the African American woman. Despite all this, the women who served during World War II did so with dedication and grace. Verna's service ended in August 1943, after the WAAC underwent a change in status through the creation of the WAC with its "duration" enlistments.

Finally, there is Hopewell resident Paige Hoagland Jr., T/5, who entered the service March 18, 1943, where he served his first front-line duty on Iwo Jima from April 24 to December 12, 1945. Stationed on Iwo Jima, Hoagland was responsible for the repair of varied equipment, including trucks, jeeps, and bulldozers. He worked close to the Japanese despite danger from rifle fire. Remarkably, Hoagland's outfit lost only three men.

The dedicated service of such women and men began to earn African Americans a long-withheld respect as soldiers and as Americans. Like World War I's progress with Black officers and combat units, World War II also had its share of burgeoning equality, as more specialized military troops were formed. The Tuskegee Airmen, for example, showed that African Americans had the intellect and ability to serve in some of the most demanding military roles.[35]

After their sacrifice and the accolades received overseas, many African American soldiers were demoralized by their treatment upon their return home. While their actions earned them the respect of some White Americans, others were threatened by this possibility of a new world order and responded with rabid violence. This was particularly evident in the South, where Black soldiers (particularly officers) were lynched, some while wearing their military uniforms. Langston Hughes perhaps said it best when he compared Germans to White southerners and suggested they were both "victims of a mass psychosis." The obvious comparison is that the way in which the Hitler regime oppressed the Jews was far too similar to the White treatment of Blacks.[36]

Hughes was right, and that truth was not lost on the returning soldiers. It was evident that, just as the Revolutionary War supported lofty ideals of liberty and equality while sanctioning owning slaves, America's horror at the suffering of the Jews under Nazi oppression fell on deaf ears and blind eyes when it came to White America's treatment of their Black countrymen and women. As for the army, it began its part by integrating the service in 1948, but that was met with considerable dissent, and several White soldiers who refused to salute or take orders from Black officers went undisciplined. Times were changing, however slowly, and African Americans were losing patience with their second-class status in both the military and civilian life.

POST-WORLD WAR II

Robert Louis "Sonny" Hunt, my (Elaine's) uncle, knows this second-class status all too well, having served in the U.S. Navy for six years starting in 1955. Uncle Sonny served on the USS *Tawara* and the USS *Independence* as a "plank owner," meaning that he went on that ship just after it was built. "We served on the east side of Greenland," he told us, "saw the Northern Lights, crossed the Arctic Circle, also crossed the equator and became a shellback" (when you cross the equator you become a shellback). In a conversation Beverly and I had with my Uncle Sonny, he told us about what life was like in the military before the civil rights movement took off. "I remember all kinds of segregation," he said. At that time, he continued, most Blacks who went into the military were made cooks and stewards. "I was lucky. I had mechanical abilities, so they taught me refrigeration and air conditioning, so I learned my trade that carried me through for the last sixty years."

When Bev and I asked him what he thought about the difference in the country now that there are more laws to protect equality, Uncle Sonny's answer was dishearteningly honest. "Segregation will never disappear. It's just done more subtle … and the Blacks are just as bad when it comes to segregation. You have a tendency to stick together for safety reasons." He continued, "Regarding discrimination, in 1951, I started Princeton High School—the White kids got chosen to college— they got picked first, a lot of the Black kids were highly educated, but never got chosen to go to college. Whatever happened in the 1930s and 1940s was still going on—things didn't start to change until the 1960s. There was no Black history for us. They only told you about George Washington Carver for Black history. Until they have a Black history class, you will never know the true story about slavery," he said, solemnly. Bev and I sat listening as he ended story, wondering: Is that one of the reasons our research is so important to us? By preserving the memories of those interred at Stoutsburg are we finally able to tell their little piece of history, and through their local story shine light on a larger American reality?

Even with all its struggles, our country has come a long way in honoring and rewarding African American veterans. Milton Ronald "Ronnie" Coleman, my (Elaine's) uncle, was drafted into the military in the summer of 1972 after graduating from Hopewell Valley Central High School. He served for three years. He then enlisted in the army as a Petroleum Laboratory Specialist and retired, with honors, after twenty years of service. Now, Ronnie lives in South Korea where he procures petroleum products for the military. Most notably, he provides quality assurance fuel support on Air Force One when the -president is traveling throughout the Pacific and Southeast Asia. Uncle Ronnie, through his military training, has risen to the head position where he is in control of all the testing and purchasing of crude oil for the military in the Asian sector of the world. Just a year apart from me in age and John's classmate: it still amazes us how much has changed just within our own lifetime.

✳

Now that my husband, John, is an adult, he has spent many years researching the accomplishments of veterans buried at Stoutsburg Cemetery or Pennington African Cemetery. And, as president of the

Stoutsburg Cemetery Association, John has led many Memorial Day services to honor our veterans. From Black Revolutionary War veterans to those African Americans listed on the Hopewell Borough Honor Roll, our little corner of America has represented itself and its patriotic zeal well.

Our annual Memorial Day tradition invites the entire community to come together the last Sunday in May. We sing and send up prayers to honor our veterans. The Memorial Day service is so important to all of us because of our love for this country: a country founded as a refuge for political and religious freedoms. We believe that this country, with all its faults, is still the greatest country on earth. It is great because of all the freedoms that we enjoy, and all of the people who have given their lives so that we can enjoy those freedoms. It is particularly true for our African American veterans, like those buried at Stoutsburg Cemetery, who were "Always ready to serve the nation that was not willing to serve them," to quote former secretary of state and four-star general Colin Powell.[37]

Though African American soldiers were once used for the most menial jobs, Blacks have now risen to the highest ranks in the military. When Beverly and I think of all the veterans buried in Stoutsburg Cemetery, we think about how we have come from unmarked graves and being buried near the outhouse to twenty-one-gun-salute funerals and lying in state. I believe our Black Revolutionary forefathers would think that their sacrifices were well worth it.

AMERICAN REVOLUTION BLACK SOLDIERS FROM THE REGION

RANK	NAME	REGIMENT	SOURCE
Private	Pompey Black	2nd New Jersey (Col. Shreve's Regiment)	IRW 1:221
Private	James Casar	1st New Jersey	IRW 1:443
Private	John Casar	1st New Jersey	IRW 1:443
Private	John Cato	4th New Jersey	IRW 1:452
Private	John Ceasar	4th New Jersey	IRW 1:546
Sub	Samuel Charlton	New Jersey Line	AAAIP, p. 127
Private	Oliver Cromwell	2nd New Jersey (Capt. Lowery)	IRW 1:640
	Cudjo (for his master Benjamin Coe)		
	possibly named Cudjo Clark	5th Massachusetts	IRW 1:652, 511
Fifer	Negro Cuff fifer	3rd New Jersey	IRW 1:652
	William Cuffey	2nd New Jersey	IRW 1:635
	Jacob Francis	New Jersey militia/Col. Phillips	IRW 1:975
	Cato Johnson	Spencer's Additional Regiment	IRW 2:1455
Private	Dick Negro	1st New Jersey	IRW 3:1973
	Black Prime	2nd New Jersey Crane's Troop of Horses	USNAMR
	Negro Sambo	4th New Jersey	USNAMR
Private	William Stives (Stivers)	3rd New Jersey	IRW 4:2609
Private	Samuel Sutphin (Sutphen)	New Jersey line(1st Reg Somerset City 1776-8) (sub for Casper Berger)	Strykers, p. 878
Fifer	Negro Titus	1st New Jersey	USNAMR
Private	Amos Tomson	1st Regt. Burlington Militia/2nd New Jersey	IRW 3:274
Private	Peter Williams	New Jersey Line	IRW 4:3014

IWR = White , Index to Revolutionary War Service Records, vols. 1–4.

AAAIP = African American and American Indian Patriots of the Revolutionary War (Washington, DC: National Society Daughters of the American Revolution, 2001)

USNAMR = U.S. National Archives Muster Rolls

Strykers = Stryker's Officers & Men (New Jersey, Adjutant-General's Office, Official Register of the Officers and Men of New Jersey in the Revolutionary War.)

BATTLE OF TRENTON

RANK	NAME	REGIMENT	SOURCE
	Pomp Devereux	Glover's 14th Continental	
	Scipio Dodge	Baldwin's 26th Continental, New Hampshire	USNAMR
	Hanobel	Baldwin's 26th Continental	IRW, 2:1187
	Sipeo	Baldwin's 26th Continental	IRW, 4:2484
Private	Nathaniel Small	Baldwin's 26th Continental, Massachusetts	IRW, 4:2497
Private	Luther Jotham	Baldwin's 23rd Continental, Massachusetts	IRW, 2:1486
Private	Thomas Semor	Bailey's 23rd Continental, Massachusetts	IRW, 4:2412
	Primus Hall/Prince Hall	Massachusetts	USNAMR
Private	Peter Jennings	1st, New Hampshire	IRW, 3:1442
	Philip Rodman	Lippitt's Rhode Island	IRW, 3:1442
	Primus Coffin	New Hampshire	AAAIP, p. 53
Private	Dick Fortune	Durkee's 20th Continental, 1st Connecticut	IRW, 1:961
Private	Cesar Cipeo	Durkee's 20th Continental, 1st Connecticut	IRW, 1:497
Private	Samuel Pompey	1st Connecticut	IRW, 3:2154
Private	John Pompey	1st Connecticut	IRW, 3:2154
	Abraham Pharoah	Connecticut	IRW, 3:2122
Private	Cudgo Shephard	1st Connecticut	IRW, 3:2442

IWR = White , *Index to Revolutionary War Service Records*, vols. 1–4.

USNAMR = U.S. National Archives Muster Rolls

POST–AMERICAN REVOLUTIONARY BLACK SOLDIER FROM REGION

NAME	DATES	SOURCE	DESCRIPTION
Aaron Schanck	b. c. 1772 to d. 1836	*FAG:* #119863083	too young for American Revolution, no record of war service

FAG: Find A Grave, database and images (https://www.findagrave.com, accessed 27 April 2018), memorial page for Aaron Schanck (unknown: 19 October 1836).

Find A Grave Memorial no. 119863083, citing Stoutsburg Cemetery, Hopewell, Mercer County, New Jersey, USA; Maintained by gazelle (contributor 48200756).

STOUTSBURG CIVIL WAR VETERANS

NAME	DATES	REGIMENT	STOUTSBURG CEMETERY	PENNINGTON AFRICAN CEMETERY
PIra S. Bergen	dates unknown	Company H, 127th U.S. Colored Troops, Infantry	known but unmarked	
Raymond Bergen	b. unknown to d. 1918	New Jersey Fireman U.S. NRE	FAG: #119864497	
George Boldin	dates unknown	8th U.S. Colored Troops Infantry, Battle of Olustee		FAG: #42726124
William H. Boyer	dates unknown	Company E, 29th Regiment, Connecticut Colored Volunteer Infantry	FAG: #42726132	
George Dillon (Dillion)	b.1838 to d. 1888	24th Regular Troops	FAG: #119865433	
Lewis Fisher	b. unknown to d. 1895	Company F, Regiment, U.S. Colored Troops Infantry	FAG: #119864755	
Charles Jennings	dates unknown	Company G, 14th Regiment Rhode Island Heavy Artillery		FAG: 42726192
Samuel Montgomery	dates unknown			known but unmarked
John Naz	dates unknown	Battery G 11th U.S. Colored Troops	known but unmarked	
Tracy Peaterson/Peterson	dates unknown	Company H, 127th U.S. Colored Troops	known but unmarked	
George Reasoner	b. unknown to d. 1893			FAG: #42726243
William H. Reasoner	b. unknown to d. 1889	Corporal, Company E, 11th, U.S. Colored Troops Arrillery	FAG: #119865356	
Samuel I. Ridley	dates unknown	Company E, 127th, U.S. Colored Troops Infantry	FAG: #119864085	
James Schenk	dates unknown	Co 41st US INF, Battle of Olustee	FAG: #119863400	
Jonathan Stives	dates unknown	Company M, 3rd Regiment, New Jersey Cavalry	FAG: #119864006	
Aaron S. Truehart	b. unknown to d. 1954	Company H, 127 U.S. Colored Troops Infantry	FAG: #119864248	
George Williamson	b. unknown to d. 1908	Company F, 8th Regiment, U.S. Colored Troops		FAG: #42726316
John VanZandt	dates unknown	Company G, 41st Regiment, U.S. Colored Ttroops	FAG: #119863667	

FAG = Find A Grave, database and images, accessed April 27, 2018, https://www.findagrave.com

known but unmarked = known inhabitants whose graves are no longer marked

WORLD WAR I SOLDIERS BURIED IN STOUTSBURG

NAME	RANK	BRANCH	DATES	REGIMENT	SOURCE
Jesse Barksdale	Private	Army	b. 1889 to d. 1937	807th Pioneer Infantry, Company A	*FAG,* #45304330
Edmond Brokaw	Private	Army	b. 1897 to d. 1959	63rd Pioneer Infantry, Headquarters Company	*FAG,* #45304285
Virgia D. Hoagland	Private	Army	b. 1887 to d. 1958	807th Pioneer Infantry	*FAG,* #45304283
Oscar Hodnett	Private	Army	b. unknown to d. 1943	807th Pioneer Infantry	*FAG,* #453042781

FAG = Find A Grave, database and images, accessed April 27, 2018, https://www.findagrave.com

WORLD WAR II HONOR ROLL, HOPEWELL BOROUGH

NAME	RANK	BRANCH	DATES	SOURCE	DESCRIPTION
Howard J. Brooks	Private	Army	b. 1922 to d. 1983	*FAG*, #45304373	
Theodore Cain		Army	b. 1924 to d. 1993	*FAG*, #45304341	
Goldie Nelson "Bill" Cain	S2	Navy	b.1914 to d. 1983	*FAG*, #45304335	
Lonnie C. Geter	Staff Sergeant	Army	b. 1924 to d. 1999	*FAG*, #93334874	
Wilmer Grover, Jr.		Army	b. 1923 to d. 1996	*FAG*, #45304286	
Virdia D. Hoagland, Jr.	Private	Army	b. 1925 to d. 1997	*FAG*, #45304281 / *Ashton*	Enlistment: September 29, 1943. 731st Medical Sanitation Corps
David Kane	Private	Army	1910 to 1988	*FAG*, #45304334	Ambulance driver, 731st Medical Sanitation Corps.
Lester Fred Nevius	Aviation Machinist's Mate C	Navy	b. 1925 to d. 1981	*FAG*, #45304371 / *Ashton*	Enlistment: September 8, 1943. Mechanic on Navy planes
Elmer Earle Nevius	Private	Army	b. 1916 to b. 2005	*FAG*, #45304361 / *Ashton*	See Chapter Eight
William W. Smith	Private	Army	b. 1923 to d. 1993	*FAG*, #45304317	See Chapter Eight
Robert S. True	Technician fifth grade	Army	b. 1919 to d. 1983	*FAG*, #45304270	See Chapter Eight
Robert M. Wheeler	Army		b. 1928 to d. 1984	*FAG*, #45304358	
Nelson B. Williamson	1st Sergeant	Army	b. 1918 to d. 1995	*FAG*, #119862873	

Ashton = Ashton, Dean H. *Be It Ever So Humble.* Trenton, New Jersey: Kirkham & Guthrie. 1947.

FAG = Find A Grave, database and images, accessed April 27, 2018. https://www.findagrave.com

POST–WORLD WAR II SOLDIERS BURIED IN STOUTSBURG

NAME	RANK	CONFLICT	BRANCH	DATES	SOURCE
Gerald Grover		Vietnam	Air Force	b. 1946 to d. 2005	FAG, #45304354
Robert L. Grover	Lance Corporal	Vietnam	Marine Corps	b. 1938 to d. 2011	FAG, #101435285
Theodore F. Grover	Corporal	Korea	Marine Corps	b. 1929 to d. 1999	FAG, #45304284
Barry Brian Nevius	Private	Vietnam	Marine Corps	b. 1949 to d. 1987	FAG, #45304369
Bruce Lionel Nevius	Corporal	Vietnam	Marine Corps	b. 1949 to d. 1984	FAG, #45304370
Clarence L. Tunison		Vietnam	Navy	b. 1936 to d. 1999	FAG, #119861583

FAG = Find A Grave, database and images, accessed April 27, 2018. https://www.findagrave.com

The chapter epigraph comes from: William A. Croffut and John M. Morris. *The Military & Civil History of Connecticut During the War of 1861–65* (Boston: Ledyard Bill, 1868), accessed April 26, 2018, https://archive.org/details/militarycivilhis00lccrof.

1   "Barbarianism in New Jersey," *New York Times*, January 2, 1880, accessed February 18, 2018, https://timesmachine.nytimes.com/timesmachine/1880/01/02/98875417.pdf.

2   Nathan Perkins Sanborn, "General John Glover and His Marblehead Regiment in the Revolutionary War: A Paper Read Before the Marblehead Historical Society, May 14, 1903" (Marblehead Historical Society, 1903), accessed January 25, 2018, https://archive.org/details/genjohngloverhis00sanb.

3   Gwen Shrift, "Marblehead Regiment Was Washington's Secret Weapon in the Battle of Trenton," *Bucks County Courier Times*, December 24, 2016, accessed January 25, 2018, http://www.buckscountycouriertimes.com/c684aa5c-c6ef-11e6-bb70-c3198735ec60.html?start=2.

4   Eric G. Grundset, "African Americans of Massachusetts in the Revolution," Massachusetts Society Sons of the American Revolution, n.d., accessed January 25, 2018, http://www.massar.org/african-americans-of-massachusetts-in-the-revolution/.

5   William S. Stryker, *Battles of Trenton and Princeton* (Boston: Houghton Mifflin, 1898), 134.

6   Connor E. Seaman, *Forgotten Glory: African American Civil War Soldiers and Their Omission from Civil War Memory* (undergraduate thesis, University of Washington, 2013).

7   "African Americans and the War for Independence, Civil War Trust," Civil War Trust, Revolutionary War History, accessed December 9, 2017, https://www.civilwar.org/learn/articles/african-americans-and-war-independence.

8   John Hope Franklin and Evelyn Brooks Higginbotham, "Give Me Liberty (1763–1787)," *From Slavery to Freedom: A History of African Americans*, 9th ed., ed. John Hope Franklin and Evelyn Brooks (New York: McGraw Hill, 2011) 84–102.

9   Ibid.

10   Frank J. Williams, "Providence and Civil War. 375th Anniversary Site [No Longer Exists but Available as Archive]," Providence Rhode Island, archive, accessed November 24, 2017, https://web.archive.org/web/20131007213155/http://providenceri.com/print/archives/375th-essays-providence-and-civil-war.

11   Virgil D. White, *Index to Revolutionary War Service Records/Transcribed by Virgil D. White*, vols. 1–4 (Waynesboro, TN: National Historical Publishing Company, 1995).

12   Ibid.

[13] New Jersey, Adjutant-General's Office, *Official Register of the Officers and Men of New Jersey in the Revolutionary War, Compiled under Orders of Theodore F. Randolph, Governor, by William S. Stryker, Adjutant General. With Added Digest and Revision, for the Use of the Society of the Cincinnati in the State of New Jersey (1911)*, official register reprinted from the 1872 edition (Baltimore: Genealogical Publishing Co., 1967).

[14] Honeyman Van Doren, ed., "The Revolutionary War Record of a Somerset County Slave," *Somerset County Historical Quarterly* 3 (1914): 184–90. This is the account of the slave Samuel Sutphin.

[15] White, *Index to Revolutionary War Service Records.*

[16] Richard S. Walling, "Prince Whipple: Symbol of African Americans at the Battle of Trenton," Whipple Website, 2001, accessed November 25, 2017, http://www.whipple.org/prince/princewhipple.html.

[17] White, *Index to Revolutionary War Service Records.*

[18] "USCT History, United States Colored Troops," African American Civil War Museum, accessed December 3, 2017, https://www.afroamcivilwar.org/about-us/usct-history.html.

[19] "African Americans and the Civil War," New Jersey State Library, n.d., accessed January 4, 2018, http://www.njstatelib.org/research_library/new_jersey_resources/highlights/african_american_history_curriculum/unit_6_civil_war_african_americans/.

[20] Joseph G. Bibly, "A Salute to Forgotten Soldiers," *New York Times: New Jersey Opinion*, accessed December 8, 2017, http://www.nytimes.com/1989/05/28/nyregion/new-jersey-opinion-a-salute-to-forgotten-soldiers.html.

[21] Jennifer Thompson, "Baptism of Fire, in Defense of Colonel Fribley and the 8th USCT," *Saber and Scroll* 1, no. 1, article 7 (March 2012), accessed December 9, 2017, https://digitalcommons.apus.edu/saberandscroll/vol1/iss1/7/.

[22] Gary Y. Okihiro, *American History Unbound: Asians and Pacific Islanders* (Oakland: University of California Press, 2015), 16.

[23] George Hicks III and Carmen Weaver Hicks, African American Women and the Military, n.d., accessed February 13, 2018, http://www.buffalosoldiersresearchmuseum.org/research/women.htm.

[24] Susie King Taylor, *Reminiscences of My Life in Camp with the 33d United States Colored Troops Late 1st S.C. Volunteers* (Boston: Published by the Author, 1902), Accessed February 13, 2018, https://babel.hathitrust.org/cgi/pt?id=hvd.32044036968782;view=1up;seq=13.

[25] Hicks and Hicks, http://www.buffalosoldiersresearchmuseum.org/research/women.htm.

[26] Jami L. Bryan, "Fighting for Respect: African American Soldiers in WWI," Army Historical Foundation, accessed December 5, 2017, https://armyhistory.org/fighting-for-respect-african-american-soldiers-in-wwi/.

[27] LTC Roger D. Cunningham USA Retired, "The Black 'Immune' Regiments in the Spanish-American War," Army Historical Foundation, accessed January 27, 2018, https://armyhistory.org/the-black-immune-regiments-in-the-spanish-american-war/.

[28] Bryan, "Fighting for Respect: African American Soldiers in WWI."

[29] Ibid.

[30] Ibid.

[31] "Return of the 807th Pioneer Regiment, ca. 1919," W. E. B. DuBois Papers, series 5, Nonfiction Books, n.d., accessed January 28, 2018, http://credo.library.umass.edu/view/full/mums312-b219-i282.

[32] Bryan, "Fighting for Respect: African American Soldiers in WWI."

[33] Aileen Cole Stewart, "Ready to Serve," *American Journal of Nursing* 63, no. 9 (September 1963): 85–87, accessed January 28, 2018, http://www.jstor.org/stable/3452837.

[34] Dean H. Ashton, *Be It Ever So Humble* (Trenton, NJ: Kirkham & Guthrie, 1947).

[35] Daniel L. Haulman. *Nine Myths About the Tuskegee Airmen* (Tuskegee AL: Tuskegee University, 2011), 3.

[36] Langston Hughes, *Langston Hughes and the "Chicago Defender": Essays on Race, Politics and Culture, 1942–1962*, ed. Christopher C. DeSantis (Urbana: University of Illinois Press, 1995), 79.

[37] "Colin Powell: We've Come a Long Way, but African-American Struggle 'Not Over,'" CBS News, September 12, 2016, accessed January 28, 2018, https://www.cbsnews.com/news/former-secretary-of-state-colin-powell-national-museum-of-african-american-history-and-culture/.

Rows, left to right: (Top) Bessie Grover, Stephanye Clark, Herma Fields and Jean Marie
Second Row: Tim and Christine Stives, Earl Hubbard, Leona Hubbard Stewart
Third Row: Earl Nevius, William (Shud) Smith, Gerry Hoagland, Cora Bergen,
Bottom Row: Albert Witcher, Evelyn and Ira Brooks, Marvel Aleta Harris

CHAPTER 8

RESIDENT VOICES

NARRATIVES AND INTERVIEWS OF DESCENDANTS FROM THE SOURLAND MOUNTAIN AND SURROUNDING REGION

The deceased [William Stives], although one of that "caste of rare" descended from Africa, was a true Whig patriot "in those days that tried men's souls." He enlisted in the American army at the commencement of the Revolutionary War and continued a faithful and courageous soldier in the cause of his adopted country, during the whole seven years' struggle, for which he received a pension during his life.

—Obituary, *Emancipator*

The compelling stories of our ancestors have remained dormant for years like fragments of a puzzle whose scattered pieces were left suspended in time. These founding families, the African American families on the Sourland Mountain and surrounding region such as the Stives, Truehearts, Grovers, Hoaglands, Hagamans, Blackwells, Neviuses, and Bergens, left descendants who had their own stories to tell, stories as inspirational and touching as those of their ancestors.

Gathering the narratives and interviews in this chapter has been a crucial step in putting the puzzle pieces together. For those we interviewed, we became physically involved in their space as we ate at their tables, handled their pictures, and foretold from the tone in their voices that a difficult memory was about to be shared, a memory taken off the shelf.

There were countless times when the hour we asked to be granted turned into two or more. We were always amazed at the transformation of those who said they had nothing to say, that there was nothing they had to offer. Those would be the same people talking an hour or two later and beyond if time permitted.

We welcome you to read the stories of people who descended from some of the amazing pioneers we've highlighted earlier in this book. We've also included stories of individuals whose families migrated north to join those already established. From their own words we share with you their triumphs, tragedies, family stories, and how reliance on their unwavering faith in church and community helped them to persevere.

DESCENDANTS OF THE STIVES FAMILY

WILLIAM STIVES, 1757–1839

Town of Residence: Stoutsburg, New Jersey (formerly Hunterdon County)

Date of Written Text: August 4, 2014

Interviewer/Narrator: Timothy R. Stives (4th Great-Grandson)

Permission from: Timothy R. Stives

His Story: A Revolutionary War Soldier and fifer who joined the 3rd Regiment of the New Jersey Continental Army. William enlisted at the commencement of the Revolutionary War and served under George Washington, as well as with General Sullivan in the expedition against the Indians.

Introduction: One of the original African American settlers on the Sourland Mountain, New Jersey, William, along with his wife, Catherine Vanois, together raised ten children.

February 1778. The Continental Army is encamped at Valley Forge, just northwest of Philadelphia. A young Black man, William Stives, about eighteen years old, makes his way to the camp and enlists in Captain Cox's Company of the 3rd New Jersey Regiment. He will spend the next five years in George Washington's army. He will be in many battles and see much fighting, first as a fifer and later as an infantryman. Eventually, after the war, he will make his way to the Sourland Mountain.

In the same company is another soldier about a generation older than William. Samuel Stivers is in the hospital at Valley Forge, suffering from wounds received the previous autumn at the Battle of Brandywine. He is from Newark, or possibly Second River, New Jersey. Samuel will die of his wounds on April 1, 1778. His widow, Rachel (Van Winkle) Stivers, will receive a widow's pension after the war.

I am a direct lineal descendant of William Stives. He is my great-great-great-great-grandfather. I was born in Trenton and spent most of my life living in the Trenton and Princeton area. My father was born in Princeton. My father, grandfather, and great-grandfather are buried in the Princeton Cemetery on Witherspoon Street. My great-grandfather was born on the Sourland Mountain.

In the Revolutionary War service and pension records of William Stives there is a note stating "there has been considerable difficulty in determining what spelling to use for the name of this man, as he uses the spelling Stivers in his pension claim, but in 1839, his son, in speaking of himself and the widow, used the spelling Stives. Most of the other references also used the spelling Stives."

The service and pension records further state that he was born in 1760 and that he was a musician in Captain Richard Cox's Company, 3rd Regiment, New Jersey Continental Line. He enlisted in February 1778 for the duration of the war, and he was promoted to private in May 1779. On January 1, 1781, he was transferred as a private with Captain Cox's Company to the 1st Regiment, New Jersey Continental Line. On April 11, 1781, he was detached to Captain Aaron Ogden's Company of Lt. Colonel Francis Barber's Battalion of Light Infantry and in camp at Head of Elk, Maryland. On May 20, 1783, he was transferred to Captain Nathaniel Leonard's Company of Colonel Matthias Ogden's Regiment. He was discharged from service at Newburgh, New York, on June 5, 1783.

William was in the Battle of Monmouth on June 28, 1778, and the Battle of Newton, New York, on August 29, 1779. He was present with Major General Sullivan's Expedition against the Indians in 1779. He fought in the Battle of Springfield, New Jersey, on June 23, 1780, and was present at the surrender of Lord Cornwallis at Yorktown, Virginia, on October 19, 1781.

My father never talked much about his family. One day in the early 1990s my cousin Richard, who lived around the corner in Princeton Junction, told me that he was going to take me on the "Stives cemetery tour." He took me to the Princeton Cemetery and showed me the graves of my grandfather and my great-grandparents, followed by a stop at St. Paul's Cemetery to show me the graves of various great-aunts and great-uncles. Then he said we had to go to Hopewell. We drove "up the mountain" and I saw, for the first time, the Stoutsburg Cemetery. In the cemetery were the graves of Mary and Jonathan Stives. Who were these people? Richard didn't know. My genealogical odyssey had begun.

The earliest record indicating when William Stives first came to the Sourland area is the record of his marriage. William married Catherine Vanois, of Somerset, on November 15, 1789. The ceremony was conducted by the Reverend William Frazer at St. Andrew's Church in Ringoes, New Jersey. St. Andrew's was rebuilt in 1867 in Lambertville.[1]

Genealogy is a frustrating endeavor. There will always be unanswered questions. For example, we do not know anything about the origins of Catherine Vanois or her life prior to the date of her marriage. For that matter, we do not know anything about the origins of William Stives before his enlistment in February 1778. There are clues, but making assumptions without proper documentation, or relying on the Internet, is dangerous in the genealogy business. The clues, in my opinion, led to Samuel Stivers and the colonial village of Second River, New Jersey, which today is the town of Belleville.

Roxanne Carkhuff, a local historian, genealogist, and long-time member and officer of the Hunterdon County Historical Society, wrote a piece which I was handed. It appears to be from the *Somerset County Genealogical Quarterly* about the early settlers of the Sourland Mountain, and a specific area referred to as Rock Mills. On the piece of paper, it states "William Stives and his wife, Catherine, may have been two of the earliest, if not the first settlers to this area of the Sourland Mountains. They were married by Rev. William Frazer at Ringoes in 1789 and shortly thereafter the couple were living on the Mountain. Stives was a free black who, through his service in the Revolutionary War, qualified for a government pension."

I first met Roxanne Carkhuff one afternoon while doing research in the New Jersey Archives Library in Trenton. When the librarian learned I was doing genealogical research on people from Hopewell, he said,

"Well, in that case, you absolutely have to meet Roxanne Carkhuff. She's sitting right over there." When I introduced myself, she said, "You know, of course, that you are the descendant of a Revolutionary War soldier?" At that point, I did not know that, so she sent me over to the microfilm drawer and within thirty minutes had taken my research back to 1760. Finally, before she left that day, she told me I absolutely had to meet Earl Nevius, the caretaker of the Stoutsburg Cemetery, and his wife, Virginia. A great friendship was about to begin.

William and Catherine Stives had ten children. The census records of East Amwell Township and court records of the estate of their son James (examined by Roxanne Carkhuff) provide us with some information about them. (Note: There may have also been a son William.)

1. **Cornelius** - born 1792. Married Elizabeth McIntire. Died in East Amwell in 1866. *This is my great-great-great grandfather.*

2. **Harriet** - born 1796. Married Samuel Peterson. *(Virginia's ancestor.)*

3. **James** - born 1799. Unmarried. Died in East Amwell in 1844.

4. **Stacy** - born 1803. Moved to Alma, Allegany County, New York. Died in 1878.

5. **Stanford** - born 1805. Moved to Fairfield, Iowa.

6. **Letitia** - born 1808. Married Joseph Mackintire in 1824. In 1850, living in Roxbury Township.

7. **Procena (Prosena)** - born 1810. Married John Arnold.

8. **Elizabeth Ann** - born 1811. Married Eli Middleton. Moved to Newtown, Pennsylvania.

9. **Elisha** - Married Hannah Mackintire 1817. Moved to northwest Pennsylvania.

10. **Catherine** - Married Francis Middleton.

Shortly after meeting Roxanne, I took her advice and telephoned Earl Nevius. I introduced myself, and Earl replied he would be happy to help me with my family research. He offered to take me on a tour of the graves in the Stoutsburg Cemetery. Then he said, "Let me give the phone to my wife. I think she can help you more than I can." When Virginia came on the phone, she said, "Mr. Stives, why don't you come over to the house and I'll tell you everything I know about my Uncle Johnny Stives." Her Uncle Johnny Stives? Later, I learned Virginia and I were distant cousins. She is also a descendant of William Stives.

Land records found by Roxanne Carkhuff show William Stives purchased a number of parcels of land in the Sourland Mountain area, all in the Township of Amwell, Hunterdon County. The first two were conveyed to William Stives by Ralph Drake and Jane his wife. The earliest was dated July 11, 1791 and the second was on June 29, 1798. The third property was conveyed by Isaac Stout to William Stives on May 5, 1806.

It would be impossible to overstate the contribution Roxanne Carkhuff has made to our knowledge of the early settlers of the Sourland Mountain and many of the people buried in the Stoutsburg Cemetery. During the time I was actively doing my research, I retained her services and she provided me with a wealth of information on my ancestors. While it is all public information, professional genealogists know where to find it, how to interpret it, and how to present it in an understandable manner. Much of the information you will find on websites today regarding William Stives and his descendants was originally done by Roxanne Carkhuff. She was the person who spent countless hours tracking down the details in local libraries and archives.

William Stives was a member of the Old School Baptist Church in Hopewell for forty years. A book titled *Town Records of Hopewell, New*

Jersey by Lisa C. Gedney,[2] published in 1931, contains a section that has abstracts from the record book of the Old School Baptist Church. There are two entries referring to William:

Page 153: 21 September 1799 (William Stiver, a Black Joined church).

Page 169: 24 August 1839, William Stives, deceased, an aged colored member.

William Stives appeared before the Hunterdon County Inferior Court of Common Pleas for the August 1820 term, making a declaration to qualify for his Revolutionary War pension. At that time, he gave his age as sixty, placing his birth at around 1760. In 1820, his assets consisted of 22 acres with small improvements, 2 horses, 2 cows and a calf, 2 hogs, and 7 sheep. A farmer, he had a lame leg for a number of years and suffered from rheumatism. His wife, Catherine, age fifty, placing her birth around 1770, was in tolerable health but was crippled in one hand. Children still living at home were Stacy, age 19, Letitia, age 12, Prosena, age 10, and Betsy Ann, aged 9.

It did not take long for me to realize that everybody in Hopewell knew Earl and Virginia Nevius, as well as their daughter, Beverlee Nevius Tucker. All three, along with Roxanne, took a great interest in my genealogy research, and we had many discussions over a period of two or three years. Virginia was particularly enthusiastic and in 1993 insisted that my wife and I attend the Memorial Day service at the Stoutsburg Cemetery. It was there I first met Beverly Mills and Elaine Buck.

When William died in 1839, his obituary appeared in the *Emancipator*, a New York newspaper at the time. I have reprinted it in its entirety because it is beautifully written and shows that William was a very respected member of the Hopewell community:

Another Revolutionary Pensioner gone. Died near Hopewell, New Jersey on the 24th, William Stives, aged 82, a respectable member of the Baptist Church for the past 40 years. The deceased, although one of that "caste of rare" descended from Africa, was a true Whig patriot "in those days that tried men's souls." He enlisted in the American army at the commencement of the Revolutionary War and continued a faithful and courageous soldier in the cause of his adopted country, during the whole seven years struggle, for which he received a pension during his life. He was in several battles against the British in which he showed distinguished bravery. He was also with General Sullivan in his expedition against the Indians. His deportment in private life was well worthy of imitation, both as a man and a Christian.[3]

Despite all of our research, we have never been able to determine definitively where William Stives is buried. There was no mention of interment in his obituary or any record of burial in any library. No tombstone has ever been found in any local cemetery. He could be buried in the Stoutsburg Cemetery, he *could* be buried in an unmarked grave in the Old School Baptist Church Cemetery, or he could be buried at the old Stives homestead on top of the mountain. As of this date, no one knows for sure.

It may have been Roxanne who first came up with the idea, why not place a memorial stone in the Stoutsburg Cemetery in honor of this Revolutionary War soldier who had been so long forgotten? Earl and Virginia thought that would be entirely appropriate. So, as his descendant, I personally arranged to have a stone carved. There was only one spot to place it—right next to the graves of William's two grandchildren Mary and Jonathan Stives.

There are many men who served their country honorably buried in the Stoutsburg Cemetery. There are graves of Civil War veterans as well as men who fought in both world wars, Korea, and Vietnam. If, indeed, William Stives is buried in Stoutsburg, and I like to think he is, then he is in good company. May he continue to rest in peace.

BESSIE BROKAW GROVER, 1900–1978

Town of Residence: Skillman, New Jersey

Date of Written Text: Date Unknown

Interviewer/Narrator: Bessie Grover

Permission from: Dolores Varner (Granddaughter)

Her Story: Bessie Brokaw Grover writes about her family and growing up on the Sourland Mountain.

Introduction: Bessie was a descendant of the Stives, Peterson, and Brokaw families, some of the original African American settlers on the Sourland Mountain. The Bessie Grover Park, located on Camp Meeting Avenue in Skillman, was named after her because of her heroic effort of saving her family members from a house fire in 1974.

This is the story of my life, Bessie Grover. I was born on the Sourland Mountain in the year 1900. I was one of eight children, which was five girls and three boys. I was the middle girl to two older sisters and two younger sisters. We were raised on a farm of about forty or fifty acres where we raised all kinds of vegetables and fruits such as apples, peaches, grapes, and pears. We had cows, horses, pigs, chickens, ducks, geese and grew all kinds of grain. We were very happy even though we did not have fancy food to eat. We made our own bread and butter and killed our own pigs. We cured hams and also smoked them. My grandfather [meaning her great-great-grandfather, Friday] was a slave who was brought. Aaron Truehart was my grandfather and his brother's name was William Truehart. The name Truehart was given to them from their slave master because they [meaning Friday] had such a true heart. Aaron Truehart married Catherine Amanda (Peterson), who became Truehart. William Truehart never married.

PAUL ARNOLD, 1903–1979

Town of Residence: Hopewell, New Jersey

Date of Written Text: April 19, 2017

Interviewer/Narrator: Kevin Lonergan and Beverly Mills

Permission from: Kevin Lonergan

His Story: Paul Arnold, known as "Beetle," was raised in Hopewell and was a descendant of the Stives family.

Introduction: Beetle was known as one of the best African American baseball players from this region. As a member of the Brooklyn Royal Giants, he played against some of the most well-known players, both Black and White, ever known in the history of baseball. Paul was voted to be an All Star in the 1935 East-West game.

In the 1960s if you were to take the 12:55 bus, like I used to do, out of Hopewell to Trenton you would undoubtedly see Paul (Beetle) Arnold sitting by himself on the bus. Whether you were going to shop, take in a movie, or just hang around town Beetle Arnold would be on that bus. I was always going because I was had a modeling job at Litt Brothers Department store every Saturday afternoon. I was a teenage model; couldn't wait to get through the afternoon so that I could have my meager pay which would be promptly spent on cosmetics, records, or fake hair, and not necessarily in that order. Whenever I got on the bus and saw Beetle he was never without his cap, and if you gave him a quick glance you might have thought it was just a lone White man riding the bus. He looked similar to my maternal grandfather, Garland, and I used to comment on that. But it was Beetle Arnold, a light-skinned Black man born and raised in Hopewell. Beetle's reputation as a baseball player was well known, and he was a former member of the infamous Pennington Allstars, a local Negro League team that played throughout the early 1920s. They were practically unbeatable. In my house I have a team picture from 1919 that includes Paul Arnold grinning with a wide grin on his face, pale vanilla in a sea of chocolate brown.

Paul was the son of Paul Arnold Sr. and Katherine Arnold. His dad, Paul Sr., owned and operated the Hopewell Barber Shop on Broad Street where he advertised "special attention given to ladies' and children's hairdressing and shampooing at customer's home or shop." His dad was a descendant of William Stives, a Revolutionary War veteran, who served under George Washington and was one of the first Blacks to settle in the Sourland Mountain area.

The old-timers used to say that Beetle Arnold was one of the best baseball players ever and would have been drafted to the majors if the leagues weren't segregated. On April 20, 1927, the *Hopewell Herald* reported that Paul Arnold was going to play with the Brooklyn Royal Giants. The article further reported that 1926 was a very successful year for Paul and Hilldale, a well-known colored team in the country, had bid for his services. Paul chose Brooklyn instead and on May 11, 1927, the *Hopewell Herald* reported that Paul had signed with the Brooklyn Royal Giants, which at that time was the second-best colored baseball club in the country. It reported that on the opening game of the Eastern league Paul played the outfield and batted in the lead-off position. The Giants were defeated by Hilldale, 8 to 1, but it was Paul who made the only hit! On August 10, 1927, the *Herald* also reported that many from

Hopewell attended the Brooklyn Royal Giants game against Trenton with the "expectation of seeing Paul 'Sonny' Arnold in action."

On April 19, 2017, we posted a Friday Memory on Facebook about Paul Arnold's skill and reputation as a baseball player,[4] and I was immediately contacted by Walter Swanson, a former resident of Hopewell, now living in Michigan. Walter used to work in the pharmacy that Beetle sometime frequented. Walter was excited to share one of his experiences with Beetle.

I worked in the Hopewell Pharmacy as a part-time stock boy while I was in high school. Mr. Arnold was not a regular visitor to the drug store, but a frequent one (if that's a distinction). I remember him as a gentleman who was happy to chat with anyone—including me. I enjoyed our chats. They may have been about anything, and sometimes about baseball. It was the pharmacist, George Neely, who told me that he was a bit of a superstar in the Negro Leagues. I then began to press him on specifics. I remember him mentioning Satchel Paige, Josh Gibson, and Jackie Robinson but also the personal playing styles of Babe Ruth and Lou Gehrig. He had apparently played with them in off-season games.

My Beetle Arnold story is that once at the Golden Nugget Flea Market in Lambertville, I bought a Babe Ruth watch fob: a tin badge pressed into the shape of a baseball player at bat, with a short loop of leather that was supposed to attach to a pocket watch. I used it as a key chain. I was so proud of this—mainly so I could show it off to Mr. Arnold. When I presented it to him, he looked at it quietly for a minute, handed it back to me, and said, "That's not Babe Ruth." "Waddaya mean," I said? "Ruth didn't bat like that. No. That stance looks more like … uh, Bobby Murcer. Yeah, that's Bobby Murcer. That is exactly how Murcer stood at the plate."

Never mind that this cheap tin souvenir was probably pressed before

Bobby Murcer was born, but because of the detail of the stance, Mr. Arnold was adamant that it was a Murcer watch fob!

Not long after we posted our Friday Memory about Paul Arnold, we were also contacted by a member of the Hopewell Valley Historical Society telling us there was a local man, Kevin Lonergan, who had a bundle of correspondence written by Paul Arnold. The correspondence was found in a barn that Kevin cleaned out that had formerly been on the Arnold property. We immediately contacted Kevin, who showed us an amazing number of letters written by Beetle while he was on the road with the Brooklyn Giants. So interesting were these letters, we asked Kevin to contribute his compelling story.

Paul "Sonny" "Beetle" Arnold was the youngest of five children, born to Paul and Katherine "Kate" Arnold. He was born in 1903 according to the 1910 census. In 1901, Paul's father hired T. Howell to build the family a new home in Hopewell Borough, which stands at 27 West Broad Street. Paul's father passed away between 1900 and the 1910 census.

Paul was 5'9" tall and weighed about 160 pounds. He batted lefty and pitched righty. He was signed with the Philadelphia Hilldale Giants in 1926, then part of the Negro Leagues. He lived in Newark for a period of time and then later resided in his childhood Hopewell home. In 1927 he played with Brooklyn Royal Giants. Paul was a hardworking player, as can be seen in the many allusions to him being injured and physically roughed up, found in correspondence between himself and friends of the time period. He also played amateur football but stayed professionally active in baseball. He played with the New York Royal Giants in 1928, prior to the Great Depression.

Teams disbanded due to corruption and economic tensions between 1929 and 1932, and Paul signed on with the Newark Browns in 1932. In 1934, he joined the Newark Dodgers, an Independent Negro league team that became part of the Negro National League. He finished out his professional career here through 1936.

Paul was an enthusiastic player. One story notes Sonny trying to catch a fly ball destined to be a homer and knocking himself unconscious catching the ball. The article says that hundreds of fans ran down to the field to resuscitate and congratulate him for saving the game from being a loss.[5]

One highlight of Paul's career was the East-West game of 1935. He was voted alternate center fielder for the All-Star team by the fans in 1935. Literally 10,257 fans wrote in and voted for him to play as an All Star. The game took place at Comiskey Park in Chicago, Illinois. There were 25,000 fans attending the game. It was broadcasted over the radio. The game was a dead heat until the eleventh inning. Paul played against the likes of James Thomas, "Cool Papa" Bell, Josh Gibson, Walter Fenner "Buck" Leonard, Willie "The Devil" Wells, George "Mule" Suttles, and William McKinley "Sug" Cornelius. Paul was pulled in as relief center fielder for Martin Dihigo Llanos in the bottom of the 11th, who subsequently went in for relief pitching. The first pitch to Mule Suttles became an amazing hit that sailed over Paul's head into the crowd, drove home 3 runs, and ended the game 11–8 in favor of the West. That was Paul's last professional game.

It is also noted that he played against Babe Ruth multiple times in Trenton, in an effort to create a fan base for the leagues. The pitchers were urged to let Ruth hit, but from the commentary it seems that most pitchers disapproved of this practice.

Paul was a literate and passionate person and player. He devoted his life to baseball. He played, coached, and loved the sport. He loved to imbibe in spirits and they never doused his passion for the game. His teammates have said directly how fast he was, how well he hit, and how Sonny always brought light to the game.

OCTAVIA BROKAW BROWN (1914–1960)

Town of Residence: Skillman, New Jersey

Date of Written Text: Date Unknown

Interviewer/Narrator: Transcribed from the writing of Octavia Brown, a sister of Bessie Grover

Permission from: Dolores Grover (Octavia's Great-Niece)

Her Story: Octavia Brokaw Brown: "How I Found God"

Introduction: As a descendant of the Stives, Peterson, and Brokaw families, Octavia was raised in Skillman and worshipped at the Mt. Zion AME Church in Skillman, New Jersey. She suffered for years from a debilitating illness but, in spite of it all, Octavia took pen in hand and wrote, "I feel this may be an inspiration to some other lost soul." Octavia Brown was a sister to Bessie Grover and was a member of the Brokaw family who worshipped at the Mt. Zion AME Church in Skillman. Below are excerpts from her written testimony.

When I first walked into Mt. Zion AME I had a feeling of coming home. As I sat through the sermon, I could see my mother being there for this was her church. She loved it dearly. Here I had my last look at her beloved face. The memories stirred. For here I went to Sunday school.

I could have made Mama's last days a little happier, perhaps, but I could not get her an extension of time. However, not understanding this, and with a chip on my shoulder for anyone who tried to reach me, I proceeded to do all things, that is called sin. I clung to all material things. Each one in turn kept failing me. I was in the hospital twice, came home but I couldn't last. In October 1951 I went to the doctor, he took my temperature, 104, and put me in a hospital. In a couple days they said I had trouble in my chest and they were sending me to another hospital. When they asked me who they should notify in case of my death, I said, "Call the undertaker. They still bury people, don't they?" The devil sure had me hopping. I entered Roosevelt Hospital October 18, 1951. After various examinations they said I had trouble in both lungs and I had to stay six months to a year.

I found keeping busy was best. I became a reporter for our hospital magazine, I took over the duties of preparing the altar for services of all faiths and helped the minister to serve communion. In 1955 they suggested an operation, removal of the left lung. I had my operation, healed up, and knew I had it made. But up came complications. I had developed fluid and became bedridden again. So like Job I became sorely afflicted. From 1953 to 1957 I had five operations; I weighed eighty pounds, and nothing helped. The doctors gave up. Everyone prayed for me, ministers, deacons, Catholic sisters, a priest and rabbi, all came to pray for me. I prayed night and day. I was still a very sick person and helpless, but my faith was growing. I sat with my head hung down for I was too weak to hold it up. I prayed aloud for the first time. When I first raised my head and said, "Be still and know that I am God," the nurse ran out. She came back with the doctor and I was sitting so still, I guess they were both frightened. During this time a cool breeze passed through my room and touched me. I picked up my Bible and there it was, the 46th Psalm. I sat so still, the doctor felt my pulse, nurse took my temperature, and they said she is almost normal. I said, "Yes, you know what, I am going to get well." I was able to leave the hospital after six years.

When I met Reverend and Mrs. James right away something clicked. I knew this was what I had waited for. It being God's will he lead my heart and feet home. Our Heavenly Father has seen fit to return me to the hospital when I wrote this. But I will be baptized in Skillman, and I shall wait on God.

MARGARET "PEGGY" HUGHES TUNISON, 1938–

Town of Residence: Skillman, New Jersey

Date of Interview: February 20, 2016

Interviewer/Narrator: Elaine Buck

Permission from: Peggy Hughes Tunison

Her Story: Peggy Hughes Tunison is the daughter of Puritan Brokaw and Charles Hughes. She is a descendant of the Stives, Brokaw, and Hughes families.

Introduction: The Hughes family were known to be early entrepreneurs and landowners who experienced a horrific tragedy that nearly destroyed their family.

My mother, Puritan Ellen Brokaw, was born February 15, 1902, and married my father, Charles E. Hughes, who was born in Camden County, North Carolina. My father lived in Elizabeth City, North Carolina, in his early teens and then came to Skillman. He was on the run, but no one is sure why or who was after him. My father resided and worked on Parvin Strykers farm, which was located on Route 601 in Blawenburg. Dad's first marriage was to Eleanor, a beautician, and they lived on Camp Meeting Avenue, in Skillman. During the 1920s Eleanor died, and he married my mother, Puritan. My mother had been a waitress at the fancy restaurant in Hopewell, which is now the Historic Hopewell House.

My father started Charles Hughes Taxi Service that served Hopewell, Skillman, Belle Meade, and Princeton areas, but he also did special runs to New York City. My mother also drove the taxi. They had four or five cars and a bus. Dad was always at the train station to meet the trains that stopped in Skillman and also delivered mail to Zion. My parents operated the taxi service business for over thirty years, and my mother continued to run it until 1956, which was after my dad's death. My mother died the next year in 1957 at only fifty-five years old. She died from cancer of the bowel, and we think the cancer may have been caused by a piece of steel that hit her in the back during the train wreck.

Let me tell you what I remember about the Mt. Zion AME Church property. My maternal grandmother, Virginia Brokaw, belonged to the Mt. Zion AME Church, which I understand was built by the Africans back when it was located in Zion. My father helped move Mt. Zion to its current location on Hollow Road. I was told the land the church is on belonged to my father, because Scudder True, who lived next door, never completed the sale of the property. A White man from Hopewell named Sam Reasoner would go buy properties for Dad because my dad had saved a lot of money and began buying properties. Daddy would give Sam the money and then he would transfer the property to my father. My father set up his brother, Ernest, in property along with several other people who wanted to buy land. The Hughes house on Camp Meeting Avenue, their family homestead, was one of the houses Daddy bought and the one next door where one of my sisters, Josie, lived. He also brought the True family house, but I was told that Scudder didn't pay him the last $1,200 so I believe that Scudder never owned the property. My father bought all three houses.

Our family always used Castoro from Hopewell as our lawyer, so in 1953 when my dad died the property went to my mother, Puritan Brokaw Hughes. When Mom died in 1957 the property went to me and my two sisters Josie and Jane.

When I was ten years old my other two sisters, Ellen and Aquilla, were killed in 1948 in a train wreck. Ellen was nineteen and Aquilla was thirteen. The Reading Railroad Dinky didn't switch tracks at the right time and the train derailed while my two sisters and Mother were traveling on it. The train was coming from Bound Brook to West Trenton and wrecked right outside of Pennington. The car overturned on the side my sisters were sitting, and somehow my mother managed to climb out of the wreck. I remember hearing the family talk about how my sisters were thrown from the train and their bodies were mangled. My mother, Puritan, was in shock because she was going up and down the tracks to find their body parts to put them back together before the police arrived. In the paper it also said she went running across the field to a farmhouse for help. This accident nearly ruined my father, and he went downhill a little each day. My mother had to be the one to keep the taxi service business going. I remember my mother saying, "We have to keep going!" We didn't get much money from Reading Railroad and I've kept all the newspaper articles about it throughout the years. [Stoutsburg Cemetery records show Ellen & Aquilla Hughes, October 5, 1948. Interred by Judkins Funeral Home (now Hughes Funeral Home.)]

STEPHANYE CLARKE, 1970–

Town of Residence: New London, Connecticut

Date of Written Text: November 23, 2016

Narrator: Stephanye Clarke

Permission from: Stephanye Clarke

Introduction: For years Stephanye Clark was anxious to have more information about her ancestry so she could pass it along to her children and grandchildren. One day she was presented with startling information that she is a descendant of William Stives, a Revolutionary War veteran, who lived in the Sourland Mountain region.

Her story: Home is usually described as a place. For me, it is also a place: a place in history, a place in family, a place you are of—not necessarily that place where you live. Being able to give *that* place to my kids has always been a source of anxiety and desire.

Thanks to a mailing from my big sister (and several messages via Facebook), I went from having little to no connection with any of my own family history to learning that I am a descendant of a war hero, an *American* hero. And just like my own father, he was now *my* hero. Here's how I remember it starting. In early December 2015 my older sister, Collette Ferguson, reached out to me to say she had a "package" for me and asked for my mailing address. Fast forward to a couple weeks later, I received the package that also included a beautifully written letter from her to me. In this letter she detailed her journey to finding something out about our family history. I kept reading until I hit the jackpot—the resting place of our fourth great-grandfather, Private William Stives, Revolutionary War veteran. What my big sister didn't know is that for years, as a mother, I have struggled with not having any oral history to share with my daughters. I wanted to be able to tell them about some of our ancestors—how resilient they were. I mean, obviously, whomever we have descended from endured quite a bit … but I hadn't had any stories. Both sets of my grandparents passed away when my parents were young, and we lived so far from everyone. Secretly, and sometimes not so secretly, I wanted to be able to share more with my daughters—to give them something to share with their children. But until this letter from my big sister, the best I had was stories of my mother as a college student in the Jim Crow South. Although those stories were riveting, I had always wanted more … and now I had it! She even sent along a document that showed the family tree.

I also have to thank my lifelong friend Scott for sharing something he had discovered, that my ancestor had been in Valley Forge with George Washington! He had been encouraging me along my journey, and when I sent him a link about the cemetery he texted me right back saying, check out the second article under *"in the news"* section—the one with the photo gallery. And so, I did and saw "Two Women Seek the Truth About a N.J. Burial Ground and Slavery in the Garden State." That sealed it. I went back to the home page, found out their contact information, and emailed Sharon (Elaine) Buck and Beverly Mills and then saw another article about them writing a book about the heroes buried at the Stoutsburg Cemetery.

I received a response right away from Elaine and made arrangements to travel to New Jersey on the weekend of September 23–25, 2016. Elaine also told me that she, John, and Beverly had just met with some other Stives descendants a couple weeks prior and that we just missed them.

My oldest daughter and my grandson drove up from Virginia Beach to meet me and my youngest child to learn more about our family. We met with Elaine, John, and Beverly and started our journey. We toured Hopewell, New Jersey, and saw the church William Stives attended, saw land he owned, and finally visited the Stoutsburg Cemetery. I got out of the van, walked over to the marker bearing his name, and lost it! Here I was, face to face with the marker of my fourth great-grandfather and it was overwhelming. The minivan we came in contained three generations of his descendants—me, my two daughters, and my grandson, Liam. Even though Liam is far too young to understand or remember what happened, as we drove by the land our great-grandfather owned he pointed out of the window like he saw or knew something!

I am grateful to have met John, Elaine, and Beverly. I learned that William Stives was awarded a Badge of Merit for his service and saw a copy of his discharge papers signed by George Washington and so much more. As exciting as all this is it's also a bit scary. They shared photos of members of the White side of my family—all of us descended from William and his son, Cornelius.

Truthfully, I've been a bit leery to reach out to some of our Stives relatives because I imagine there may be some resistance to meet or connect with Black relatives. But that won't stop me from reaching out to other relatives.

DESCENDANTS OF THE TRUEHART FAMILY

HERMA MAE HUBBARD FIELDS, 1907–1994

Town of Residence: Trenton, New Jersey

Date of Written Text: March 8, 2017

Interviewer/Narrator: Beverly Mills (Granddaughter)

Permission from: Garland Fields (Son)

Her Story: My grandmother Herma was the oldest daughter of Herbert Hubbard and Sarah Matilda Hoagland Hubbard. Her first name was a blend of her parents' first names. My grandmother, a descendant of the Truehart, Bergen, Hoagland, and Hagaman families, was born and raised in Stoutsburg on the Sourland Mountain and at age sixteen took over the household after her mother's sudden death from an asthma attack.

Introduction: Herma possessed the bold spirit of her father, Herbert Hubbard. My grandmother was always determined to be in charge of her life and did not let the fact that she was an African American woman, who had not completed school, defeat her in any way. After raising her children, my grandmother attended school in Philadelphia and earned a beautician's license, which enabled her to open her own business in 1948.

As the firstborn grandchild of Herma Hubbard Fields, family members have said that out of all the grandchildren I, Beverly, take after our grandmother the most.

My maternal grandmother, Herma Mae Hubbard, was born on May 14, 1907, to Herbert and Sarah Matilda Hubbard. She was the fifth child born into the Hubbard family, who lived on the Sourland Mountain. As their firstborn girl, Herb and Matilda could not resist naming their daughter Herma, the perfect blend of their first names.

Herma, whom we all called Mom, grew up in a musical family where her father and brother, Earl, both played the violin. Instead of the violin, Mom decided to take up the alto sax and as a teenager played in an all-male band that played around the region. Mom was out playing with the band when she came home to the news that her mother had suddenly passed away from an asthma attack. My grandmother Herma Mae was only sixteen.

As was the tradition with most women in 1925, Mom got married at the young age of eighteen to Garland Fields of Somerville, New Jersey. However, when the Depression set in, times were particularly tough for the young Black couple, who rented housing from local farmers to work as sharecroppers. To help financially, Mom did the best she could in between her twelve pregnancies by doing domestic work and occasionally working in factories. Sadly, these twelve pregnancies only realized four children who lived to adulthood.

When Mom approached middle age, she realized that for the most part her marriage had unraveled. It seems she got tired of depending upon my grandfather and had had enough. I often think of the bravery it took for my grandmother to take such a big step in the 1940s to enroll in the Apex Cosmetology School in Philadelphia. Mom was going to do whatever it took to become a hairdresser and open her own business.

When my grandmother opened her shop in 1948, she operated her business out of the front two rooms of the house and left the remaining rooms for the family's living quarters. As a child in the late 1950s and early 1960s, I would regularly visit Mom with my own mother at her shop on Montgomery Place in Trenton, New Jersey. I can still envision the green and white house where you could see Mom through the front window standing on her feet for up to twelve hours a day doing hair. As youngsters my cousin Bonnie and I would run errands to Bill's Corner store for cigarettes or sodas or whatever the customer would ask us to buy for them. It usually took quite a while for the ladies' hair to be done because back then any respectable Black woman had her hair straightened with a hot comb before having it curled. The smell of hair from the red-hot straightening comb is still in my mind, a smell that would linger long into the evening hours after the shop had closed.

One thing about Mom, who didn't drink a drop: she sometimes smoked Tareyton cigarettes and loved gossiping. She was a very hard worker who rewarded herself with a brand-new shiny black Chrysler Imperial in 1955. And it wasn't until after I was grown that I figured out that her boarder, Frank, the man with his tiny mustache and smoking jackets, was actually her boyfriend, something she kept secret for years because she never divorced my grandfather.

People still tell me they remember my grandmother pulling up in her swanky Chrysler to do hair in Hopewell, Pennington, the local funeral parlor, or wherever she was needed with her hot combs and curling irons in hand!

WILLIAM EARL HUBBARD, 1908–2002

Town of Residence: Pennington, New Jersey

Date of Written Text: February 10, 2017

Interviewer/Narrator: Beverly Mills (Niece) and Elaine Buck

Permission from: Stanley Stewart II (Nephew)

His Story: Earl was a son of Herbert and Sarah Matilda Hubbard and brother to Herma Hubbard Fields and Leona Hubbard Stewart. Raised in Stoutsburg on the Sourland Mountain and a descendant of the Trueheart, Bergen, Hoagland, and Hagaman families, Earl Hubbard was determined to learn to play the violin even though no one would teach him. He was so determined to learn how to play the violin he made his own instruments.

Introduction: Earl was quoted as saying, "When you love music it gets into your blood like everything else and you can't get it out." Earl created the Earl's All Girl Chorus and was a musician and member of the Bethel AME Church for decades.

William Earl Hubbard, who went by Earl, was born 1908 on the Sourland Mountain to Herbert and Sarah Matilda Hubbard. As a young person Earl had the desire to learn how to play the violin, however, back in those days, he was denied access to lessons because teachers refused to teach "colored" students. In fact, it would take Earl another seven years before he found a teacher who was willing to give him lessons at 25 cents a lesson for fifteen minutes.

While Earl pursued his craft, he was able to find another teacher willing to give him lessons, but the cost was way too steep, at $1.50 a lesson. At that time Earl was only making $4.50 a month cleaning at the Trenton Train Depot. The only thing he was able to do was take lessons whenever he could by scraping together enough money to take a lesson, but he was only able to do this for two years.

Fortunately, help came from another source that would enable Earl to once again take lessons. He had met a doctor's wife who was in need of repairs on her home. The wife told Earl that if he would do the necessary repairs she would make arrangements for him to audition to take conducting lessons with the Temple University Orchestra. Earl auditioned and was accepted. Amazingly, Earl was able to finish the entire four-month course, which turned out to be the same time needed to finish the house repairs. By this time Earl was an exceptionally skilled musician and would have turned professional if it wasn't for the fact, in most cases, he was the only Black violinist.

In 1986 the *Pennington Post* (no longer in print) interviewed Earl about his love of music. In the article he was quoted as saying, "When you love music it gets into your blood like everything else and you can't get it out. Half your education in music is going and hearing the best. By reading and seeing them, you learn. Of course, you learn your own style."

Elaine recalls speaking with Catherine Terhune (Kitty), a well-known pianist from Hopewell, New Jersey. She remembered hearing the story of how Earl and Kitty went to Philadelphia to play with the Philadelphia Symphony Orchestra. Earl was there to play the violin, and Mrs. Terhune was to accompany him on the piano. Upon their arrival, however, they were told to sit in the very back of the room, the assumption being that they were an interracial couple. When the announcer called for Earl Hubbard and Catherine Terhune, the performers, they were found sitting in the very back next to the bathroom. As they came forward, with their heads held high, to everyone's surprise it was that couple who had been ushered to the back of the room! According to the story, the announcer quickly apologized and attempted to seat them at a table in the front, to which Earl and Kitty politely replied, "No thank you, we will stay seated in the back where you placed us."

LEONA FLORENCE HUBBARD STEWART, 1913–2003

Town of Residence: Pennington, New Jersey

Date of Written Text: June 22, 2017

Interviewer/Narrator: Beverly Mills (Great-Niece)

Permission from: Stanley Stewart II (Son)

Her Story: My aunt Leona Hubbard Stewart was the youngest child of Herbert and Sarah Matilda Hubbard and a descendant of the Truehart, Bergen, Hoagland, and Hagaman families. Leona was born and raised in Stoutsburg on the Sourland Mountain along with her siblings, Herma and Earl. While in Pennington Leona lived in one of the oldest historic homes in Pennington for over fifty years. It is in this house where she raised three children after the sudden death of her husband, Stanley Stewart.

Introduction: Leona was a woman who had impeccable style. For many years she was a deaconess at the Witherspoon Presbyterian Church where she would always invite someone to her home for one of her famous "lunches." Leona was known to greet her visitors with a warm fire, delicious food, and a libation or two.

It wouldn't be an exaggeration to describe Leona Stewart as a Renaissance woman. Anyone who visited her home or had the good fortune to be invited to dinner or to one of her legendary after-church "lunches" would be treated to her impeccable style and taste. Leona Stewart was my great-aunt, my maternal grandmother's baby sister.

She was born to Herbert Albert Hubbard and Sarah Matilda Hubbard on June 2, 1913, in Stoutsburg, New Jersey, where she was raised with her older siblings, brothers Earl, Hervey, and Basil (Hervey and Basil passed away), and sister, Herma.

Aunt Leona married Stanley Stewart of Pennington, New Jersey, and was the mother to three children, Janice, Stanley II, and Jeffrey. I can still remember being about four years old when our next-door neighbor, Annabelle Stewart, who was also Leona's sister-in-law, came with bad news that her brother, Stanley, had been tragically killed in a car accident. This was in the early 1950s, and Leona was left a young widow to raise her children alone. To make ends meet Leona worked in private homes in Princeton, New Jersey. It wasn't until later in life that she made the decision to take secretarial courses so that she could get a job working in an office. Being the person she was, Leona graduated with honors and eventually ended up as a counselor for the New Jersey State Home for Girls, from where she retired. For many years she was also a dedicated member of the Witherspoon Presbyterian Church where she served as a deaconess.

For the majority of her adult life Leona remained in the Pennington home, a two-story colonial with Dutch doors, located on South Main Street. The home, one of the oldest in Pennington's original early African American settlement, was also one of the locations that hosted services for followers of Richard Allen's newly founded African Methodist Episcopal Church in 1816. Church history recounts that AME parishioners took turns hosting in various homes until the Bethel AME Church was built in 1847 next door to Leona's house. Another interesting feature about this house is that it was the "summer home" briefly owned by Dooley Wilson, the actor who played Sam the singing piano player in the 1942 movie *Casablanca*.

I remember when I was a little girl the neighborhood ladies, which included my mother, my grandmother, Mrs. Stewart, who lived next door, and a few other ladies up the street, had an unspoken competition among them; whose wash was first to be out on the clothesline? My mother would be on the phone with my grandmother with the gossip for the day, "you sure had your wash out early today, but it looks like

Leona had hers out first." This seemed to go on for quite some time, and as much as they tried Leona always seemed to beat them to the clothesline. Finally, not able to stand it anymore, my mother asked Leona how it was possible that she had her wash out before anyone else in the neighborhood, to which Leona, with a little smirk on her lips, replied, "Because I put it out the night before!"

Aside from beating everybody to the clothesline, everybody who knew Leona would talk about her culinary skills. With a big wicker basket in the crook of her arm, Leona would walk through the neighborhood delivering bread she had just baked. I warmly remember the days I would visit Leona in her cozy house to see what she was cooking or just to sit and talk because there was always a delicious aroma coming from her house. She was skilled in making all kinds of food, and I believe my interest in cooking began from tasting dishes such as her outstanding beef stroganoff! It was also a favorite time for us to sit and chat during the winter months when she had a fire blazing in her fireplace that took up most of the living room wall. I recall the wide-planked oak floors, the Dutch doors that separated her living room and dining room, and the comfortable wing chairs placed in a nook near her bookcase. Every evening she would pour herself a glass of scotch that was accompanied with an unfiltered cigarette. In all my years of knowing Aunt Leona I never witnessed her in a pair of pants, her preference being an A-line or wrap-around skirt and blouse topped off with a cardigan sweater.

ROBERT SPENCER TRUE, 1919–1983

Town of Residence: Pennington, New Jersey

Date of Written Text: August 14, 2017

Interviewer/Narrator: Patricia True Payne (Daughter)

Permission from: Patricia True Payne

His Story: A man known for his integrity and character, Bob True was respected by many in his community and workplace.

Introduction: A descendant of the Truehart family (before some family members shortened the surname to True), Bob was a great-grandson of Aaron Truehart, Civil War veteran with the 127th U.S. Colored Troops, one of the troops present at Appomattox.

My father, Robert Spencer True, was born in Skillman, New Jersey, to Spencer and Mae True on October 8, 1919. My father lived in the Skillman-Pennington area all of his life. I was told that it was the True family who were instrumental in donating the land for the Mt. Zion Church to be relocated on Hollow Road right next to the family home.

Everybody always called my father Bob, who married my mother, Hazel Nevius, in 1940. Together they had three children: Patricia Corinne, my two brothers, William Spencer and Gerald Scott, and me.

Our family grew up on South Main Street in Pennington, New Jersey. I remember when my aunts and uncles and cousins would come over, the kids would run up and down the front staircase and then down the back stairs and again through the living room and dining room until they were out of breath. The grown-ups would pay the kids no mind because they were busy laughing, talking, or playing cards while they ate and drank.

My father worked for Montgomery Township for thirty years and was very highly regarded, so much so that the township named their maintenance building after him when he passed away. Dad was also a police lieutenant in the Pennington Fire Department, a member of the Mitchell Davis Post #182 in the American Legion, and an honorary member of the Somerset County Police Chiefs' Association. For years my father was active as a long-standing member of the Stoutsburg Cemetery Association.

My father possessed a gentle, kind spirit with a smile and sense of humor that was infectious.

✴

DESCENDANTS OF
THE BLACKWELL FAMILY

WILLIAM WALLACE "SHUD" SMITH, 1923–1993

Town of Residence: Pennington, New Jersey

Date of Interview: May 2003

Interviewer/Narrator: Beverly Mills (Daughter of William Smith)

Permission from: Beverly Mills

His Story: How Shud Won the Big Game for the Pennington All-Stars (as told to Beverly Mills by her uncle Arthur "Dick" Clark)

Introduction: My father, William Smith, grew up his entire life nick-named "Shud" and is the proud descendant of Frost Blackwell and Nancy Vanvactor Blackwell, who were both enslaved in the local area during the Revolutionary War. Always the consummate athlete and according to his uncle, Dick Clark, my father was told by a baseball scout that had he not been a Black man he would have been signed to a major league team. This was prior to Jackie Robinson breaking the color barrier.

Not too long after World War II there was a baseball team in the Hopewell/Pennington, New Jersey, area called the Pennington All Stars. In case some are not familiar with baseball in that era, the team was made up of a group of young Black guys who just wanted to play ball. Nothing more, nothing less. However, this was pre–Jackie Robinson America so never mind these guys just returned from serving in World War II and were newly married Black guys rearing young families, in those times society was what it was. According to witnesses this is how Shud won the game.

The hotshot team from Hopewell was all White and at the top of the league. The Pennington All Stars, however, wanted to play this team in the worst kind of way but the White team was not interested in playing the Black team and made it perfectly clear. As the season wore on and since they were at the top of the league, they finally consented to play the Black team, the Pennington All Stars.

The night before to the big game the All Stars got together with their manager, Mr. Hoagland, to discuss who was going to pitch the game. Since Mr. Hoagland had two sons, William and Chester, whom they called "Nin," who were currently on team, he wanted William to pitch the game. According to Uncle Dick Clark, who as Shud's uncle was only a mere four years older, said he felt obliged to speak up and tell Mr. Hoagland that Shud should pitch the game because of his mean fastball. But Mr. Hoagland had other ideas. He said he thought William should pitch because William was more experienced and Shud could play shortstop, which was his usual position. The manager's decision upset everyone, but they had no choice but to go along with it.

When the day of the big game finally arrived, Mr. Hoagland did exactly what he said he was going to do, put William in to pitch. Well, William pitched as well as he could but after pitching 3 or 4 innings the White team was up by about 7 runs and the All Stars were giving up and started to feel demoralized. They thought the "big game" was pretty much over. Finally, in what seemed like an eternity, Mr. Hoagland called Shud in from shortstop to pitch. He made this decision with not a moment to spare because by this time Shud had time to sweat and stew and get really mad! Shud stepped to the plate and began to pitch what old-timers say "looked just like bullets!" That's how mean his fastball was. Shud threw so hard and fast that when the opposing team got up to bat they were so scared of Shud's fastball they started to back away before even trying to swing! The Hopewell team didn't score another run for the remainder of the game and the Pennington All Stars ended up winning the big game!

LOIS GETER, 1928–

Town of Residence: Trenton, New Jersey

Date of Interview: August 8, 2015

Interviewer/Narrator: Beverly Mills and Elaine Buck

Permission from: Lois Geter

Her Story: Lois Geter is an educator who broke ground hired as an African American teacher. She lived her life with a firm belief in the value of education.

Introduction: Lois is the proud descendant of Frost Blackwell and Nancy Vanvactor Blackwell, who were both enslaved in the local area during the Revolutionary War.

I am the daughter of Fairfax and Margaret Seruby, whom everyone called "Mag." My grandfather was Samuel B. Seruby, who married Roxanna King, whose family originally came from Virginia. Roxanna was a mulatto because her mother was a White woman who had come from County Cork, Ireland. My grandpa and grandmom were legally married but I don't know how this was able to take place. Going back another generation, my great-grandmother Josephine Blackwell, who was Samuel's mother, married into the Seruby family who lived on South Main Street in Pennington. Josephine was a sister to Beverly's great-great-great-grandmother Nancy, who married Joseph Smith Sr.

My grandfather Samuel worked at the Pennington Prep School, which back then was called the Seminary. He also worked at the Stover's store in Pennington. It was one of my grandfather's duties to take the horse and wagon to Trenton to get groceries for the week; it took him all day to do and he'd go on Saturday. The officials at the Pennington Prep School didn't tell anybody but my grandfather needed some more math knowledge, so he went to school at night to study math. As a Black man back then he wasn't allowed to attend school during the day with the White students.

On my mother Mag's side of the family my grandfather died of the flu by the time my mother was nine years old. He left his widow with eight children. I believe my grandmother died of a broken heart because she died not long after her husband's death.

As a result of the death of my maternal grandparents, Horace and Annie Booker Cain, all eight children had to be farmed out to different families. Originally, they were all supposed to go to an orphanage, but the day the orphanage administrators came, family members and neighbors pitched in and each took a child to raise. Many of these people lived in the Sourland Mountain area near the Stoutsburg Cemetery. For instance, the Moores, a White family, took in one of the oldest boys, my Uncle Jack. The Moore family lived at the last farmhouse on the right-hand side of the road going to the cemetery. Jack was to be a helper and was able to go to school. Another brother, my Uncle Dave, went to live with the Benjamin Dyer Family, a Black family. The house, which was in Pennington, was beautiful with a stairway with an engraved newel post and stained glass. My grandmother, Roxanna

Seruby, lived next door. The house had tennis courts and well-known Black tennis players used to come there and use the courts. Tragically Mrs. Dyer, who was my godmother, was killed when she went shopping to buy me a tricycle. She was hit by a car and didn't survive.

As for some of the other children, my Aunt Florence was adopted by the Henry Hodnett family, Aunt Mabel went to live with cousins in Cranbury, and my mother, Mag, went to live with Tom and Beulah King in a house near the Driver family on South Main Street in Pennington.

The day I got married to Lonnie Geter it rained very hard and was one of the hottest days of the year. The wedding reception was at the Carver Center in Trenton, New Jersey. After the reception everyone came up to our family house in Hopewell to continue the party. My husband, Lonnie, and I changed clothes and left for our honeymoon. The guests from the reception, even though they had eaten, were hungry again so they came up to the house in Hopewell and my mother struggled to find more food to feed them. They came back for several days!

In my career as a teacher I got my first teaching job in Hamilton Township, New Jersey, and was the third Black teacher ever hired there. I was married at this time and left after six and a half years because in those days if you became pregnant you had to stop working for a least a year. I stayed home to raise my family for a number of years and then became a substitute teacher at Stokes School in Trenton, New Jersey, and Bethany Lutheran School in Ewing, New Jersey, where I was the first Black teacher hired at Bethany. Back then when they advertised for teachers they posted an ad in the paper requesting that a picture be sent with your application. Since I knew they never had any Black teachers, I intentionally didn't send my picture when I applied.

I have kept a list of everyone who was buried in the Stoutsburg Cemetery and the Pennington African Cemetery. My paternal grandparents, Samuel Blackwell Seruby, who was blind by the time he died, and Roxanna King Seruby, are both buried in the Pennington African Cemetery. When my grandfather died it was a very bad winter and they had to keep his body at the funeral home in Pennington until the weather got better. The funeral home, Blackwell Funeral Home in Pennington, buried White and Black people alike and still have funerals to this day. Also buried in the Pennington African Cemetery is Samuel's brother, Joseph, who was an officer in Company D, 24th Regiment of the U.S. Colored Troops in the Civil War. My great-uncle Archibald Campbell Seruby, known as "Spader the Peanut Man," is also buried in the Pennington African Cemetery. I've kept an article from the Sunday *Trenton Times*, dated September 25, 1994, about Spader that described him as a "hawker of peanuts with a flamboyant style, dressed in a black top hat, black frock coat and wearing an eye-catching tie. He sold peanuts for five cents a bag at sporting events in the local area." Uncle Spader was also a veteran of the Spanish-American War and died at age fifty-eight.

CONSTANCE DRIVER WHEELER, 1930–

Town of Residence: Trenton, New Jersey

Date of Interview: October 1, 2015

Interviewer/Narrator: Elaine Buck and Beverly Mills

Permission from: Constance Driver Wheeler

Her Story: Constance Driver Wheeler, known as "Connie," grew up in Pennington, New Jersey, and is descended from Frost Blackwell and Nancy Vanvactor Blackwell as well as the Driver family, who migrated from Virginia. Connie remembers the ladies of the Bethel AME Church coming to her house to sew aprons for a fund-raiser from scraps of old dresses on her mother's pedal sewing machine. Connie was sixteen or seventeen years old when her mother, Helen, gave her some of these homemade aprons, which she has graciously donated to the Stoutsburg Sourland African American Museum.

Introduction: The Driver family members were long-standing parishioners of Bethel AME Church in Pennington. Connie is a granddaughter of William Allen, the man who found the remains of the Lindbergh baby. Here is the story she told Beverly and Elaine.

I was born in 1930 and got my first bath from an old pitcher that used to be in the house where I grew up at 218 South Main Street in Pennington, New Jersey. My parents were Addison and Helen Smith Driver and my brothers and sisters were Jennie, Addison Jr., Dorothy, and Alvin.

On one side of our house our neighbors were the Caffee family. Rose Caffee was a beautician, who at that time was married to her second husband, Horace, who I remember was very tall. He was the brother of Rose's first husband, John, who died young when he was in his thirties. Horace and John were twins, and when John died Horace and Rose started a relationship and eventually married. Both brothers were very fair and could easily pass for White men. I understand that some members of the Caffee family actually passed for White and when they came to visit made sure that anyone who knew them as White would not see them visiting in the Black neighborhood. Holly and the twins were the sons of Rose's first husband, John, and Freddy, Richard, Muriel, and Shirley were Horace's children. The whole neighborhood went into shock when Harold, Arnold's twin, drowned at the Jersey shore when they were just teenagers. Living right next door, Shirley and I became best friends and we graduated together from Pennington High School in 1949. Our class theme was "We Are the '49ers!"

On the other side of our house lived the Cain family, Jack and Mabel and their children, Colleen and Clifford. Our houses were divided by a driveway and close enough so when Mommy wanted to talk to Mabel all she needed to do was raise up her window and whistle. Mabel would hear the whistle and would come to her window where they would hang out of their windows and talk about whatever it is they had to talk about!

Most of the ladies in the neighborhood either went to Bethel AME Church or the First Baptist Church, which was around the corner. Ladies from both churches were always trying to raise money through different fund-raisers. One of the fund-raisers of the Bethel AME ladies were the aprons they made from scraps of old dresses. I remember how they would get together at someone's home or at church to sew them, some hand stitched and some done by machine. The aprons were sold for either five or ten cents! I remember when they came to my house to sew they would congregate in the kitchen and work on an old pedal sewing machine that was set up there. They also held a rummage sale each summer, and in those days the ladies passed hand-me-down clothes from household to household.

Other fund-raisers held at Bethel were the church dinners. One that a lot of people remember as the most successful was their famous chicken and waffle dinner where the ladies always wore white aprons when they cooked. First, they would make sure to brine the chickens, which were regular fryers that they would boil with fresh celery and poultry seasoning. Once the chicken was boiled, they cooled it and chopped it into cube-sized pieces. I remember how their gravy was as smooth as silk—it was more like a cream sauce than a gravy on top of a homemade waffle.

At the Harvest Home dinners, the ladies could really shine when it came to their specialties. For instance, if it came down to who was going to make a particular dessert, it was very territorial. First the menu would usually be ham, chicken (sometimes roast beef but usually that was too expensive), homemade succotash, harvest beets, mashed potatoes and gravy, and homemade rolls. Everybody knew who was going to make what. Anna Mae Hoagland always made the homemade root beer, Sally Hoagland made the banana cake, Birdie Clark the coconut cake, and Mommy would make her apple pie. The kids would bob for apples and everybody had so much fun. They were great times!

*

DESCENDANTS OF THE HOAGLAND FAMILY

GERALDINE (GERRY) HOAGLAND, 1930–

Town of Residence: Hamilton Township, New Jersey

Date of Written Text: February 15, 2018

Interviewer/Narrator: Beverly Mills and Elaine Buck

Permission from: Geraldine Hoagland

Her Story: A descendant of the Hoagland family, Geraldine was one of eleven children born to Paige and Anna Mae Hoagland. The Hoaglands were the only African American family who lived on Princeton Avenue in Hopewell Borough, New Jersey.

Introduction: Geraldine was a long-standing Sunday school teacher who taught at Bethel AME. Present-day adults who used to be her students remember how she would pick them up in her shiny Chevrolet Impala. Gerry, who preferred to stay single, maintained that it was important that children be educated in religious instruction.

I came from a household of eleven children born to my parents, Paige and Anna Mae Hoagland. People wonder how we all fit into the house when we were growing up on Princeton Avenue in Hopewell—all of us, Liz, Paige, Gertrude, Thelma, Doris, William, Freddy, Kenny, Connie, Arlene, and myself. Since I was one of the younger ones in the family I barely remember when the older ones lived there. I can remember that the boys had a room, the girls had another, and my parents had their own.

I graduated in 1949 and went to school with the other Black kids from the area that mostly came from Columbia Avenue, the main street for the African American community. I remember the Nevius kids: Earle, Peggy, Verna, Lester, Hazel, Dorothy, and Edna. Across from the Neviuses were the Hunt kids: Robert (Sonny) and Dolores (Toots). The Bartlett kids were Bobby and Earl while the Young family had Marion and her cousins Patsy and Dorothy. Across from the Bartletts were the Waldron children who were Edie, Alice, Emma, Herbert, Dick, and Archie. Next to the Waldrons were the Staton kids, Sarah and Emmanuel. Next door to the girls from the Young family lived the Bernard girls: Betty, Frances, and Nancy. Across from them were the Carter kids: Carrie, Reggie, John, Irene, Bobby, and Boyd. My cousin Virdia Hoagland lived on Model Avenue a few blocks away from the "Black" section of Hopewell. My cousins Sonny and Marlene Terry, who also went to school in Hopewell, lived in our house at a different time than when most of us grew up in the house.

My mother, Anna Mae, did housework and also worked in the kitchen of the elementary school across the street from our house. The one thing about my mother was that she was a no-nonsense woman who did not allow anyone White to mess with her children.

Our house happened to be right next door to St. Michael's Orphan Asylum, where I can remember watching children being dropped off and seeing them and their parents cry as they left. I never forgot that because it was such a sad thing to see.

After I graduated I worked for thirty-one years for RCA and traveled to work past Somerville, New Jersey, every day. After I left there I still was used to working so I got a job with the post office and ended up retiring from there.

I've always had a firm belief in God and often wondered why the Lord has kept me here for so long. What has been his purpose? I've always been a church-goer and started out going to Sunday School at the First Baptist Church in Hopewell. From there I joined Second Calvary Baptist Church because when I got baptized I wanted to be fully immersed in the water and not sprinkled on my head, which was the custom of the Methodists. I joined Bethel AME in 1962 because my parents, who had previously been going to Second Calvary, were also members of Bethel. I've been a member ever since.

I always believed that children need to be instructed in religious education so that's why I became a Sunday School teacher. The kids used to get a kick out of me picking them up in my brand-new Chevy Impala to bring them to church. It's too bad that kids don't come to church like they used to anymore, but then again parents today won't even send them.

*

DESCENDANTS OF THE BERGEN FAMILY

CORA BERGEN NEVIUS, 1892–1948

Town of Residence: Hopewell, New Jersey

Date of Written Text: October 21, 2011

Interviewer/Narrator: Louis Peyton Clark (Grandson)

Permission from: Louis Peyton Clark

Her Story: A descendant of the Bergen and Nevius families, Louis Peyton Clark traces his grandmother's ancestry to the family homestead in Maine.

Introduction: Louis Peyton Clark is the oldest grandson of Cora and Elmer Nevius. Always called "Peyton" by the family, Peyton recounts what he learned about the ancestry of his maternal grandmother, Cora Bergen Nevius.

I have traced the lineage of my mother, Edna Mae Nevius Clark, back to England.

My mother's mother, and my grandmother, was Cora Bergen Nevius, whom I called Nana. She lived on Columbia Avenue in Hopewell, New Jersey, and died when I was twelve years old. I remember her well because she took care of me several weeks each summer up until the time of her death. Her husband and my grandfather, Elmer Levi Nevius, worked on the railroad until retirement. Grandpa was a very quiet man and though he lived longer than Nana, I do not remember much about him. Grandpa had a brother named Billy who was a policeman in Philadelphia and was married to Aunt Katherine. They had one daughter, Barbara. I remember they often visited family who lived both in Hopewell and Pennington. I can remember how aggressive and outgoing Aunt Katherine was, and when she came to town everyone would change their plans to cater to her needs. Aunt Katherine ruled! She insisted that everyone in the family of my generation should go to college.

When I checked the 1910 census, it indicated that Grandpa and Uncle Billy had three sisters. Their father was Thomas Nevius, and his mother (their grandmother), Hannah McIntyre Nevius, was living with them. Both Thomas and Hannah were listed as widowed. I was the oldest grandchild of Cora and Elmer Nevius and remember we would have Christmas at their house; I would receive presents from my two uncles, Earl and Lester, and my aunts, Dot, Verna, Peggy, and Hazel. They were great family gatherings. After my brother Syed and Allan, Aunt Dot's son, were born, Nana had several years of illness and did not feel up to having us all together at one time.

Nana had two brothers, Wesley and Raymond Bergen. Their mother, Minnie Bergen (1873–?), was White and their father, James Bergen (1853–?), was Black. Minnie and James married in 1894 and lived in Pennington. Wesley would occasionally visit his sister Nana. I remember seeing him but do not remember ever talking to him. Her other brother, Raymond, was killed during World War II.

James's father was Phillip Bergen (1820–?) and his mother was Elizabeth (1825–?). Since James's parents were all born before the end of slavery, I am searching slave records to find our origins.

Minnie Bergen's maiden name was Butterfield; she came from Farmingdale, Maine. I do not know how she met James Bergen. Minnie's father was Hiram Butterfield (1836–?) and her mother's name was Mary Dobbins (1839–?). Hiram's father was John Butterfield and his mother's name was Judith Whittier (1809–?). John Butterfield's father was Ephraim Butterfield Jr. (1772–1848), and his mother was Zipporah Robinson (1775–1853). Ephraim Butterfield Sr. was born in England in 1734 and came to Dunstable, Massachusetts, with two brothers, Abraham and Isaac. Ephraim moved to Farmingdale, Maine, where several generations lived until Minnie married John Bergen in New Jersey.

I am told the Butterfield home in Farmingdale, Maine, still stands.

HERBERT ALBERT HUBBARD, 1875–1947

Town of Residence: Stoutsburg, New Jersey

Date of Written Text: August 2014

Interviewer/Narrator: Stanley Stewart II (Grandson)

Permission from: Stanley Stewart II

His Story: My memory of spending summers with my grandfather Herbert Hubbard, who taught me discipline and held me accountable when I did not do my chores.

Introduction: My grandfather Herbert Albert Hubbard was the son of Kate Hubbard and a member of the Bergen family (though I have never been sure of the connection). He was the first African American graduate from Rider University but ended up working as a sharecropper on a large farm in Hopewell owned by the Pembleton family.

Here's what I remember about "Pop," which is how we all addressed him. I was born on July 5, 1937, and lived in Princeton, New Jersey, at 94 1/2 Leigh Avenue. Pop lived on a farm at the edge of Hopewell and was a sharecropper working for a White family named the Pembletons. It was a seventy-acre dairy and vegetable farm where all milk was sold to Borden Dairy, which supplied the entire area with milk and dairy products. Many of the cows on Pop's farm were housed at Borden's facility, which I believe was in Hightstown, New Jersey.

I remember me and my sister, Janice, spending summers on the farm in Pop's care as Daddy worked at the post office in Princeton and my mother, Leona, worked at the GM Plant in the Trenton area painting airplanes during World War II.

I remember the summers from 1943 through 1947 because we had chores like feeding the chickens, dropping hay from the loft, feeding the cows in the barn, and weeding the vegetable garden, which was quite large. I remember one day I was supposed to weed the garden, but I went off and had a grand time playing and did not complete any of my chores.

Well, when it came supper time I showed up to eat only to be informed by Pop that I had not done any work and therefore I could not eat. So, I went to bed early and hungry but was up early the next morning getting my chores done!

There were seventy cows on the farm, which included the twenty-five or thirty that were kept at Borden's Dairy. These cows were milked twice a day at 4:00 a.m. and 4:00 p.m. seven days a week by Pop, my dad, and Uncle Garland, who was my Aunt Herma's husband.

There were three horses on the farm: two draft horses, George and Sarah, who were used for plowing the field, and the third horse, Patcoolie, who was a black and white pinto. Patcoolie was on the wild side and would bite you if you got too near him. Needless to say, we didn't ride him very much!

There was also a bull named Ferdinand on the farm that was struck by lightning and died. This happened during the war when meat was rationed along with most everything else. Every family had a ration book with stamps for various items such as coffee, sugar, flour, meat, and even shoes of which you could get only two pair per year. Back to Ferdinand, he was dragged to the barn skinned, dressed, and sold to the local A&P food store. I also remember that Pop slaughtered a hog every fall. They would hang him up by his hind legs and slit his throat to catch the blood in a bucket. Someone we would stir the blood to keep it from coagulating so that it could be used in making blood sausages. No part of the pig was ever thrown away! During the war years food for a lot of folks was in short supply, but I remember the pantry on the farm as being like a wonderland. There were jars of just about everything that could be grown and canned along with smoked hams and sausages and such. I still can remember the smells that emitted from that place.

Pop's wife, my grandmother Sarah Matilda, gave birth to my mother,

Leona, on June 2, 1913, but my grandmother died nine years later. Pop did his own cooking and normally ate right out of the frying pan (which at the time I thought was pretty cool). He had a woodstove in the kitchen that never went out summer, winter, spring, or fall. There was always a pot of something simmering on the back.

The side of the Pembleton house where Pop lived was one big room downstairs and two bedrooms upstairs. There were no bathrooms or toilets in this side of the house. There was an outhouse out back with seats for two. There was a Sears Roebuck catalog tied to a nail for toilet paper. The instructions from Pop were to use the shiny pages in the summer time and save the thin pages for winter as the shiny pages were too cold! We normally got a bath every Saturday night in a large No. 10 wash pan in the kitchen. Our water came from a well out front, while the Pembleton side of the house had indoor plumbing that included running water, a kitchen sink, a bathtub, and a flush toilet. They very seldom, if ever, stayed at this house.

There was a tomato canning factory at the back end of the farm and Pop took several wagon loads at the end of every summer. We baled hay for the cows and raised corn for the hogs. We worked from sunup until it was dark. There was a radio in the house where we used to get weather reports and sometimes listen to music and the news.

If Pop wanted to go into town, he would hitch up the horse and buggy because he did not like riding in cars and didn't even use the tractor on the farm. He'd much rather use his horses, George and Sarah, to do all the plowing, his reason being that horses don't get stuck! I remember that Pop always shaved with a straight razor of which he had several because he would not go near or use an electric razor.

In the winter months, when we lived in Princeton, we would visit Pop two or three weekends out of the month until 1947 when my brother Jeffrey was born, and we moved to Pennington. After we moved to Pennington we did not visit the farm that much.

When the Pembleton family sold the farm it virtually left Pop homeless, so he moved to Pennington with his oldest daughter, Herma. He became very ill with stomach cancer, which then was called "consumption," suffered a lot, and passed away.

After I received my cousin Stanley's story about Pop, I could not help but wonder about the story my grandmother Herma had always told about Pop, that he was the first "colored" man to graduate from Rider College. We had all grown up hearing this and Mom, as she was called, could sometimes slightly embellish a story. But for some reason I could not shake the nagging feeling that I needed to check her story out, just in case she hadn't embellished.

One warm September day I attended a presentation at the William Trent House in Trenton, New Jersey, to hear a lecture on slavery in the Lawrenceville, New Jersey, region. Afterward I was able to speak with one of the presenters, Brooke Hunter, an associate professor at Rider University. After getting her contact information, I spoke with Professor Hunter and told her the story my grandmother claimed about my great-grandfather and asked if there was someone who could investigate. Professor Hunter put me in touch with a fellow associate professor, Robert Congleton, who is also a librarian as well as the university archivist at Rider University.

Without hesitation I called Professor Congleton and gave him the story. "Could my grandmother possibly have been telling the truth because she was known to tell stories," I explained. Professor Congleton, who said to call him Bob, asked if I would give him a little time to investigate but that he would get back to me either way. About a month later, while sitting at my office at work, the phone rang and on the other end was Robert Congleton. As soon as I answered I detected an air of excitement in his voice as he quickly got to the point. "Well, your grandmother was telling the truth. Your great-grandfather was indeed the first African American graduate from the Trenton Business School in 1894 and earned a degree as a Stenographer." Bob invited me to his office to talk more about this exciting discovery and to show me a copy of Rider's 1894–95 handbook that had my great-grandfather's name listed. He then offered to write a story about Pop since Rider was celebrating its 150th anniversary. I didn't hesitate and immediately scheduled a date to meet with Bob. As a result of this meeting, an article was written by Adam Grybowski of the Alumni Department for the fall 2015 edition of *Rider Magazine*. Below is the article as it appeared.

"FIRST IN CLASS"

Herbert Hubbard: A Brilliant Penman and Skilled Musician was Rider's First African American Graduate

After a startling entrance into business and an equally un-usual exit, Herbert Hubbard worked for most of his life on a seventy-acre dairy and vegetable farm run by a white family named Pembleton.

Despite working as a sharecropper, Hubbard, who was black, had an education that prepared him for white-collar work. In 1894, he graduated from Trenton Business College, a forerunner to Rider University, making him the University's first confirmed African American graduate. Upon graduating, he would find employment that conflicted with the mores of post–Civil War America, cutting his promising professional life short.

The naming of Hubbard as Rider's first confirmed African

American graduate came this fall after the University's archivist, Robert Congleton, and Hubbard's great-granddaughter Beverly Mills met to discuss the issue. Hubbard's status was a family legend for generations.

"Over the years, I've been asked time and time again: Who was the first African American to graduate from Rider?" Congleton says. "Now, I have an answer."

It is possible that, prior to Hubbard, Rider may have graduated African Americans who passed as white students unbeknownst to school officials, Congleton says.

Hubbard's name appears in the annual bulletin published by Trenton Business College to advertise courses and requirements, share tuition costs, list current students and recent graduates. A brilliant penman and skilled musician, Hubbard is listed as an 1894 graduate, but because the publication did not include photos, it was impossible to distinguish the race of students without further details.

Born June 7, 1875, Hubbard was the only child of a woman named Kate who worked as a housekeeper for a wealthy Hopewell, N.J., family, the Stouts. Kate, who was a single mother, died when Hubbard was a boy, though it remains unclear his exact age at the time of her death.

After Kate died, J. Hervey Stout and his sister, Sarah, raised Hubbard. Both single, they lived together in a house on what is now Broad Street. The siblings were distinguished for maintaining "one of the most hospitable homes in the Hopewell valley," according to a book of early Hopewell history, *Pioneers of Hopewell.*

"I don't know if they did it because of a sense of loyalty to Kate, who had been there a long time, or if they saw something worth investing in," says granddaughter Mills. "Maybe it was both."

According to family stories, Hubbard was a self-taught musician who not only played the violin but made the instrument too. He passed his musical gifts on to his son William Earl, who was a well-known local musician for some fifty years. Hubbard's musicianship was secondary only to his penmanship. "Apparently, his penmanship was absolutely extraordinary, and he would drill his children, impressing upon them the importance of good penmanship," Mills says.

Mills and Congleton believe the presence of a wealthy patron was instrumental in Rider admitting Hubbard. "Someone would have had to not only advocate for him but pay for him," Mills says. "The Stouts must have seen something special in him."

If this is true, Hervey is the likely candidate. He appeared at several significant events in Hubbard's life, Mills says. When Hubbard married Sarah Matilda Hoagland in 1897, Hervey served as a witness. Hubbard named his first son, who died at a young age, Hervey. "Hervey obviously cared about Herb," Mills says. "If he didn't, he wouldn't have done these things."

Before the Civil War, opportunities for free blacks to pursue higher education in the North were limited and virtually nonexistent in the slaveholding South. In response, many historically black colleges were founded with the primary mission to educate African Americans. More opportunities arose for blacks following the Civil War, when private colleges enrolled more African Americans than public institutions, often preparing them for professional jobs.

Booker T. Washington, the president of the Tuskegee Institute, led the shift toward educating blacks with the goal of securing them jobs in manual labor, where more jobs existed. For instance, in the 1890s, while Hubbard was studying at Rider, New Jersey opened a Manual Training & Industrial School for Colored Youth (known as the "Tuskegee of the North") in Bordentown. "This segregated residential high school provided vocational training for African American men and women in manual labor jobs," says history professor Brooke Hunter.

At Trenton Business College, Hubbard likely studied the standard curriculum of penmanship, shorthand, stenography, public speaking, and other subjects related to business. Bucking the trend led by Washington toward manual labor, Hubbard used his gifts to transcend contemporary expectations for African Americans—a feat he accomplished, but only for a limited time.

According to Mills, Hubbard told his children that he worked for three years after graduating, saying that he was employed in the back room of two offices (most likely a bank and an insurance company) to keep out of sight from white clients who may have been offended by seeing a black man in such a position. "He would be the one penning specific documents, but the business owners couldn't ever show that a black man was writing them," Mills says.

Hubbard and his wife would have three children after the death of Hervey: William Earl, Herma (a combination of his first name, Herbert, and his wife's middle name, Matilda), and Florence Leona. In 1898, a year after he was married, Hubbard was no longer employed in business but instead, at the age of 23, became a sharecropper for a local family. The exact nature of this transition is unknown. "The only thing I can think of is that farming was a sure shot and he had to provide for his family," Mills says. "It couldn't have been easy for him."

Hubbard began working on the farm in 1898 and lived in a section of the Pembleton house with two bedrooms upstairs and one large room downstairs. The Pembletons had indoor plumbing and running water, but not Hubbard. He received water from a well and used an outhouse behind the home.

Despite lacking modern amenities, the farm provided a living. "I remember the pantry on the farm as being like a wonder-land," says Hubbard's grandson, Stanley Stewart II, who was born in 1937. "There were jars of just about everything that could be grown and canned, along with smoked hams and sausages and such."

The farm sold its milk to nearby Borden Dairy. Stewart explains that cows were milked twice a day, seven days a week—first at 4 a.m. and then again at 4 p.m. When not completing the work himself, Hubbard received help from his son and son-in-law.

Hubbard worked on the farm until around 1947 when the Pembletons sold it. The sale left Hubbard "virtually homeless," Stewart says, and, as a result, he moved to 233 S. Main St. in

Pennington to live with his oldest daughter, Herma. Hubbard died in Pennington on July 11, 1948, from stomach cancer. He was 73.

Hubbard was buried in Stoutsburg Cemetery, where Mills currently works as secretary. She has been conducting research for a book about the contribution of African Americans to the Hopewell region, and her great-grandfather's story is one she hopes to tell. "He's just one person out of many who has an absolutely fascinating story," she says. "So many of them were extremely talented people and the economic engine of the region. If they were born today, who knows what they would have accomplished."

Rider Magazine (Fall 2015): 14–17
(reprinted with permission)

DESCENDANTS OF THE GROVER AND NEVIUS FAMILIES

EARLE NEVIUS, 1916–2001

Town of Residence: Hopewell, New Jersey

Date of Written Text: March 3, 2017

Interviewer/Narrator: Carol Nevius Waldron (Daughter)

Permission from: Carol Nevius Waldron

His story: Carol Nevius Waldron remembers her father's strong work ethic and how he was the first African American mail carrier in Hopewell Borough, New Jersey, and caretaker of the Stoutsburg Cemetery.

Introduction: My father, Earle, was a descendant of the Nevius family whose roots go back to the early 1800s on the Sourland Mountain. He was a landowner and entrepreneur whose work ethic was one of his most recognized traits. My father took over the responsibility as caretaker of the Stoutsburg Cemetery from his father, Elmer Nevius. Both my dad and grandfather worked for years to bring the cemetery up to pristine condition after years of neglect.

My father, Earle Nevius, was born on August 2, 1916, to Elmer Levi Nevius and Cora Mae Bergen Nevius. My dad's siblings were one brother, Lester, and sisters Dorothy, Hazel, Edna, Verna, and Peggy.

My dad was an avid reader who strongly believed in education. When he joined the U.S. Postal Service in 1950 he was the first Black mail carrier in Hopewell Borough. Dad faithfully delivered Hopewell's mail for thirty years and was a familiar figure in the community where everyone knew him as "Mr. Nevius, the mailman!" My parents were married for sixty-five years and lived the majority of that time in our house on Columbia Avenue in Hopewell Borough. I was raised in that house along with my sister, Beverlee, and my twin brothers, Bruce and Barry.

I learned that in Dad's younger years, before he joined the army, Dad held a variety of jobs that included a job as a railroad hand, a short order cook, and golf caddy. While in the army he was stationed at Fort Belvoir, Virginia, and went on to receive an honorable discharge in 1943. My uncles, Bob and Albert, always talked about Dad's entrepreneurial spirit and how he started his own ice delivery business in Hopewell Township and in the Sourland Mountain area.

After retirement Dad actually took time to relax by playing golf and traveling with my mother, Virginia Cary Nevius. For as far back as I can remember my dad was the caretaker of the Stoutsburg Cemetery on Provinceline Road in the Sourland Mountain. This was a responsibility he took over from his father, Elmer. I also remember the meticulous records my dad kept along with any documents, deeds, or maps associated with the cemetery. He was always the go-to person for people who called our house looking for a plot for their loved ones. It was just like my dad to be careful to make sure not only to pass along all the cemetery records but also to pass along the torch of caretaking the cemetery to his grandson Baron Holland and his nephews Glen Nevius and John Buck.

Anyone who knew my dad always said the same thing. He was a man to be taken at his word because he meant what he said and said what he meant!

ALBERT THOMAS WITCHER, 1921–2013

Town of Residence: Hopewell, New Jersey

Date of Written Text: April 7, 2017

Narrators: Susan and Angela Witcher

Permission from: Susan Witcher and Angela Witcher

His Story: Daughters Susan and Angela remember their father's words, "It's our heritage, you see. You've got to come from somewhere!"

Introduction: Albert Witcher was a gift to the Hopewell Valley community. Throughout his entire life he cherished the African American history of this region. A man with remarkable memory to the end of his life, he was a witness to an earlier time. Through his selfless devotion to doing what is right, Albert was instrumental in preserving the Pennington African Cemetery.

It's hard to adequately recognize how much our father, Albert Witcher, contributed to the legacy of the African American experience in central New Jersey. Everyone who knew him was aware of his pride and dedication to home and community. Nowhere was this pride more evident than in the care he gave the Pennington African Cemetery. His outgoing personality, remarkable memory, and hard work made him an integral part of the historical narrative of our region. In 2004 he was awarded the Griot Award by the Kitchen Table News in recognition of his work in preserving African American history. As a griot, or storyteller, he maintained a tradition of oral history for the Pennington and Sourland Mountain regions.

He was born on August 7, 1921, to Albert Vernon Witcher and Stella Grover Witcher, and had two sisters, Marion and Edith. He grew up in Pennington, spending time with relatives in Skillman, visiting neighbors, working on local farms, and playing baseball. He was a 1939 graduate of Central High School, was drafted into World War II in 1943 where he served in the army with the military police, and married our mother, Verna Lee Nevius of Hopewell, in 1948. They settled into our family home in the Sourland Mountain region, which came from our mother's Bergen ancestors. In the early years of their marriage the house had woods that reached almost to the back door. Dad removed rocks and mowed further back until we finally had a backyard. He used this same energy to plant a field of vegetables that was admired by all who passed by for decades. No one else could coax that many vegetables out of the "mountain grit." By 1960 Albert and Verna were able to add an addition to the home. They remained married for fifty-three years and raised three children, Susan, Tommy, and Angela.

Dad took care of home by building a career at United Engine Rebuilders. He worked his way up from doing piecework to becoming a salaried employee. He enjoyed business and held positions in management and sales. He took pride in landing major accounts with companies such as American Airlines and Frito-Lay.

Although Dad worked many hours he always found time for community service. He was a member of the First Baptist Church of Pennington since childhood and served on the Trustee Board for many years. He enjoyed being a member of the Sourland Planning Council and committed himself to being president of the Pennington African Cemetery Association.

The Pennington African Cemetery was one of his greatest passions. The cemetery was purchased in 1863 by Bethel AME Church trustees for Black residents. Dad knew many of the interred. Grandparents, uncles, cousins, and friends were buried there; and he labored to take care of it his entire life. He felt strongly about our tradition of volunteers taking responsibility for the upkeep of the cemetery. As a boy he went there with Granny to tend to his grandfather's grave. Together they would walk from their home on Crawley Avenue in Pennington with a hoe or rake and make sure the area around his headstone was neat. He attended the funeral of Charles Jennings (U.S. Colored Troops, Rhode Island), who was the oldest Civil War veteran living in Pennington when he died, bantered with Archibald (Spader) Seruby, a snack vendor known as the Peanut King, who was a veteran of the Spanish-American War, and paid his respects to Georgie Stewart, a schoolmate who died when she was seventeen.

In 1990 he was interviewed by the *Pennington Post* to talk about his years of work in maintaining the cemetery and the financial struggles he encountered by bearing most of the expense. When asked about the years he had spent caretaking the cemetery Dad simply replied, "It's our heritage, you see. You've got to come from somewhere! There has to be some pride in what belongs to you. Oh, it's been tough at times for us to be able to take care of the cemetery, but it's been kept up. You cut the grass, you get the equipment that's needed, you do what needs to be done. It's a place that just wouldn't exist if somebody didn't go in there and do something."

By this time the cemetery had moved from being actively used for burials to becoming a historic burial ground. The challenges that the Pennington African Cemetery Association faced became more complex. In addition to maintaining the grounds and paying respect to the deceased, it became necessary to push back on aggressive development that resulted in the blocking of the entrance to our driveway and our losing a row of mature trees and one of the access points to the cemetery. Under his leadership the Pennington African Cemetery Association staked out the boundaries and raised awareness in the Pennington community. He oversaw a grant application for capital improvements for fencing and gave tours and interviews to anyone interested in learning about the cemetery.

As members of the Pennington African Cemetery Association, we remain dedicated to the preservation and maintenance of the cemetery, not only to honor our father's memory but to honor the memory of all the interred who helped build our community. It's the right thing to do.

DESCENDANTS OF FAMILIES WHO MIGRATED TO THE SOURLAND MOUNTAIN AND SURROUNDING REGION

ADA WALDRON HIGHTOWER, 1896–1974

Town of Residence: Hopewell, New Jersey

Date of Written Text: June 30, 2017

Interviewer/Narrator: Elaine Buck

Permission from: Elaine Buck (Great-granddaughter)

Her Story: Elaine Buck remembers her grandmother, the daughter of slaves, who migrated north from Virginia to seek a better life.

Introduction: Ada and George Hightower were pillars of the First Colored Church in Hopewell, New Jersey, and served there for many years. The Hightowers were an integral part of the Black community on Columbia Avenue in Hopewell and were among the earliest African Americans to live on this street.

I honor my great-grandmother Ada Waldron Hightower (Grammy), who was born in 1896 in Bannister, Pittsylvania County, Virginia (near Lynchburg). Ada is the daughter of Lizzie Womack and Abraham Waldron, both former Virginia slaves. She married George Hightower and from that union they had twelve children.

Slavery had ended, and Ada and George survived as sharecroppers on land in Virginia that belonged to the Hayes family. On this land, the family was able to raise their own vegetables, chickens, pigs, and a cow, which kept the family fed. However, since they were sharecroppers the landowner generally reaped all of the financial profits.

All the Hightower children worked in the tobacco fields along with the adults from sunrise to sundown. Schools were segregated, one-room school houses with poor-quality used books. But there really was no time for schooling especially when the crops needed harvesting. Unfortunately, little hope of economic prosperity was a reality in the Jim Crow South.

During the Great Migration era, George and Ada made their way to New Jersey in search of a better way of life. They resided in Trenton for a while where Grandpop George worked at one of the pottery factories in Trenton. At that time Trenton was the home of one of two major pottery centers in the United States.

Grandpop and Grammy purchased a home in Hopewell Borough on Columbia Avenue. Ada's brother William, her sister Mary, and her sister Jennie also had homes on the "Avenue."

The Hightower family attended the First Colored Baptist Church of Hopewell, which was later named Second Calvary Baptist Church, where they served faithfully until they went on to be with the Lord. Grandpop George died in 1964 and is buried in the church burial ground on First Street along with Ada's parents, Abraham and Lizzie Waldron.

Grammy died on March 8, 1974, at the age of seventy-seven and is buried at Stoutsburg Cemetery in Hopewell Township on Province-line Road along with her sisters, Mary Barksdale and Jennie Terry, and her daughter (my grandmother), Queen Hester Hightower Coleman.

MARVEL ALETA CLARK HARRIS, 1915–2015

Town of Residence: Burlington, New Jersey

Date of Written Text: 2012

Interviewer/Narrator: Douglas Harris (Son)
(Excerpted from his book *The Marvel Chronicles*)

Permission from: Douglas Harris

Her Story: My mother, Marvel Clark Harris, was the eleventh child born to Henry Ballard and Pinky Coles Clark, who migrated from Virginia and settled in Pennington, New Jersey. Mother was born during a blizzard and was a sickly child. According to the doctor, my mother was not expected to live into adulthood. For sixty-two years my mother was married to my father, Milton Harris, where they raised two children, my sister, Marlene, and me. Mother died two months after reaching her 100th birthday.

Introduction: My mother was an exceptional woman whose life I chronicled in a book titled **The Marvel Chronicles**. My mother acknowledged that God led and directed her throughout her entire life. My cousin Karen Clark once observed, "When Aunt Marvel comes in a room, Jesus walks in with her." Aunt Marvel was our family historian, and we are pleased to be able to share her words.

My father, Henry Ballard Clark, was born in Gretna, Virginia, in August 1873 to Henry and Louisa Morehead Clark.

My mother, Pinky Coles, was born on January 18, 1873, in Chatham, Virginia, just a few miles from my father's birthplace. Pinky was the daughter of Susie Belle Gregory and Milton Coles, both former slaves. Susie Belle's mother was a dark-skinned Asian Indian from Madagascar, the island off the coast of Africa. Pinky's paternal grandmother, Delila Coles, was part Indian and part African American. Her paternal grandfather was a full-blooded African.

I was the eleventh child born to my parents, but more significantly I was the seventh daughter of a seventh son. My birth was dramatic. I was born at home in Pennington, New Jersey, on December 13, 1915, in the middle of a blizzard. I was a sickly child. At the time of my birth, Woodrow Wilson was president, Henry Ford had produced his millionth Model T, Frank Sinatra was one day old; slaves had been free fifty years, segregation was the law of the land, discrimination against "coloreds" was rampant, education beyond grade school was for the elite, women could not vote, and the United States was in the midst of World War I. Our family physician, Dr. Abbey, told Mother I wouldn't survive past ten years old. But Mother was determined to prove him wrong.

I was called Margaret by my first-grade teacher, who had never heard of the name "Marvel." The name Margaret stayed with me all the way through high school. I missed just about all of fourth grade. My illnesses came one right after the other and I had to go to a specialist as many as three times a week. I was out so many days I had to repeat fourth grade. Four years later, though, I was doing so well the principal and my teachers decided to see if I could skip eighth grade, which I did. When I was fourteen, I was hired by a White woman in town to help her with household duties, primarily preparing meals. She came to school seeking a "colored girl" to help her. I would leave school at 3:00 p.m., go to Mrs. Britto's, do my homework, prepare and serve the evening meal to the family, eat my meal in the kitchen, clean up, and go home. When I graduated from high school, I won an award for having the best grades. It was quite an honor, especially for a colored girl in a predominantly White school.

Despite this honor, my photo, along with photos of all the other African American students, were in a row at the bottom of the page [in the school yearbook]

Because of my good grades, I was accepted at Douglas College, a women's college affiliated with Rutgers University, but I could not attend because it was the middle of the Great Depression. There was no money.

As far as my career was concerned, for a short time I worked as a beautician, but the majority of my work history was with the Department of Motor Vehicles where I was employed for over twenty years.

Throughout my life my focal point has been my church and belief in the Lord. Presently I am a member of the Second Baptist Church of Burlington where I have been for seventy years.

IRA BROOKS, 1917–2001

Town of Residence: Hopewell, New Jersey

Date of Written Text: February 22, 2017

Interviewer/Narrator: Catherine Fulmer Hogan (Granddaughter)

Permission from: Evelyn Brooks

His Story: Catherine Hogan talks about the life of her grandfather Ira Brooks, who migrated from Maryland and became an African American landowner on the Sourland Mountain.

Introduction: The consummate family man, Ira Brooks was one of the most beloved individuals who lived on the Sourland Mountain. Always ready to help anyone in need, Pop Pop and his wife, Evelyn, reared ten children and lived a rich, full life providing food for their family from the "sour" land.

My Pop Pop, Ira Brooks, moved to Skillman, New Jersey, in 1931 at the age of fourteen. In 1948, Pop Pop and Nana, my grandmother, Evelyn, purchased twenty-eight acres on Mountain Church Road and raised ten kids. This was a big deal for a man of color to own that many acres in Hopewell Township. My grandmother told me that she was really the one who struck the deal to buy the land.

When Pop Pop moved to Skillman at the age of fourteen he held a number of odd jobs such as chauffeuring for local families. It was because of his chauffeuring job and his frequent trips to Tuckahoe, New York, that he was led to Mrs. Looney's boardinghouse where his future bride was living. My Pop Pop only stood at a mere five feet three inches tall, but with all of his charm he was a giant of a man. Ira and Evelyn started courting and were married on November 24, 1940, and four years later they came to New Jersey to settle on "The Mountain."

In the early part of their marriage, Pop Pop, Nana, and their three oldest children first lived on Wertsville Road across from Minnietown Lane. Everybody on the mountain knew Wertsville Road because it was one of the main roads that led further up the Sourland Mountain, to Flemington, and to points beyond. Minnietown Road, a side road off Wertsville Road where Hillbilly Hall sits on the corner, was where mixed couples used to live back in the early days when Black folks first came to the mountain. The people were nicknamed "minnie dots" and lived in tiny two- and three-room cottages that were barely big enough to live in.

In the early 1950s, Ira was known by everybody as "Brooksie" and later even "Pop Pop." He started a towing and hauling business to earn extra money for his ever-growing family. He started doing this part-time at first and then full-time after he retired from the Pennsylvania Railroad where he worked for twenty-eight years. Pop Pop continued to tow and haul with his wrecker until 2000, which was nearly a half century. Over the course of those fifty years, he rescued many people from ditches, flat tires, overheated engines, you name it. In those days Stony Brook Road was a bit of a "lover's lane" so Pop Pop would frequently pull cars out of the woods when drivers found themselves stuck in the mud. There are so many people to this day that tell our family about how Pop Pop came to their aid with his chains and that old wrecker of his!

ARTHUR HORACE "DICK" CLARK, 1918–2008

Town of Residence: Pennington, New Jersey

Date of Written Text: 2012

Interviewer/Narrator: Douglas Harris (Nephew) (excerpted from his book *The Marvel Chronicles*)

Permission from: Douglas Harris

His Story: Arthur (Dick) Clark was the youngest out of the twelve children of Ballard and Pinky Coles Clark, who migrated from Virginia and settled in Pennington, New Jersey.

Introduction: An avid sports fan, Dick, as he was known, excelled in several sports in high school and was chosen as one of the first inductees into the Hopewell Valley Sports Hall of Fame. The father of six children, Dick began his career at Howe Nurseries as a supervisor before working his way up to landscape designer. Dick was the first African American school board member in Hopewell Township, New Jersey, and was cofounder and first president of the Hopewell Valley Association of Equal Opportunity, an organization devoted to improving race relations in the community.

My uncle Dick was the twelfth and youngest child born to Ballard and Pinky Coles Clark. His sister Marvel, my mother, remembered that when he was born he had bright red hair wound into tight little curls, or more accurately, tiny little knots.

My grandfather Ballard wanted to name him Dick so he called him by that name even though my grandmother Pinky had named him Arthur. So, he was known as Dick his entire life with most people thinking that was his real name. Pinky was in her forties when she gave birth to Dick and wasn't fast enough to chase after him when he ran away from her. So, she would tell his sisters, my mother, Marvel, or my aunt Frieda to run after him and bring him back. My mother said that she and Frieda were both good runners; they could easily catch him while Mother waited on the porch with a switch or strap in hand.

In his younger years, Uncle Dick loved sports and was quite an accomplished athlete and had earned eight varsity letters before graduating in 1936. Later, he was honored as one of the first inductees in the newly established Hopewell Valley Sports Hall of Fame.

In 1940 Uncle Dick married Winifred Crews from Trenton, New Jersey, and raised six children on Dublin Road in Hopewell Township in a house across the street from where he was raised. During his career he worked for Howe Nurseries for thirty-six years where he started out as a laborer and worked his way up to planting supervisor, landscape salesman, and finally as a landscape designer. To further his career aspirations, Uncle Dick completed landscaping courses at Cook College and enrolled in a Dale Carnegie sales course. He was also a landscaping instructor for an adult education course at the local high school in Pennington, New Jersey.

Being the trailblazer that he was, Uncle Dick served as the first African American school board member of the Hopewell Township School District and was cofounder and first president of the Hopewell Valley Association of Equal Opportunity, an organization that was devoted to improving race relations in the community. Always community minded, Uncle Dick served on the Board of Directors for the YMCA and was a member of the Mercer County Juvenile Justice Conference, a committee that dealt with juveniles with domestic court issues.

Throughout his life Dick was a lover of farming, and many times when we would come to Pennington to visit we would find him toiling in his garden where he grew sumptuous vegetables and flowers alike. And, as if that wasn't enough, Dick was always looking for something else to do. So, in his seventies and eighties, he took a job working part-time job at the local Getty gas station getting up at the crack of dawn to pump gas. Uncle Dick did not live as long as his sister, my mother, Marvel, who died at one hundred; he died at age ninety.

EVELYN DUNN BROOKS, 1921–

Town of Residence: Hopewell, New Jersey

Date of Interview: August 29, 2015

Interviewer/Narrator: Elaine Buck and Beverly Mills

Permission from: Evelyn Brooks

Her Story: Evelyn Dunn Brooks describes living in a boardinghouse in

New York to building a life on the mountain with her husband, Ira, and ten children.

Introduction: People from the region have always thought of Evelyn Brooks as the lady on the mountain with all the kids. Evelyn and her husband, Ira, farmed the "sour" rocky soil on the mountain to feed their brood. Known for her quick wit and intelligence, Evelyn and Ira (known as "Pop Pop") were known for their selflessness. Evelyn has been a Second Calvary Baptist Church "Mother" for several years, and it is not uncommon for her to dance up the church aisle to this very day while being "slain in the spirit."

In 1998 a *Trenton Times* article titled "Brooks Family Legacy Impressive" was written by Rev. Willie J. Smith about Evelyn and Ira Brooks.[6] In this article Evelyn Brooks described how she was nineteen the first time she saw Ira when he came to Bronxville looking for a room. Ira was a houseman and chauffeur for Marie Buckley before moving to Bronxville from Princeton in 1938 or 1939. In those days hired help could live near the people they worked for but could only board in places that took in people of color. Because the boardinghouses in the Bronxville area were all full, Ira's employer consulted the local police on where Ira could go. This recommendation ultimately led him to the same boardinghouse where Evelyn was staying. Intrigued by the story, Elaine and Beverly thought it only fitting that Evelyn Dunn Brooks, who was ninety-four at the time, be the first person interviewed for their oral history. After her cup of tea was fixed, she launched into her story.

I grew up in Bronxville, New York, and before I married I used to go to the Savoy Ballroom in New York to see many acts. I recall seeing Chick Webb and also Ella Fitzgerald when she was just starting out as a singer. Ella was a foster child who ran away from home to be in the talent show at the Apollo Theater in Harlem. The first time she didn't win but the second time she won first place. I think because she was a foster child Chick took pity on her and so he took her under his wing to help her get her career started.

My husband, Ira, didn't come to Hopewell until he was about fourteen years old. He came from Sparrows Point, Maryland, where he was living with his aunt who ran a boardinghouse. Alex Brooks, Ira's uncle, was the first to settle in the Sourland Mountain. It was Ira's father, Samuel, who came to Hopewell searching for his brother, Alex, whom he knew was somewhere in the area. This was during the depression and Sam had no other way to get here so he walked the entire way from Maryland to New Jersey with a buddy. Sam and his friend ended up parting company in Delaware because he found out that his friend wanted to rob somebody. To earn money to buy food, Sam got a job chopping wood for a lady in Delaware. The woman wanted him to stay and work for her, but he was bound for New Jersey. As he traveled, Sam went to the police station in whatever town he was passing through because by nightfall he wanted to be locked up for the night to make sure he could get a meal and make it through the night alive. Sam made sure he always kept five cents in his pocket so, in case he was stopped, he would not be picked up for vagrancy. The nickel was his protection from that. When he finally arrived at the Battle Monument in Trenton he asked if anyone knew his brother Alex Brooks. He was told that someone heard that Alex lived in an area called Stoutsburg, which was just outside of Hopewell. Sam caught the trolley and was united with his brother. Alex also ended up buying land off Provinceline Road, a main road that runs up to the Sourland Mountain.

We were married in 1940 and first lived in Hopewell Borough on Columbia Avenue before we moved to a home we rented directly across the road from Hillbilly Hall. The house was owned by Cora Bergen

Nevius, the wife of Elmer Nevius, and we rented for $25 a month. One Sunday, which happened to be an Easter Sunday, a Jewish man came past and asked us if we were looking for a house of our own, which we said we were. The man took us up to Mountain Church Road to a ten-room house on twenty-eight acres. We bought the house in 1948 for $5,000 but the man had to hold the mortgage and agreed that we pay him $50 per month. The taxes were $48 a year. At that time, we were one of only three families living on Mountain Church Road. I remember how nice the farmers were to us and would leave extra produce on our front porch because in those days people were always helping each other.

I still remember some of people and places that were on the mountain back then. There was the Conover family, who lived on Route 518; Mr. Conover was very fair and looked like a White man. I had heard that he came from a plantation that used to be on Amwell Road. There was also a Black man that I remember who lived there with the Conovers who played the violin. It was either Sam or Dorey, I don't remember which one; both were well-known Black violinists who were always in demand.

Hopewell had its own deal of prejudice back then. I remember there used to be a bar called Derby's Tavern where some of the locals, both Black and White, would go even though it didn't have a good reputation. A local Black man, George Cain, used to go with the tavern owner who was a White woman, which caused a scandal. Then there was the Arnold family from Hopewell, who were really Black but could all easily pass for White. Arlene Arnold, the daughter in the family, was a hairdresser who only catered to White women. I asked her one day if she would do my hair and she told me, "I don't do Black folks' hair but if you want your hair done come at night to the back door!"

I also remember Ashton's restaurant, where the Hopewell Bistro is now, which was owned by the Van Doren family. It was around 1942 or 1943 and I was waiting for a taxi to take me home, so I decided to buy some ice cream for myself and my firstborn, Calvin, who then was about two years old. I went to sit down with the baby and was told I could not sit at the counter. I asked them was it okay that I buy their ice cream, but I couldn't sit at their counter? They told me I could not sit at the counter and would have to wait on the front porch. After that I didn't bother to go back ever again and made sure I told all my Black friends.

JOHN KIRBY HUGHES SR., 1926–2013

Town of Residence: Trenton, New Jersey

Date of Written Text: December 12, 2017

Interviewer/Narrator: Audrey Hughes Randolph

Permission from: Audrey Hughes Randolph (Daughter)

His Story: John Kirby Hughes Sr. was the son of Ernest Walter Sr. and Pearl Barnard Hughes. Ernest and his wife, Pearl, hailed from Camden County, North Carolina, and migrated to New Jersey in the 1920s.

Introduction: He recognized the value of a life lived and provided "Going Home" services for African Americans through the Hughes Funeral Home.

My father, John Kirby Hughes Sr., was born in Skillman, New Jersey, on April 16, 1926. John K. Sr. was affectionately known by everybody as "Jack." The Hughes family, along with the Harrisons, are cousins descended from African American families who have lived on the Sourland Mountain on Camp Meeting Avenue and Hollow Road since the late 1800s.

My father was educated in the Montgomery Township and

Princeton public schools in New Jersey. In his high school yearbook, Dad declared his "singular" intention was to become a funeral director and an entrepreneur. But like many men of his generation his goals were temporarily postponed when he entered the U.S. Army during World War II where he served with distinction. At the conclusion of his military service, Dad attended Howard University in Washington, D.C., and the American Academy of Funeral Science in New York City, where the studied business and mortuary science. After graduation, Dad subsequently served apprenticeships at Newsome Funeral Home, the Rodney Dade Funeral Home, and the Judkins Funeral Home, all located in Trenton, New Jersey.

Having lived through the embroiled era of segregation, Dad and my mother, Carolyn Yeager, understood the need for the establishment and success of African American businesses. Inspired and encouraged by family and friends and also influenced by the echoing spirit of the civil rights movement, my parents realized their dreams of entrepreneurship and service to the greater Trenton area and surrounding communities by establishing the Hughes Funeral Home in 1959, all the while raising a family that included myself (Audrey) and my siblings Carolyn, Margaret, Carlton, John, and Jerome.

Keeping in the spirit of the civil rights era, as well as their own well-defined business values, my parents recognized and embraced their responsibilities to the families they would serve. They were dedicated to providing and assisting in the recognition of the value of a life lived and to facilitate meaningful ways for the families and community to celebrate the memories of their loved ones. My father's beautiful smile and his humble spirit brought comfort to many souls during times of bereavement.

The original business model established by my father continues to be upheld and is now being well managed by his children and grandchildren, who continue to serve the community with excellence by holding fast to the exceptional business ethic their father and grandfather instilled in them. My father's greatest pride was his family.

Aside from operating the Hughes Funeral Home, my dad was an active member of the Aaron Lodge No. 9, Princeton, New Jersey, the Ophir-Consistory No. 48, and Khufu Temple No. 120.

My father joined our mother in heaven when he passed away on April 12, 2013, just four days shy of his eighty-seventh birthday.

JACQUELINE HARRISON SMITH, C. 1930–

Town of Residence: Skillman, New Jersey

Date of Interview: January 22, 2018

Interviewer/Narrator: Elaine Buck

Permission from: Jacqueline Harrison Smith

Her Story: A daughter remembers her father and other local African American men working for the Reading Railroad, walking the railroad tracks to make sure they were secure.

Introduction: They were known as the keepers of the railroad track. These local African American men, with ties to the Sourland Mountain, made sure that the tracks were clear of anything that would cause an accident.

Did you know that there was a time when people were actually keepers of the Reading Railroad tracks? That people actually had the dangerous task of walking the tracks that went through Skillman to make sure everything was safe before a train came along? That was the responsibility of African American men with ties to founding families from the Sourland Mountain: Archie Harrison, Wilmer Grover, and Elmer Nevius. Archie Harrison's youngest daughter, Jacqueline "Jackie" Harrison Smith, remembers hearing stories of her father and other local African Americans working on the railroad. Archie Harrison, Wilmer Grover, and foreman Elmer Levi Nevius from Hopewell were employed by the Reading Railroad and performed their duties so well they virtually prevented disasters that could have changed the course of history. As a track walker it was their responsibility to inspect the track for any potential problems such as blockages, railroad separation, or anything that may arise that would interfere with the safe passage of the train and its passengers. This stretch of railroad tracks once carried President Franklin Delano Roosevelt. The standard signaling equipment used, a red globe signaling lantern and a clear globe lantern, were required devices by the Reading Railroad and were used at night. The Harrison descendants still have Archie's lanterns in their possession.

One of the original African American settlers in the Sourland Mountain area, Archie, his wife, Annie, and their family resided on Hollow Road where the home still stands. Archie Harrison was an unassuming man who was a leader and cofounder of the First Colored Baptist Church of Hopewell, now known as the Second Calvary Baptist Church in Hopewell Borough, New Jersey.

One of Jackie's fondest memories was how the "Dinky" train, which was a one-car train, came through Skillman and would keep going unless you pulled the switch on the side of the Skillman Station building. Her brother Thad would pull the switch to stop the Dinky so that they could go to the movies in Hopewell.

This special but unknown task performed by these African American men, Archie Harrison, Wilmer Grover, and Elmer Nevius, would by today's standards be considered part of national security. I believe it's never too late to salute these local heroes and recognize their sacrifice and potential danger they willingly placed themselves in.

JAMES CHARLES JENNINGS, 1949–2015

Town of Residence: Lawrenceville, New Jersey

Date of Interview: April 11, 2015

Interviewer/Narrator: Elaine Buck and Beverly Mills

Permission from: Shana Jennings-Williams (daughter)

His Story: Great-grandson of Charles Jennings, the oldest living Civil War veteran in Pennington, New Jersey

Introduction: James Charles Jennings and his ancestors were lifelong members of Bethel AME Church in Pennington, New Jersey, where they served as church administrators and musicians. The family operated a general store in Pennington from 1924 to 1955. The Jennings family was also related to William Allen, the man who discovered the remains of the Lindbergh baby.

Beverly Mills and Elaine Buck interviewed James Charles Jennings, mostly known as "Charlie," at his home on Fackler Road in Lawrenceville, New Jersey, on April 11, 2015.

Charlie proudly showed a picture of his grandmother, Lillian Jennings, who could have easily passed as White. There are stories that she actually did when she traveled alone just for the experience. Lil, as she was called, was the aunt to Alphonso Smith and sister to his mother, Cora. Cora was Beverly's great-grandmother and could have also passed for White like her sister Lil.

Charlie mentioned he did not have much history on his dad's side.

He said there had been a rift that left his grandmother Lillian ostracized from the family so they didn't speak. He remembered another person who was ostracized from the family who was Helen Driver's mother, whom they called little Helen Allen. Charlie said he had no idea what happened, but Helen just wouldn't leave the house and stayed in all the time.

Charlie talked about Bethel AME Church history and showed us a picture of Bethel as the original Hopewell (Pennington's) first Black congregation built in 1847. That's how it had been referred to. Charlie proudly showed a sword and two guns owned by his great-grandfather, Charles S. Jennings, who was in the Rhode Island Regiment of the Civil War. The sword was the one he wore with his dress uniform, items that had been passed down to his father. Charlie was told that on Memorial Day his great-grandfather would display his Civil War gun and other items in front of the general store on South Main Street in Pennington, New Jersey. For many years his great-grandfather had the distinct honor of being the oldest living Civil War veteran in Pennington and marched in the Memorial Day parade.

Charlie recalled the day his dad, Donald, and Albert Witcher reminisced about cow drives down Main Street in Pennington. The cows would come into the train station and they would be marched down the street. Charlie also talked about sitting on Howard Hoagland's porch at night: the men would be on the Hoaglands' porch and the women on another and everybody would be telling stories. One story was about the day that Sadie Dunn, a member of Bethel AME who lived on South Main Street, got shot. They were having Bible study at the church and Mabel Sample, Sadie's next-door neighbor, went to get Sadie to go with her to church. The only thing was Sadie's common law husband didn't like her going to church all the time and told her not to go. Mabel told Sadie, "Don't listen to what he says," so Mabel grabbed Sadie and they left. Suddenly, Sadie's man came out of the house with a shotgun and shot her! According to Albert they deputized a couple Black men to go arrest him; luckily Sadie recovered.

Charlie said that when he was a little boy he, along with neighborhood kids Jeffrey Stewart, Fred Boyer, and Tommy Witcher, took a pack of cigarettes from the Jennings store. They walked back where the horse was kept in the barn, which was full of hay, and started smoking cigarettes and flicking ashes around! It was a miracle nothing burned. Beverly reminded Charlie about the story of when she and Jeffrey Stewart actually burned down a little structure they called the "playhouse." Jeffrey was giving Beverly a lesson on how to strike matches and suddenly ignited some things the older kids had stored in there. Beverly said her mother was hanging laundry and they had somehow gotten past her without arousing suspicion. So, Jeffrey said, "When you go past your mother just skip like we're just playing." Beverly and Jeffrey ran upstairs and hid under the bed and could hear fire trucks coming. When Beverly's mom saw the smoke, she figured it out and quickly called the fire department!

Charlie told us he had another story for us but warned us that it might be considered on the racy side! He told us about how he was sitting on the front porch of grandmother's house, which was next door to Reverend and Mrs. Milton. He said he heard Mrs. Milton say to her husband, who was the pastor of the Bethel AME Church down the street, "Reverend, did you take the trash out?" Getting no answer, she asked him again. "Reverend, did you take the trash out?" But still there was no answer. Finally, about ten minutes later and out of patience she said, "Reverend, if you take the trash out I'll have something good for you later on!" To which he heard Reverend Milton say, "I was going to get that anyway!"

Charlie's grandfather worked at Lawrenceville School, and we also asked him what he knew about formerly Black-owned land in the

Sourland that has been lost. We told Charlie about the large amount of land once owned by the Truehart family and how Lindbergh came to Billy Truehart's house and demanded to buy his property, only to be turned away. That brought up a family story that Charlie heard of how Lindbergh wouldn't even shake Bill Allen's hand and "treated like a dog." (Bill Allen was Charlie's relative who found the remains of the Lindbergh baby.) Charlie said that throughout the years people have tried to say that Bill Allen received reward money for finding the baby but, to his knowledge, he never received a dime. He said that Elinor Ganie, his deceased daughter, also maintained that her father never received a dime.

Charlie said that as far as the information he had about the Jennings side of the family is concerned, they originated from the South, he believed from one of the Carolinas. On the Houston side, his grandmother Lillian's family, they were all free Blacks from Somerset County but still could only work menial jobs. Charles told us a story about his great-grandfather Charles Jennings, who was a veteran of Rhode Island's 14th Regiment who fought in the Civil War. He said he great-grandfather told the story of how he was on a train going south to Louisiana with his regiment. What they didn't know was there was a plantation owner who armed his slaves to get them ready to fire on the train. The plantation owner told his slaves there was a train coming to take them all further south. As the train went by a field the slaves opened fire on the Black soldiers sitting on the train. Charlie said his great-grandfather was miraculously spared but he never got over the death and carnage that he witnessed on that train.

We were careful that we didn't wear out our welcome, to which Charlie said, "Well you're just going to have to come back for part two because there's more to talk about and to show you."

Sadly, Charlie died less than two months later.

Nevius Family Enjoying a Night at the Apollo Theatre, Harlem, New York

1 Henry Race and William Frazer, "Rev. William Frazer's Three Parishes, St. Thomas's, St. Andrew's, and Musconetcong, N.J., 1768–70," *Pennsylvania Magazine of History & Biography* 12, no. 2 (July 1888): 212–32, accessed November 28, 2017, http://www.jstor.org/stable/20083262.

2 Lisa Cokefair Gedney, "Town Records of Hopewell, New Jersey," in *The New Jersey Society of the Colonial Dames of America: Old School Baptist Church, by Authority of the Board of Managers of the New Jersey Society of the Colonial Dames of America* (Hopewell, NJ: Little & Ives, 1931).

3 "William Stives: A Revolutionary Patriot," *Emancipator* 4, no. 25 (October 17, 1839): 100.

4 Beverly Mills and Elaine Buck, "Today, Friday's Memory Goes to Paul (Beetle) Arnold," Facebook: Elaine Buck and Beverly Mills, Authors, If These Stones Could Talk, April 19, 2017, accessed February 19, 2018, https://www.facebook.com/ifthesestonescouldtalk/photos/a.806465616160806. 1073741828.804297839710917/859231084217592/?type=3.

5 "Paul Arnold Catching a Flyball," *Hopewell Herald*, October 1, 1924.

6 Willie Smith, "Brooks Family Legacy Impressive," *Trenton Times*, November 25, 1998.

The Minstrel Revue, full page advertisement, reprinted with permission from *The Hunterdon County Democrat*, March 3, 1932, Volume CVII, Number 135

CHAPTER 9

RESIDENT STORIES

"I NEVER KNEW THAT ..."

If there is a book that you want to read, but it hasn't been written yet, you must be the one to write it.

—Toni Morrison, American novelist (1931–)

In 1976, under the Gerald Ford administration, our nation decided to carve out twenty-eight days to celebrate Black History Month, an expansion upon the idea of "Negro History Week" introduced in 1926 by pioneering African American professor Carter G. Woodson.[1]

Some can say this was America's first attempt at making a concerted effort to educate fellow Americans, Black and White, to commemorate the vast contributions African Americans have made in forming American society.

In our local region, when we observe the African American contribution, it's hard not to acknowledge how blessed we are to live among miles of beautiful landscape, stately homes, good school systems, and sufficient amounts of open space. These idyllic surroundings, though, may hamper us from seeing the other side of our history, challenging parts of history that nonetheless played an integral role in shaping our region into what it is today.

We bring to you "I Never Knew That," a chapter in which we highlight local stories about people, places, and events in the Sourland Mountain region and surrounding area, all stories that we never knew. As you proceed, you may find our first four stories to be the most challenging to read because of their disturbing content. We bring these unvarnished stories, however, to illustrate that in spite of how painful they may be to read, they represent an essential way interpreting difficult history—to know about the good and the bad.

We begin with a story of how Elaine's innocent day at the beach evolved into receiving information about a horrific discovery steps from her own backyard. She shares her devastation upon learning the secret that a neighboring house had been holding for years. From this Beverly calls upon relatives to help her remember why there was a bullet hole in her house and how her great-grandfather was targeted in this decades-old mystery. In the same vein, Elaine recounts her outrage on discovering that a member of the National Alliance, an organization that shares the same ideology as the Ku Klux Klan on racial purity, was seeking public office in Hopewell. From here Elaine continues with another story of how our local community leaders and businesses, as recently as the 1930s, endorsed and celebrated local "minstrel shows"—a public-theater performance dating back to the 1830s. Who would have thought that local communities delighted in the entertainment of White people who put on vaudeville skits by dressing in comical clothing, blackening their faces, exaggerating their lips with white paint, and speaking in an illiterate manner.

For the remaining stories both of us recognize local people we believe were not sufficiently acknowledged for their achievements, people not celebrated as they should have been. Fitting this description is the story of William Allen, a man who lived in Pennington, New Jersey, who discovered the remains of the Lindbergh baby and found himself thrust in a limelight he did not expect or ask for. We then highlight a connection between the Academy Award–winning movie *Casablanca* and one of the oldest homes in Pennington, New Jersey, while we bring you the inspiring story about a prominent educator from the Hopewell Valley School District who won a state title—only to have it denied. We then end this chapter with an uplifting story about a Hopewell family's visitation from a world-famous African American member of the Baseball Hall of Fame.

"UGLY TRUTHS ABOUT THE LOCAL KU KLUX KLAN PRESENCE"

Told by: Elaine Buck

Town: Hopewell, New Jersey

Date: 2016

Introduction: How a day at the beach revealed secrets about the Klan presence in my neighborhood and further discoveries about the strength of the organization.

I couldn't wait for the day to come. Each summer I looked forward to a day trip to the Jersey shore with a group of ladies I have grown very close to. I call them my "favorite Bible Study ladies" because each Friday we spend a couple hours receiving spiritual fuel to sustain us through the week. I felt close to the women who had banded together to offer support to each other through all the challenges life had thrown our way.

Finally, the day arrived, that special time we carved out to ride to the

Jersey shore. It was just me and my favorite ladies, but I referred to it as "Elaine's Beach Day."

The weather couldn't have been more perfect, that day in August 2016 when we set out for Ship Bottom, New Jersey (Long Beach Island), and we arrived in plenty of time to enjoy the day. We stepped onto the beach and we could feel the August heat of the sand under our feet. We chose a spot that would give us just enough privacy but not too far from the boardwalk or the ladies room. We placed our beach towels and blankets down and after getting situated, with our chairs and sunglasses in place and sunscreen carefully applied, it seemed as if we collectively let out a sigh of relief. Our relaxation time had officially begun!

After a day of basking in the sheer delight of the sun and enjoying the company of the ladies, on our car ride home suddenly, to my amazement, I was asked by my friend what I knew about the presence of the Ku Klux Klan in Hopewell. She knew my research partner, Beverly, and I were writing our book on the African American presence in this region.

I looked directly at my friend, who also happened to live the next block over from my home in Hopewell. Frankly, I didn't know what to say because I certainly didn't expect to be asked such a question particularly on this day.

It's not that I didn't want to talk about it, just the opposite. When Beverly and I started our research, we knew we had to brace ourselves for potentially uncovering information that would be difficult to process, information that would undoubtedly stir up emotion. And as much as we thought we were mentally prepared for what we might discover on our journey, at times it was so painful we would literally have to stop reading in order to collect ourselves. Unfortunately, those occurrences happened more than we could have imagined.

I looked at my friend and told her that the only information I had about the KKK in the area amounted to what I'd read in *Family Burying Grounds, Montgomery Township, Somerset County, New Jersey,*[2] a book written by Walter C. Baker.   But now she piqued my curiosity and I wanted to know why she would ask me that question. She told me that in 1984, when she bought her house on Prospect Street in Hopewell, her husband decided to check the attic to see if there was anything up there that might have been left behind. Never in their wildest dreams did they expect to uncover what they found: her husband made his way up to the attic, but he quickly returned holding a black oilcloth bag, his face white as a ghost. They were not prepared to find an official KKK hood complete inside the oil cloth, the sweat stains and official number still visible on the yellowing fabric.

I stared at her not knowing how to respond. The only thing I could do was ask if she could show me the hood because I needed to see it with my own eyes. Then my mind started to process what I had just heard. How is it possible that this hood had been worn by someone who literally lived right around the corner from my home? I immediately thought about my family, how my husband, children, uncles, cousins, and friends walked past that house every day on their way to Hopewell Elementary School. I thought about my mother and my husband's mother, both of whom attended this school along with all the Columbia Avenue children from the "colored section" who walked past this same house on their way to school.

The day when I finally laid eyes on that hood, I felt like I had looked into the true face of evil. I felt the sting of deception as I thought of all the wonderful people that make the town of Hopewell what it is; I began to wonder if the person who placed this hood on his head and proclaimed his allegiance to this unholy organization actually worshipped in our churches. I thought about how this guileless, evil imposter lived right among us, all the while undoubtedly pondering depraved, malicious, unholy, deceitful, hateful thoughts.

Knowing that this vile, demonic, atrocious, heinous, loathsome, barbarous, black-hearted, ruthless, bigoted, cowardly reprobate matriculated in my town makes me ill. Did his wife share his view, I wondered? Did he have children to pass along this wickedness?

I feel the grief of my ancestors who endured the cruel, brutish, inhumane treatment at the hands of the KKK and their "Invisible Empire." I think about how this organization gleefully used my people's death as a spectator sport, attracting crowds of onlookers who came with picnic baskets to watch someone be castrated, burned alive, and then hung from a tree. It's incomprehensible that this same sentiment is still alive and well as these groups hide behind the guise of nationally known groups such as the National Alliance today. This hatred is in our midst and it is a cancer in our society. It reminds me of a Bible verse that addresses this type of hatred and malevolence.

It is 1 Thessalonians 5:5, where it says, "Ye are all children of light, and children of the day; we are not of the night, nor of darkness."

When I showed Beverly the book by Walter Baker, citing the KKK burial in New Jersey, she read it and looked at me in amazement. "You mean this took place right here in Blawenburg? The cemetery that we have passed countless times in our travels?" "Yes," I said. But there was more for her to read.

I handed Beverly a 1923 article from the *New York Times* about KKK burials in New Jersey that appeared in Walter Baker's book. The first paragraph of the article began by acknowledging that the origin of the cemetery could not be documented. However, it went on to mention some of the oldest headstones found in the cemetery and the family names associated with the deceased, names that are prominent to this day. The point of the article was that Blawenburg Cemetery was believed to be the first cemetery to hold a Ku Klux Klan funeral in the State of New Jersey. It described the number of Klan members who came to attend this religious service and how they initially gathered at a garage across the street before descending upon the cemetery dressed in full KKK regalia. It talked about the order of the service, how they placed an American flag on the casket before a reading from Romans 12. The ceremony concluded with instruction from a spokesperson to continue working for the "betterment of the country." It ended with a bugler sounding taps before they departed.

As Beverly and I continued researching we came across other articles, to our surprise, that appeared in our local newspaper at the time, the *Hopewell Herald.* It seems like the year 1924 was a very busy year for the Klan in this region.

A couple months later, on April 23, 1924, the *Hopewell Herald*'s headline read "Klan Holds Easter Morn Services." Once again, at midnight, the skies were lit up in the Hopewell area, with a blazing burning cross opposite the residence of W. B. Secor, in the field owned by A. C. Bond. Apparently, this midnight meeting was how many chose to bring in the Easter holiday. The article described how automobiles lined the sides of the road for over a mile from each direction of the meeting place. The field was packed with over 300 Klan members, including women.[3]

Barely a month later, a third article reported that a thirty-foot-high cross had been burned near the H. A. Smith Manufacturing Company plant. This cross drew many onlookers who were apparently hoping to "witness a Klan ceremonial," but the crowd was disappointed: since there was no sighting of any Klan members, the crowd watched the cross burn slowly but "no one made an attempt to disturb it."[4]

The most unsettling article for me was the one titled "Klan Holds Easter Morn Services," which described how, on April 30, 1924, four hundred people, with sixty in Klan robes, packed the Hopewell United Methodist Church. The building, too small to accommodate this type of crowd, turned hundreds of people away. The doors and windows were opened to accommodate the onlookers. On this day forty men and twenty women presented themselves in full Klan regalia complete with robes and hoods. Other attendees—who were believed to be part of the Klan—were not dressed in the ceremonial garb. It is believed that the invitation was extended to all patriotic and fraternal groups for that evening service. After the regular service, Pastor Rev. W. B. Magsam graciously allowed the Klan time to explain the principles of their organization, while they passed out cards for anyone interested in gaining admission.[5]

My thoughts immediately went to Jim Davidson, who has been involved with the East Amwell Historical Society for a number of years. I thought if anyone would have information about the KKK in this region Jim probably would. Throughout the years, our professional relationship with Jim had grown as our research deepened, and we considered Jim to be our friend. So, it was not uncomfortable for me to call him, as a friend and fellow colleague, for his input on such a sensitive subject.

When we spoke, Jim offered to send me an article written in the *Hunterdon County Democrat* about a Klan clubhouse in East Amwell titled "Clubhouse Being Erected by Klan-Members in Regalia Appear at Ceremony on Larison's Corner Site." Along with sharing the article, Jim was quick to mention there are still presently many local family names associated with the founding of the Klan. Below is the article as it was written about local Klan activity in this area.

So rang the headlines in the June 16th, 1927 edition of the *Hunterdon County Democrat*. Yes, the KKK was alive and well in East Amwell and throughout Hunterdon County in the late 1920's. The local branch of the Klan was organized as the Hunterdon County Protestant Club, but there was no mistaking ... its affiliation. Members in full regalia arrived by automobile for the cornerstone-laying of a 40 x 60 building to be their local "clubhouse". This building still exists but not for its original purpose.

The KKK existed throughout the country in a huge resurgence of "Americanism" in the 1920's. Most people, from seeing movies, think the Klan was in the south and only against Blacks but that is only part of the story. They were against Jews, Catholics and foreigners as well. My father would tell me stories of growing up in Worcester, Mass. where he saw Klansmen with ax handles beating on Catholics who moved into the area.

While born in the South the Klan quickly spread northward. The first KKK in New Jersey was formed in 1921. New Jersey had its own Grand Dragon and King Kleagle. One of the bastions of the Klan was in nearby Zarephath at their Pillar of Fire Church (still in existence). It was here that the national KKK periodical, "The Good Citizen" was published. At a rally in Bound Brook in 1923 over 12,000 Klansman showed up. In New Jersey the Klan's protests were against "the Hebrew and Roman Catholics." In Wall Township they even had a Klan resort.

In 1925, 800 Klansmen, in regalia, held a rally on East Main Street in Flemington. I found that they even marched in several parades down Main Street. About twenty years ago when new owners moved into a house on Rt. 202 directly across from the Klan "clubhouse", they found an underground tunnel going under Rt. 202 from their barn to the Klan building. In the tunnel they found a hoard of Klan memorabilia, including literature, regalia and crosses. In fear, they burned them all.

The *Democrat* article mentions all the names of the locals on the club's incorporation papers, but I won't print them here—the names are still very familiar in the area. The interesting thing is that the building is still around—The Calvary Presbyterian Church on Rt. 202 just north of Larison's Corner.[6]

✳

"WHY THERE WAS A BULLET HOLE IN MY HOUSE"

Name: Beverly Mills

Town: Pennington, New Jersey

Date: May 26, 2017

Introduction: When researching the KKK presence in the Hopewell Valley and surrounding region, a memory started to resurface. A call to my uncle explained why there is a bullet hole in my house.

While continuing to research with Elaine into the KKK presence, what we found particularly stunning was that not one newspaper article expressed outrage over the Klan movement that seemed to be sweeping the state in the 1920s. While the evidence was overwhelming that the Klan had taken a significant foothold in our local area, I had completely forgotten that the KKK had—within my lifetime—made a personal visit to one of our homes.

One day a conversation with Elaine about the Klan and its prevalence in our region seemed to jog a childhood memory: something about a bullet hole in the dining room wall of my house. I was a child of only about four or five and had only a dim memory of what had happened. I decided to speak to my uncle, now in his eighties, about the bullet hole and where it came from. I called my uncle, who always went by the nickname Gump, to see if he remembered why there was a bullet hole in my house. So, one day while we were sitting at Elaine's dining room table I called Gump to find out what he remembered.

"Am I imagining this or is there actually a bullet hole in my house?" I asked Gump. I went on to say how I remembered my great-grandfather standing and pointing to a spot in the upper corner of the dining room wall. It was always there, that indented area in the wall high near the ceiling.

Gump was just a teenager at the time my great-grandfather told the story. He told Gump that one evening, while getting off the trolley coming home from his job in Trenton, New Jersey, he started to walk up the street when the conductor yelled to him, "Hey Joe, is that your house on fire up there!" To his shock there appeared to be something burning in the front of his house. Gump said Joe ran toward his house and soon realized the Klan was running around his house—which is now my house—located on South Main Street in Pennington, New Jersey. The fire appeared to be a makeshift cross. Gump continued with the story: Joe screamed for his wife, Ethel, to get his shotgun, because he intended to start shooting to defend his home. The Klan ran circling the house and Joe attempted to take aim to fire through an open window. Instead of firing through the window he hit Ethel's china cabinet where the bullet gouged out part of the wall, leaving a deep indentation.

I asked Gump if he had any idea why the Klan descended upon my home, but he said he didn't know why.

※

WHY I CONSIDERED RUNNING FOR THE HOPEWELL BOROUGH COUNCIL

Told by: Elaine Buck

Town: Hopewell, New Jersey

Date: May 26, 2017

Introduction: I knew I had to do something the day I discovered that a local resident, running for Hopewell Borough Council, was also a member of the National Alliance. There was no way I could let this person be a representative in my town.

Discussion about the Klan also brought up an experience I had as an adult in 2005 when I challenged a member of a White supremacy group known as the National Alliance.

To say I was shocked is an understatement when I learned that one of the members of the National Alliance was living right here in the Borough of Hopewell. This man had just been appointed to fill an interim vacancy on our local Borough Council before officially running in the November election. Before this occurred, an article ran in a local newspaper exposing him for his involvement in the National Alliance (NA) where he suggested that Hopewell become an "all-White" town.[7] The article reported he had counted the number of Jewish, Black, and Asian people that were currently living in Hopewell Borough. I immediately knew that as one of the twenty-three Black residents mentioned, I had to do something to keep this person off the Borough Council. In no way would I allow this man to make me uncomfortable and unwelcome in a town where I have lived all my life, and where my family and my husband's family have lived since the 1800s.

Emergency council meetings were held, and petitions were circulated to see how we could have him legally removed from the council. What was especially stunning to me was when I heard that some council members didn't see a problem with this person being on council.

A week or so later, while going to the post office with my son Aaron, we were approached by a reporter from the *Trenton Times*, who asked if we had ever had any racial problems in the borough. We answered that, while we were students at Hopewell Valley Central High School, there was always someone who attempted to get away with calling us a racial slur, or make some off-color joke, but as a rule people kept their comments and feelings to themselves.

The very next day my neighbor, who was so excited he could barely talk, stopped by to tell me he had just come through town and had seen a Channel 6 news truck along with a host of other news reporters, swarmed around the "National Alliance guy." The neighbor went on to say that the "National Alliance guy" was standing in front of the John Hart monument in front of the Old School Baptist Church. I grabbed my car keys, while telling my husband that I was going to speak with that man. I corralled two neighbors, who were also good friends, and away we went!

It was my intent to tell this guy that he should step down, NOW! Without hesitation I walked up and interrupted him, just as he was telling the reporters he had no intention of stepping down from his position on the Borough Council, saying it was his civic duty and right to serve.

I approached with my hands on my hips, oblivious to the cameras rolling and reporters writing. Hopewell Township police were sitting in their cars watching the peaceful interview. However, when they saw me coming they decided to get out of their cars.

I introduced myself as one of the twenty-three Black people who lived in the town that he wanted to be "all White." I looked into his eyes, which I remember were a beautiful shade of blue, and told him

I had no intention of leaving this town. I asked him if he was really a deacon at the Hopewell Presbyterian Church and, if so, that he should be ashamed of himself. I then asked him who his grandparents were, because I not only have lived in this town all of my life, I just about know everyone in the town. Little did he know his grandparents were good friends of *my* grandparents through church affiliations. I told him his grandparents would be ashamed of him and the stand he was taking. I told him that when I was reading water meters in town his grandmother's house was always my last stop, because she always invited me in to have a cool drink at her kitchen table. I told him I knew where he lived because it was the same house his grandparents had lived in, and that I now live in my grandparents' home.

I told him I read his writings on the National Alliance website that described him as "The David Duke of the North." I stared him right in his eyes and told him that I was the self-proclaimed "Harriet Tubman of the North" except I wasn't going underground!

By this time, I could see that talking to him was fruitless, because I was getting nowhere. Before I walked away I told him that if he didn't step down that I would run against him in November and that I would win because of my ties in the community. The reporters recorded the whole confrontation. The next day I woke up to a picture of me with my hands on my hips and pointing my finger in his face on the front page of the *Trenton Times, Asbury Press*, and papers as far away as New York City. In spite of my experience with a White Nationalist, these movements, whether you call them White nationalism, White supremacy, or neo-Nazism, are still alive and still growing.

*

"LOCAL BUSINESSES SUPPORTED
MINSTREL SHOWS AS RECENTLY AS THE 1930S"

Told by: Elaine Buck and Beverly Mills

Town: Hopewell, New Jersey

Date: 2016

Introduction: Minstrel shows were so popular in the Sourland Mountain region and surrounding area they would draw men, women, and children.

While researching for this book, we have heard different people talk about New Jersey's reputation for being a southern-sympathizing state. In fact, it was New Jersey that cast the majority of the popular vote to Lincoln's opponent in the 1860 presidential election.[8] New Jersey's attitude toward African Americans was abundantly clear not only in its growth of Klan membership statewide but in its support of minstrel shows.

The appeal of the minstrel was incumbent upon the portrayal of the African American man as lazy, childlike, and dim-witted. According to David Pilgrim, an expert on racist memorabilia, "One of the most popular characters was the 'coon' whose caricature was one of the stock characters among minstrel performers. Minstrel show audiences laughed at the slow-talking fool who avoided work and all adult responsibilities. This transformed the coon into a comic figure, a source of bitter and vulgar comic relief."[9]

Again, who would have known that local minstrel shows were so popular in this region and were proudly advertised in local newspapers.

When we present programs in schools, most students have no frame of reference to envision a minstrel show or the subject matter featured in this form of popular theater. Most popular from the late nineteenth to the mid-twentieth century, the appeal of minstrel shows was not lost in our region. We have come across newspaper ads for upcoming minstrel shows replete with stereotypical drawings of African Americans with blackened faces, chalk-white lips, and top hats. In fact, minstrel shows were so popular in Flemington in the 1920s and 1930s that the advertisements screamed: "'The Minstrel Revue,' A riot of fun, music, jokes, skits and spectacular scenes at the F.H.S Auditorium, Friday, March 10, 1911."[10]

The sponsors listed in the newspaper practically filled the entire page; they were lumber companies, general stores, restaurants, jewelers, car dealerships, gas and water companies, doctors, and beauty shops, all celebrating the event. The ad ended urgently stating, "All seats must be reserved," 500 seats reserved free of charge and 200 seats reserved for 25 cents extra. Children's tickets sold for 35 cents at the box office on the night of the show.

✳

"BILL ALLEN FOUND THE REMAINS OF THE LINDBERGH BABY— IGNORED BY CHARLES LINDBERGH"

Told by: Karen Lovett and Michael Ganie

Town: Pennington, New Jersey

Interview: 2016

Permission: Karen Lovett and Michael Ganie

Introduction: Bill Allen's grandson Michael Ganie and great-grand-daughter Karen Lovett reminisce about how "people tried very hard not to celebrate him." They acknowledge that, to this day, the public has little to no information about the role Bill Allen played in finding the remains of the Lindbergh baby.

One of the most remarkable narratives to include in this section is the story about William Allen. During our presentations, people literally stare at us with open mouths when we mention that William Allen, a Black man, found the remains of the Lindbergh baby. The surprise is even greater when I mention he lived right up the street from me, Beverly, and my family on South Main Street in Pennington, New Jersey, and that his daughter Elinor and my mother were best friends growing up.

The Lindbergh baby kidnapping has often been called "The Crime of the Century." For decades books, documentaries, and various suppositions have been dedicated to solving the mystery of this kidnapping. Theories have been presented to answer the question of what really happened to the beloved twenty-month-old son of Charles and Anne Lindbergh. "Lucky Lindy," one of the most revered and admired men in America, garnered all the attention the public could muster. History continues to be kind. But how much does anyone know, or care to know, about William Allen or Mr. Bill as I called him?

William Allen was born in Buckingham County, Virginia, on September 19, 1889. Bill, as he was always called, came to the Philadelphia area when he was just eleven years old.[11] He married Helen Jennings Smith and lived in Pennington where they raised their children in a tiny cottage with two rooms downstairs, two upstairs, and an outhouse out back. As I child I remember Mr. Bill always had a pack of Redman chewing tobacco in the pocket of his shirt. He would chew and spit while tinkering on cars parked in the back of his yard.

Bill's connection to the Lindbergh case happened purely by chance. On May 12, 1931, while on the job, Bill had to relieve himself and asked his coworker Orville Wilson to pull the truck over. Once they stopped, which was off Princeton-Hopewell Road, Bill walked only about fifty feet into the woods and, to his amazement, spied the badly decomposed remains of a child. The remains were subsequently identified as the Lindbergh baby.

I invited Karen Lovett, Bill great-granddaughter, and Michael Ganie, his grandson, to my house. I wanted them to talk to me about their Bill because I understood that Michael and Karen had always wanted to set the record straight about their famous relative.

"They tried very hard not to celebrate him" is how Karen described what happened to her great-grandfather with Michael, nodding in agreement. According to Michael, Lindbergh refused to shake his grandfather's hand or speak to him at all. It was reported that when Bill's son, William Jr., found out his father was in the Lindberghs' home he said to his father, "What did he say to you, Pop," to which Bill replied, "Not a damn thing. Not 'thank you.' Not 'kiss my ass,' nothing."

Michael said that New Jersey governor Harold Hoffman had to intercede to make sure Bill received $5,000 out of the $25,000 reward money because initially he had been excluded from the list of recipients. Karen and Michael both maintained the reason why it was so difficult for him to receive the reward money is because they didn't want to give it to a Black man.

Sadly, when the Depression hit, Bill lost his job and he needed to do anything he could to provide for his family. As with most people at that time he had a hard time finding work. To make matters worse, there seemed to be an embarrassing cloud that followed Bill around that was hard to explain. Finding himself in a vulnerable position, exploitive people talked Bill into touring with a circus that ended up charging ten cents for people to gawk at him.[12] Disgusted after hearing about this, Governor A. Harry Moore protested to New York police about what was happening to Bill while the circus was in New York. Upsetting so many, it caused two Massachusetts mayors to ban the circus act from their towns citing it as "contemptible commercialism."[13] However, once the public realized it was not Bill who tried to cash in on what he had discovered, he was finally offered a job at the New Jersey Home for Girls where he stayed employed until his retirement.

It's not surprising that Bill Allen's name is largely not associated with this historic event. To this day most people outside of the Allen family are unaware of what happened to Bill and how, in the twinkling of an eye, his life changed on that fateful day.

*

BEVERLY INTERVIEWED HER COUSIN STANLEY ABOUT HIS HOME IN PENNINGTON, NEW JERSEY WHERE THE ACTOR DOOLEY WILSON ONCE LIVED

Told by: Beverly Mills and Stanley Stewart II

Town: Pennington, New Jersey

Date: 2016

Permission: Stanley Stewart II

Introduction: Pennington, New Jersey's connection to an Academy Award-Winning Movie

Who knew Pennington's African American community would have a connection to an Academy Award–winning movie? Dooley Wilson, the actor who appeared in the movie *Casablanca* with Humphrey Bogart and Ingrid Bergman, had ties to Pennington, New Jersey.

According to oral history by Stanley Stewart II, in 1947 the

Stewart family—his parents, Stanley and Leona and siblings, Janice and Jeffrey—moved to 248 South Main Street, Pennington, New Jersey, which was located down the street from some of their family members. This home, one of the oldest in Pennington, was located next door to the historic Bethel AME Church, in the section of town where the original the African American community settled. It was a charming two-story brown cedar-shingled home with Dutch doors inside and out, a fireplace that took up an entire wall in the front room, and a winding wooden stairway that went to the second floor. This house is where Black AME members gathered for church service when their congregation formed in 1816 and before their church was built in 1847. Aside from the historic aspect of their home, the Stewart family certainly was not aware they were moving into the same house Dooley Wilson occupied for a time.

For people unfamiliar with the name Dooley Wilson, you've probably heard of the movie *Casablanca*. Actor and musician Dooley Wilson, whose real name was Arthur Wilson, originally came from Tyler, Texas, and had been a performer in the 1920s in Paris and London before his landmark appearance in the 1942 Academy Award–winning movie Casablanca starring Humphrey Bogart and Ingrid Bergman. Although there is little recognition of the name Dooley Wilson, people readily recognize the phrase "Play it again, Sam" when Humphrey Bogart asks Dooley Wilson to play "As Time Goes By" late in the movie. Wilson's rendition of the song continues to be memorialized to this day.

Wilson's connection to our region was very short, and no one knows why he suddenly vacated the house and moved to California. Maybe it was a career move. However, before leaving the area he made a lasting impression on another Pennington local, Elizabeth Ragsdale, who lived to be 103 and was the daughter of William Allen, the man who discovered the remains of the Lindbergh baby. She fondly recalled her time as a beautician when she was Wilson's personal hairdresser early in her career.

✳

"'QUEEN OF THE CAMPUS'—HOW LOCAL HOPEWELL VALLEY SCHOOL DISTRICT ADMINISTRATOR DORA BERRY CAME TO TERMS WITH THE DENIAL OF HER TITLE"

Told by: Elaine Buck

Town: Hopewell, New Jersey

Date: May 11, 2017

Permission: Dora Berry

Introduction: Dora Berry won the title of Miss State University of Iowa but was denied the title. In her career in the Hopewell Valley School District, Dora was one of very few African Americans hired in the 1960s.

The first impression of Dora Berry is to be immediately struck by her professionalism. Add to this her beauty, poise, and elegance, and it certainly is not farfetched to think of her as a participant in a beauty pageant. How would anyone know that Dora Berry was the first African American female to be elected Miss State University of Iowa only to be denied the title? How would anyone know that Dora was a trailblazer during a time when the standard of beauty was judged through the lens of Caucasian standards? I wanted to know how she felt about an experience that obviously had to be very hurtful. I was curious if the years that elapsed had soothed the sting or if it was still lingering.

When Dora Martin Berry arrived as a social worker in the Child Study Team in the Hopewell Valley School District in 1971, she was one of seven Black employees working in this predominantly White school district. Throughout her tenure, which spanned decades, Berry impacted the lives of scores of children who went through the school district. From 1962 to 1967 she said there were only two Black teachers on staff, one music teacher, Barbara Williams, for K–6 and George Renwick for eighth grade social studies. The principal at the time, William Schwab, was actually ahead of his time in making these hires, and this was before affirmative action. He brought in more African American staff from 1968 to 1974 at the Timberlane Junior High School and moved George Renwick to be the director of guidance. The problem was that housing was not available for African Americans and Jewish people because they were not welcome at that time, particularly in the Pennington area. This made it particularly hard to attract African American teachers to the Hopewell Valley School District.

In the 1990s I came to the Timberlane Middle School in Pennington, New Jersey, to work on a Black History project with Dora Berry. I had always had an interest in presenting African American history to local students and was usually invited to speak during Black History month. The minute I would step into the school I would hear someone calling me, usually somebody who already knew me from my kids or the neighborhood. "Hi, Mrs. Buck." "Glad to see you again." It was while we were working on the project together that Dora told me about her experience at the University of Iowa—about their refusal to acknowledge her as the first Black Miss State University of Iowa in 1955. I came across an interview with Dora conducted in 1997 as part of the African American Women at Iowa Digital Collection and the Iowa Women's Archives.

In this interview Dora reminisced about how funny it was to look back on how she took so many of her Texas traits with her to the University of Iowa. However, soon after arriving she got to know many of the other Black students on campus and quickly learned, to her dismay, how segregated the campus actually was. In fact, she recalled thinking that Iowa was really no different from Texas.

In 1955 when the Miss State University was searching for their campus queen, Dora said she decided to seek the title and campaigned as the "Yellow Rose of Texas." She said that although there were a fair number of Black students on campus she hoped would vote for her, the numbers wouldn't add up and she would be happy to settle on becoming a finalist. Never in her wildest dreams, she said, did she think it was possible that she would win the title of Miss State University of Iowa (SUI), but she did. Though the election of a Black woman as campus queen made international news, Dora found out she won the title from a reporter who called for an interview. Prior to this call, Dora didn't have a clue she was the winner since the school administrators had not reached out to her. Once the reality sank in, she knew there were a couple events approaching where it was customary for Miss SUI to represent the university. That particular year the football team was to go to the Rose Bowl and Miss SUI would also be expected to attend. However, instead of going with the team Dora was told that the Homecoming Queen from the previous year would represent the SUI. As long as Dora was at the University of Iowa, she never once represented the university as Miss SUI.[14]

At an event hosted to honor Black alumni over a half century later, Dora was given an official apology by University of Iowa president Bruce Harreld: "I would first like to apologize for 60 years plus of official neglect of your status"; "We as an institution are very proud of your accomplishments. And we're grateful that you are such an important member of our Hawkeye family."[15]

What impacted me the most from reading Dora's story was how she felt her time at the University of Iowa shaped her as a person. Before concluding the interview, Dora mentioned that she was actually very thankful for the experience and the impact was not as long lasting as some think it would have been. Although she said she has thought about it from time to time, the university's failure to recognize her was actually a "gift that's hers to keep." In fact, Dora said, "she has regarded this as a growth experience and in her opinion that is something that can never be taken away."

"AS A CHILD I THOUGHT ROY CAMPANELLA WAS MY PLAYMATE. HOW DID I KNOW HE WAS ONE OF THE GREATEST BASEBALL PLAYERS OF ALL TIME!"

Told by: Elaine Buck

Town: Hopewell, New Jersey

Date: 2016

Introduction: Roy Campanella was a 1969 inductee in the Baseball Hall of Fame. I never realized that my relative was one of baseball's living legends.

I still remember the feeling. Even though I was just a young child I can recall the excitement when the legendary Roy Campanella came to town. He came to Hopewell to visit after his paralyzing car accident in 1958. However, in the 1940s and early 1950s before the accident, there were many in town who remembered Roy Campanella's visits to our little town. It was such a big deal to have a huge star come to our small town, particularly an African American. I remember how his driver would wheel him into the front room and how amazed I was when I saw his wooden high-backed wheelchair with spoked wheels.

"Campy," as he was called, would be driven through Hopewell in his shiny black Cadillac as it made its way to Columbia Avenue, which was dusty and unpaved at that time. He came to visit my grandparents Hester and Robert Coleman, but I always thought he came to see me because he always brought me colorful lollipops and played games with me. Even though I was a small, skinny little girl, I would push him in the wheelchair all over the house.

My family was related through Campy's mother, Ida, a relative of my grandmother's uncle Caleb Womack or "Uncie" as we called him. Uncie, who came south from Banister, Virginia, was the original owner of our house on Columbia Avenue.

As a child I had no idea that this man in the wheelchair who visited my family was a baseball legend. While I was wheeling him around, how was I to know that he was reportedly one of the best-hitting catchers in baseball and had received the MVP award? It wasn't until I got older that I realized how instrumental Roy Campanella was in the history of baseball. I learned Campy played in Major League Baseball stadiums such as Ebbets Field in Brooklyn, New York. I also read that his professional career began when he was only fifteen years old, when he played for the Negro Leagues, and that he played with them until he was signed by the Brooklyn Dodgers in 1946. Campy's amazing statistics include 242 home runs and 856 RBIs.

Not only was Campy the second African American in the major leagues after Jackie Robinson, he was the man who helped the Brooklyn Dodgers win the World Series in 1955. He was named the league's most valuable player three times in his ten-year career, in 1951, 1952, and 1953. In 1969 he became the second Black baseball player to be inducted in the Baseball Hall of Fame.[16]

Roy Campanella will always hold a special place in the annals of baseball history, however, the most exciting fact to me was that he was a member of my family!

[1] Malik Simba, "The Association for the Study of African American Life and History: A Brief History," BlackPast.org, An Online Reference Guide to African American History, accessed March 27, 2018, http://www.blackpast.org/perspectives/association-study-african-american-life-and-history-brief-history.

[2] Walter C. Baker, *Family Burying Grounds, Montgomery Township, Somerset County, New Jersey* (Belle Mead, NJ: Van Harlingen Historical Society, 2008).

[3] "Klan Holds Easter Morn Services," *Hopewell Herald*, April 23, 1924, Ancestry.

[4] "Cross Is Burned in Borough Limits," *Hopewell Herald*, May 14, 1924, Ancestry.

[5] "Klan Holds Easter Morn Services."

[6] "Clubhouse Being Erected by Klan-Members in Regalia Appear at Ceremony on Larison's Corner Site," *Hunterdon County Democrat*, June 16, 1927, CII, page 49.

[7] John Tredrea, "Council Man Belongs to White Supremacist Group," *Hopewell Valley News* 48, no. 28 (July 10, 2003): 1, 10.

[8] New Jersey State Archives, "Lincoln and New Jersey: A Bicentennial Tribute by the New Jersey State Archives," State of New Jersey, Department of State, 2011, accessed June 18, 2018, https://www.nj.gov/state/archives/lincoln.html#electoral.

[9] David Pilgrim, "The Coon Caricature," Jim Crow Museum of Racist Memorabilia, Ferris State University, accessed March 28, 2018, https://ferris.edu/HTMLS/News/jimcrow/coon/

[10] "The Minstrel Revue (Full Page Advertisement)," *Hunterdon County Democrat*, 107, no. 35 (March 3, 1932).

[11] Mark W. Falzini, *Their Fifteen Minutes, Biographical Sketches of the Lindbergh Case* (New York: Universe, Inc., 2008), 119.

[12] Ibid., 119.

[13] Ibid., 120.

[14] "Interview Conducted by African American Women at Iowa Digital Collection and the Iowa Women's Archives," University of Iowa, Scholarship at Iowa, accessed March 28, 2018, https://dsps.lib.uiowa.edu/atiowa/2016/02/16/dora-martin-berry-interview-first-African-American-Miss-s-u-i/

15 "University of Iowa Apologizes for Refusing to Recognize Its First Black Miss SUI 60 Years Later," *Atlanta Black Star*, n.d., accessed February 20, 2018, http://atlantablackstar.com/2016/10/26/university-of-iowa-apologizes-for-refusing-to-recognize-its-first-black-miss-sui-60-years-later/

16 Robert McG. Thomas Jr., "Roy Campanella, 71 Dies; Was Dodger Hall of Famer," *New York Times: Obituaries*, June 28, 1933, http://www.nytimes.com/1993/06/28/obituaries/roy-campanella-71-dies-was-dodger-hall-of-famer.html; "Roy Campanella," The National Baseball Hall of Fame and Museum is dedicated to preserving the history of baseball, honoring excellence in the game and connecting the generations of baseball enthusiasts, National Baseball Hall of Fame, n.d., accessed January 16, 2018, https://baseballhall.org/hof/campanella-roy

Robert and Queen Hester Coleman

CHAPTER 10

QUEEN HESTER'S LOCAL HOME REMEDIES AND RECIPES

by ELAINE BUCK

All food tells a story.

—Queen Hester (1912-1986)

When many people think about the most outstanding event that occurred in 1912 they most likely would mention the sinking of the *Titanic*. History records April 15 as the fateful date when 1,500 people perished in the dark frosty night of the northern Atlantic Ocean. In the United States it was also an election year in which incumbent President William Taft was soundly defeated by Democratic challenger Woodrow Wilson.

But did you know that during that decade African Americans like George and Ada Hightower, my great-grandparents, were keenly aware that on average sixty-two people were lynched each and every year?[1]

During that decade George and Ada Hightower were sharecroppers who lived in Pittsylvania County, Virginia. They had twelve children.

My grandmother Queen Hester was the oldest. My grandmother was only able to go to school up until the third grade before her role changed from student to field hand and caretaker to her younger siblings. Growing up she remembers sleeping on a mattress made of corn silk and husks, and used to say, "Many a time there would be a silkworm on you when you woke up." Times were hard, but they learned how to "make do." They picked tobacco and raised vegetables as sharecroppers on the Hayes Farm. The difference between being a slave and a sharecropper was that you did not have to stay, you were "free to go," but as my grandmother put it, "we didn't leave because we didn't have nowhere to go." They toiled and worked the fields for little or no pay and shared the better part of the crops with the farmer because now the plantation owners had to rely on paid labor, which cut into their profits.

My grandmother bore five children, Willie and James Hightower, Robert Lewis Hunt, who is called Sonny, and my mother, Dolores, who went by Toots. These children came from a previous relationship prior to her marriage to John Robert Coleman of which they had one son, Milton Ronald Coleman or Ronnie. Ronnie and I have always been extremely close, and he is more like a brother than an uncle because we are only nineteen months apart. My mother, Toots, was only fifteen years old when she gave birth to me prematurely in 1953. As a baby, Hester would park me near the cookstove to keep me warm because I weighed only three pounds when I was born. My "incubator" was a six-burner pale yellow cookstove that had an Elmira Stove Company label on the oven door. It had a lid, a removable handle, a warmer oven on the top, and a double side-by-side oven on the bottom that was constantly being stoked with coal and wood that created a pile of ashes that fell to the bottom tray to be changed daily. The temperature in kitchen that served as my "incubator" would be screaming hot in the summer and comfortable in the winter.

It would have been foolish to take my grandmother's small stature for someone who was docile: she was just the opposite. Queen Hester, or "Mom," as we called her, was five foot four of pure feistiness, with a deep-rooted faith in God. She was a straight shooter who said what she meant and meant what she said. As children we remember she would give you three chances to hear what she told you to do and if you had not responded by the third time you'd be cracked with her hickory switch, which was never far from her reach. She'd then say, "I know you can't hear but I bet you can feel!"

A sadness washes over me when I think about what my grandmother and our ancestors had to endure, particularly right after Reconstruction. I recall the story about my great-grandmother's first cousin Osee Womack, who was born in Chatham, Virginia, on January 2, 1910. Cousin Osee lived for a century and told the story about her brother Henry, who had killed his sharecropper boss and had to go on the run, never to be seen again. When Osee died in 2010 at the age of one hundred, she still didn't know if he was dead or alive. But before she passed she had the honor of voting for the first African American president, Barack Obama.

Hester moved to Hopewell in the 1940s to take care of her uncle Caleb Womack, who lived on Columbia Avenue. Oral history has it that Caleb Womack was the last slave to live in Hopewell. This is the street that I lived on and was raised by my grandmother. Most of our food was grown right in our backyard because as Queen Hester would say, "All food tells a story."

ALL FOOD TELLS A STORY

On "the Avenue," as Columbia Avenue was called, we raised chickens, grew vegetables, and had peach, Italian plum, and pear trees along with a grapevine. We canned our fruit and vegetables for the winter months, for desserts, and also to be used for church dinners. We had a metal box on the front porch where "Sparky" Ralph Lanning would deposit our milk.

Occasionally during the spring and summer months one of our relatives, Otis Waldron, would come through town with a beat-up truck with wooden planks on the side that was loaded down with watermelons fresh from his trip to Virginia.

As soon as he turned the corner I could hear him chanting, "Watermelons … git your watermelons," while I was running to tell Grandmom hoping she would reach into her apron pocket, so we could buy one of the "out-of-town" watermelons. Garland Fields, or "Gump" as everyone knew him, would come through with his fish truck and there was even a "rag man" who would drive through the Avenue collecting old rags while chanting "Rags!"

There are many folks who have said that some of the smoothest wine you would ever taste was made by my grandmother. Hester, who claimed that she needed it from time to time to "calm her nerves," made peach wine and brandy from peach skins she dried out from when she made peach cobblers or canned peaches. She would lay the skins out on a baking sheet and cover them with mesh chicken wire. My job was to take the trays up the street to Aunt Mary's house where my cousin Nelson would help me climb through a window onto the flat roof over the kitchen. There we would lay them out and place a brick on the top, so "the varmints didn't eat it!" The same process would happen with the apple skins.

Grandpop raised pigs up on the Sourland Mountain across from Minnietown Road, in a clearing back in the woods on Albert Witcher's property. I was about five or six years old when every evening I would put on my boots and ride on the truck with my grandpop to slop the hogs. The little piglets would come running and snorting so excited for their supper of leftover vegetables, field greens, food scraps, or whatever we mixed together. Then one fall day when we rode up to the hog pen, my sweet, gentle Grandpop took along his rifle, which he usually stored in the dining room coat closet. When we arrived, he chose a few fattened pigs and took them aside in a separate pen. Suddenly I heard, "POW," and I realized he had shot my pigs! It was a rude awakening for me from that day forward when I realized that farm animals were not pets, they were raised to be eaten!

My former "pet pigs" were brought down off the mountain in burlap bags to our yard on Columbia Avenue. A fire pit was made, and the pigs were then dunked in a large tub of boiling water, scalded, and then the hair was scraped off. The pig was hung on a meat hook in the smoke house, gutted, and prepared to be butchered. The head would be in a bucket in the refrigerator waiting to be ground in the meat grinder, which was clamped on the kitchen table. Relatives and friends would be on hand to assist in the day-long process of smoking and curing the hams, bacon, neck bones, pork chops, and ribs.

The process would not be complete without Alma Brooks, or "Shorty" as she was called, who lived on Mountain Church Road with her husband, Sam. Every part of the pig was to be eaten and "Shorty" would help make the sage sausage links, hog head cheese, souse meat, scrapple, pig tails, and pig feet, some of which were pickled. Pig ears were layered in gelatin, refrigerated, and then thinly sliced served on saltine crackers as a snack. The skin of the pigs was used to make another snack called "crackling," which was skin deep-fried in lard until crispy and salted while hot. Cracklings were also used in a cornbread recipe which was called crackling bread. The wash tubs were filled with pig intestines, or chitterlings, and soaked in salt water, waiting to be cleaned and refrigerated but my Lord did they stink when you cooked them! Grandmom would put a potato in them while they were cooking to take away the smell, but it didn't work! We made the lard, soap, and candles from the fat of the pigs. We used every part of the pig some way, somehow!

My grandpop bought baby chicks to me and Ronnie every spring around Easter time that were fed and fattened in preparation for the dinner table. I remember getting up early each morning and going out to the chicken coop to feed them; there was an infrared heat lamp clamped from the ceiling that shone down on the chicks to keep them warm. As soon as I opened the door, they would start chirping, waiting for their feed, and once they got old enough, about four or five weeks old, I would lead them out of the chicken coop, so they could roam freely around the yard. We didn't have a fence. Somehow, they would stay in our yard until they were rounded up to go back into the coop. In preparation for our Sunday meal after church, once again, my sweet-spirited, gentle grandfather would get his chopping block, which was a huge tree stump, and his ax and wham … Grandpop would wring the chicken's neck and off went their heads. I was heartbroken running around the yard chasing my chickens with no heads!

He raised chickens on Columbia Avenue until one day in the early 1980s the Hopewell police came to the house to tell him he must stop raising farm animals in the borough. Grandpop had a chicken named Lois who rode on his shoulder while he cut grass. So he told the police officer, "This isn't a farm animal, it's my pet." So later that week, we received a phone call from Grandpop inviting us to dinner, of which we gladly accepted. What a dinner he fixed … chicken and dumplings, turnip greens, Aunt Jemima cornbread. After we ate, he looked at us with a big smile on his face and said, "Lois sure tasted good didn't she." (Away I went screaming once again!)

We would gather up the dead chickens and the next phase of the "farm to table" would begin. Grandmom would be waiting in the kitchen dressed in one of her homemade aprons that always had a pocket; she had a can of "Yellow Lily" snuff for dipping stashed in her pockets along with her handkerchief and a small change purse in case the Avon Lady or Fuller Brush man stopped by. There would be a pot full of boiling water on our old-fashioned cookstove with newspaper stretched out on the kitchen table and tin pans filled with alcohol. The large feathers were plucked out with pliers, the chickens scalded in the boiling water, then patted dry. Since it was a family affair, the next step was for the younger children: I would pluck the fine feathers with large tweezers. Grandmom would then light the alcohol-laden pans on fire so that we could singe the fine feathers. The last step was to cut the chickens in pieces, to be soaked in salt water, until it was time for the chicken breasts, wings, and legs to be fried, baked, or stewed. The giblets—which consisted of the gizzards, liver, and heart—were saved for gravy or boiled for snacking. The chicken feet were also cooked, seasoned, and stewed with onions.

Often on clear nights my great-grandmother Ada, or "Grammie," would point out the Big Dipper and remembered following the North Star to get out of southern bondage. Her sisters all dipped snuff. One sister, Aunt Jenny, had a colorful picture in an oval wooden convex glass picture frame in her living room of the *Titanic* with people floating in the ice-filled water. My aunt Mary, her sister, who lived across the street from her, was also there to join in on the conversation. There was a lot of laughing and storytelling about the old days while everyone waited for the meal, which was shared around a large dining room table. They would laugh about things like, how nice it was to have aluminum foil now. They'd laugh about how "they ate so many ashes cooking their sweet potatoes over an open pit fire," or they'd laugh about "how fast someone at the table could clean all the meat off a chicken bone."

Grammie, her sisters, and Mom all drank their Postum, which was a kind of instant coffee, and even a brewed coffee out of their saucers. They would pour the hot coffee from their cup onto the saucer and blow on it to cool it down then drink it; I'd follow suit with my tea, hot chocolate, or Ovaltine. Grandmom Hester wouldn't let me drink coffee and she'd said, "No baby, coffee will make you Black." I'm not sure what that meant because I was already Black, but okay, she was the boss!

Uncle Will, a brother to Ada, Mary, and Jenny, lived across the street and delivered coal in town from his old light blue half-ton pickup truck that my husband, John, who lived next door, thinks was a Ford. On Sundays after church at Second Calvary Baptist, the pastor and his family would gather around our bear-claw-footed dining room table, which had four leaves to seat ten to fifteen people. After the food was blessed, sometimes we each had to recite a scripture. I always tried to get away with saying the shortest scripture in the Bible such as "Jesus wept," so one day my grandfather said, "If you don't find another scripture, you're gonna weep!" Our afternoon meal usually consisted of fried chicken, glazed baked ham with pineapple slices and maraschino cherries, potato salad or mashed potatoes with giblet gravy, collard and turnip greens, string beans, beets, fried green tomatoes, diced fresh tomatoes with sugar, cucumbers and onions, homemade yeast rolls, and cast-iron skillet cornbread. Dessert consisted of sweet potato pie, ash potato pie (which was made from white potatoes), pineapple upside-down cake, pound cake served with fresh frozen strawberries and fresh whipped cream, and banana pudding made with vanilla wafers.

While dessert was being prepared, we would sit in the living room and sing hymns and gospel songs while pictures of Jesus, John F. Kennedy, and Martin Luther King looked down on us from the wall. Not to be left out was our cast-iron black and white Boston terrier doorstop that stood faithfully by the front door! My grandfather, or Dad as we called him, would sing in his deep baritone voice:

I Want to Be Ready / I Want to Be Ready
When He Calls Me,
I'm Trying to Get My House in Order
So I Can Walk, So I Can Talk,
Walk in Jerusalem Just Like John

Another good one song was:

We're Crossin Over One by One
We're Fast Approaching Life's Setting Sun
Don't Let Him Catch You with Your Work Undone
We're Crossing Over One by One

There would be lots of clapping and foot stompin' to keep time while we sang praises to God—one song leads right into another.

THANKSGIVING

Ronnie remembers our Thanksgiving meal being a feast of wild game: rabbit, squirrel, both smothered in velvety onion gravy. (Yuk!! Who eats this kind of food?) My people did and still do because there was a time when we had to eat what was available. Slaves and sharecroppers were lucky if they were given the waste to eat from the master's table, therefore they learned how to make a meal to feed large families. First- and second-generation enslaved Africans were thrown into unfamiliar territory when they were brought to the Americas, so they used roots, tree bark, and vegetation to survive. We would now consider unthinkable some of the food our ancestors had to eat.

The dining room table would be set with a beautiful white handmade lace tablecloth that was made by Grandmom, of course. Grandpop bought a set of china to serve twenty people and we used shiny crystal stemware glasses.

Our fresh turkey came from the Lee's Turkey Farm in East Windsor, New Jersey; sometimes Grandpop would get a live turkey; we fed and played with him (he was another one of my friends) only to have him slaughtered and served on Grandmom's fine china platter. My sisters, Denise and April, and I cried through the whole dinner looking at our golden brown aromatic "friend" sitting before us with seasoned Pepperidge Farm stuffing, glazed baked ham surrounded by a bounty of candied yams with miniature marshmallows, mashed potatoes, giblet gravy with turkey necks, fresh string beans with new potatoes, collard greens (seasoned with smoked ham hocks), okra corn and tomatoes, corn on the cob from the garden (both were flash frozen, cooked from the summer harvest), and, most importantly, cranberry sauce. I ate everything except the turkey that day because I just couldn't eat my friend!

Every fall we could count on the local hunters from the Brokaw family to drop off a freshly killed deer. Venison roast, loins or cutlet steaks, roasted leg of venison, would be butchered and wrapped in freezer paper, labeled, and stored in one of the two freezers for future stews and suppers. Fresh wild game has to be soaked in one or two tablespoons of vinegar overnight, rinsed and patted dry, before being cooked to take the wildness out of it. On a good day, the rugged-looking hunters would also have a pheasant or two, a goose, or a duck (all hanging upside when delivered).

CHRISTMAS

CHRISTMAS BREAKFAST

Corn fritters, fried apples, smoked bacon, sage sausage patties, grits, and eggs

Biscuits (butter and molasses)

Breakfast included Hoe Cakes (believed to be cooked by slaves over an open fire pit on the flat side of a field hoe). Hester's hoe cakes were cooked in her hot skillet.

CHRISTMAS DINNER

Roast beef and gravy, mashed potatoes

Macaroni and cheese (made with a variety of cheeses, always yellow Cooper cheese with the black skin wrapped around the outside provided by Angelo Pagano, owner of the Hopewell Village Market)

Succotash, collard greens, chow chow (made with green and red tomatoes), corn pudding

Homemade yeast rolls (made using Fleischmann's Yeast)

Desserts

Homemade Gingerbread, Jelly Cake, Chocolate Fudge frosted layer cake, peach cobbler

QUEEN HESTER'S HOE CAKE RECIPE

4 or 5 tablespoons bacon drippings

2 tablespoons flour

2 cups cornmeal

1 teaspoon salt

¼ cup milk

1 teaspoon baking soda

1 teaspoon of baking powder (Clabber Girl)

1 egg

Cook in heated greased skillet 1 or 2 minutes browned on each side (about the size of pancakes).

Served with hot blackstrap molasses (made from Uncle Alfred's sugarcane crop, imported from South Boston, Virginia)

Robert Coleman's smoked bacon (from the smokehouse in the backyard) and red eye gravy Country scrambled eggs

QUEEN HESTER'S BISCUIT RECIPE

(Duplicated by Granddaughter Denise Ewing)

2 cups of flour

1 tablespoon baking powder

½ teaspoon salt

½ cup shortening or butter

¾ cup milk

Preheat oven 375 degrees.

Put flour on wooden surface (table or cutting board) after dough is mixed—place it on floured surface—knead gently and roll out dough. Then cut dough with the mason jar canning ring or water glass—put 20 to 25 three-inch-sized biscuits on ungreased cookie sheet.

(bake time—approximately 10 minutes)

Christmas Eve was so exciting—so much so that Ronnie and I

couldn't go to sleep. We kept tickling each other and laughing until we cried. Hester would poke her head in the bedroom door and say, "Y'all better quit that sniggling and giggling, Sandy Claw coming." I was only five or six years old, so I wasn't sure who "Sandy Claw" was so I kept looking for someone with a claw to come to the window. Her deep southern accent was hard to understand. In the morning I figured it out: Santa Claus had come and put a new toy tractor for us under the tree. We rode our tractors up and down the sidewalk until our legs hurt.

Every Christmas Ronnie and I got a bag of fruit, nuts, and candy. I was thrilled when we got a pomegranate and a fresh coconut. Grandpop used the hand drill to bore a hole in the coconut, so I could drink the juice; then he took his sledgehammer and broke it open, good times!

NEW YEAR'S EVE

SAVORY NEW YEAR'S EVE RECIPES

Fried chicken

Glazed ham

Black-eyed peas *(for prosperity)*

Dirty rice

Pig's feet/Chitterlings

Turnip greens and mashed turnips

Collard greens

(we also drank the potlikker from the greens)

CRACKLING BREAD

Made with coarsely chopped homemade fried pork rinds (mix ¾ cup cornmeal, ¾ cup flour, 3 tablespoons of sugar, 3 or 4 tablespoons of bacon drippings or melted lard, 2 teaspoons baking powder, 1 teaspoon salt, ¾ cup of milk, 2 large eggs); mix together, pour into hot greased skillet, cook 4 for to 5 minutes, flip, cover, turn flame down on low, let cook approx. 5 minutes.

✳

April and Denise still have fond "food memories" of our grandmother's mouthwatering baked delicacies: Coconut cake made with fresh grated coconut (I was the coconut grater—I would be so happy that I would get to eat the inside of the coconut when we were through), coconut custard pie, chocolate cake with homemade marshmallow fluff icing (made with hand-beaten egg whites using a hand-cranked whip) (Ronnie and I got to lick the beaters), lemon meringue pie, egg custard (made especially when anyone was sick), rice pudding, bread pudding with warm sauce, canned peaches, peach cobbler, canned pears. (Denise picked up on Grandmom's baking skills.) I had many bouts with tonsillitis when I was five or six years old, so Grandmom would always make egg custard or Jell-O for me. It always made me feel better and special. (Aunt Jenny and Aunt Mary would give me a silver dollar whenever I was sick.) Since we all lived on the same street, when the older aunts, uncles, and neighbors took sick, Hester made potato soup and egg custard, which was smooth and creamy and went down easy. We didn't put our family members in a nursing home unless it was the last option. Ronnie, Cousin Nelson, and I were the "runners." We would deliver the food to our elderly family members in a picnic basket, with strict orders not to drop anything.

SUMMERTIME AND
THE LIVIN' IS EASY

I remember in the 1950s/1960s as a child about five or six years old, making homemade ice cream with my grandmother and *her* Aunt Jennie (who also lived on the "Avenue," as did her sisters Mary and Ada) for our Second Calvary Baptist Church annual Block Party (held on Columbia Avenue).

HOMEMADE VANILLA
ICE CREAM RECIPE 1

(Makes 20 fl. oz.)

1/3 cup packed light brown sugar

1 cup of milk

1 cup heavy cream

¾ cup granulated sugar

1 vanilla bean

1 tablespoon Watkins Vanilla extract

5 large free-range egg yolks

(add strawberries or blueberries or peaches or chopped pecans)

Pour milk and cream into a saucepan, place over medium heat, and stir in white sugar and light brown sugar.

Slit the vanilla bean down its length and scoop out the tiny black seeds. Stir them into the milk and cream mixture. Reduce heat and continue stirring, until all the sugar has dissolved, then remove from heat.

In a large bowl lightly beat the egg yolks. Gradually add the warm milk and cream mixture, beating gently to combine. Transfer the mixture back to the pan over low heat. Cook, stirring continuously, until mixture thickens to the consistency of custard. Then pour the ice cream into a freezer-proof container and freeze overnight before serving. Stir the ice cream a few times to prevent it from freezing into a solid block (texture should be smooth and creamy).

HOMEMADE VANILLA ICE CREAM RECIPE 2

(made using kosher salt/makes one quart)

Ingredients

3 cups heavy cream

5 large egg yolks

1 cup whole milk

¾ cup sugar

1 tablespoon pure vanilla extract

Kosher salt

Stir the cream, milk, sugar, and 1 teaspoon kosher salt in a medium saucepan and bring to a simmer over medium heat.

Beat the egg yolks in a medium bowl. Slowly pour 1 cup of the hot cream mixture into the beaten yolks, then pour back into the saucepan, whisking, and return to medium heat. Cook, stirring constantly with a wooden spoon, until mixture thickens and reaches 180 degrees Fahrenheit on a thermometer (approx. 6 to 8 minutes). Remove from the heat and strain the custard through a fine-mesh strainer into a large bowl. Stir until mixture cools to room temperature. Cover lightly with plastic wrap—chill for 3 or 4 hours. Hand churn the mixture until smooth. Place in plastic container for 1 hour in freezer. Serve and enjoy.

The homemade ice cream would be served over homemade biscuits topped with sweetened strawberries, or over gingerbread, peach cobbler, or apple pie, or in a Dixie cup with hot chocolate syrup.

The "Avenue" would be lined with sawhorses with plywood; the ladies from the Church Sewing Circle would decorate them with handmade tablecloths. Each tablecloth was made with different print—some made from curtains that were recycled into a tablecloth. Some with colorful flowers on them, some with fruit on them, and I always loved the red and white checkered cloth.

The Bartlett house driveway had the homemade ice cream sitting in a metal tube surrounded by a block of ice, which also held juicy watermelon slices. The Coleman house (our house) had an ongoing fire pit made from a metal barrel that was cut in half, metal grates were placed on the top, the other half was used for a lid; cooking roasted pig, barbecued chicken (homemade BBQ sauce), hot dogs, hamburgers, and roasted corn on the cob floating in heated homemade melted butter.

Hester's famous potato salad made with homemade mayonnaise, deviled eggs, coleslaw, baked beans, sliced tomatoes, homemade bread and butter pickles, and chow chow (made from green tomatoes). She rose early in the morning to cook while it was cool in the kitchen. She would sing while she cooked. One of her favorite songs was "No Never Alone." Now that I'm grown, I think she was singing that song about me; I was always underfoot. Grandpop made a stool for me so that I could help her cook. I loved using the egg slicer to chop the hard-boiled eggs; I used the hand-held grater to shred the carrots for the slaw. There was a sense of pride once the fine cuisine was ready to serve. I can still see her big smile and feel the love that went into the meal.

The Carter, Terry, and Washington houses had a stand (tables with two sawhorses) with pies and cakes, or bread pudding. There was also an "unofficial food contest" by the Church Ladies to see who made the best dish or dessert. (Don't dare mess up—your name would be put on the "do not eat her cookin' list" and they probably made you sit on the "mourners bench" until you repented.) Favorite beverages included luscious sweet tea, mint tea (loose-leaf tea leaves from the herb garden were tied in cheesecloth bags, placed into a large pot of boiling water, then we removed the pot from the burner to steep—removed tea bag and added sugar), freshly squeezed lemonade. On occasion Mother Genie Daniels from Crusher Road would make homemade sweetened sarsaparilla (root beer) from dried sarsaparilla roots for flavoring. These drinks would be ladled out of the large metal pot with a block of ice and served in mason jars.

The unpaved dirt street with no curbs was filled with children running, playing tag, having wheelbarrow races, wooden stilt races, jumping rope, double Dutch, bike races, hopscotch, water balloon and "chicken" fights (a piggyback game), baseball games, horseshoes and quoits clinked in the background. Lots of squealing and screaming went on when you got nailed in the back with a fast-moving water balloon. I always rode on Ronnie's back when we played the "chicken fight" game. He was sure to ram me into somebody so that we would knock them down. Mother May I? Simon Says, and of course Hide and Seek were organized by the older kids. The Terry house had a smooth-surface cement porch where all the kids played a game of jacks. Gloria and Francine were the champs. My hands were too small. I could only make it up to "sixies." Some cheatin' went on and we didn't have a problem callin' you out about it!

In the early spring and all summer long Robert and Hester went fishing every day that they could. Uncle Ronnie and my sister Denise would go along for these excursions. They fished mostly private (secret) ponds like the Timm's Farm in Hopewell Borough, Amwell Lake, Aunt Molly Road, or Stoney Brook. They would come home at dusk just in time to spread the newspaper out on the back porch in order to clean their catch. Sometimes 50 to 100 fish. Mostly sunfish, bass, trout, and on a good day catfish, a snapping turtle, or hopefully an eel. While cleaning the bounty of fish, Grandpop would smile his big bright smile, and say, "Once he hits that hot grease, his own momma won't recognize him," and we'd laugh until our bellies hurt.

OCEAN FISHING

We usually went ocean fishing off of the Belmar or Asbury Park Pier. We stayed at a bed & breakfast in Asbury Park. A nice Black lady served a half cantaloupe with strawberries every morning. We caught mackerel (to be salted and stored in the large crock), blue fish, whitings, porgies, spots, and blowfish. I almost ran off the pier when they caught a blowfish and it blew up like a balloon right in front of me.

FRESHWATER FISHING

We caught sunfish, catfish, trout, bass, and shad (which was baked). The fish eggs (roe) were saved, dipped in egg, dredged in flour, and fried, served with scrambled eggs for breakfast along with the fried fish and grits (of course).

Once they caught a snapping turtle and got it back to the "Avenue," Grandmom would take her three-foot-long metal rod and put it in front of the snapping turtle's mouth; he would snap down on it (after being transported in a metal pail in a burlap bag by now he was not happy); she'd pull his neck out and whack his head off with the sharpened ax. Then we started guard duty—we followed that headless turtle all day. Headless chickens!! Headless turtles!!! Life on a farm ain't easy.

Grandmom told us the turtle wouldn't die until nightfall and we just had to see this with our own eyes. She was right!! At nightfall the turtle finally died; she removed the skin from his shell, soaked the meat in vinegar water overnight, and made the best snapping turtle soup ever made. AND on a really good day Ronnie, Johnny (who is now my husband), and our cousin Nelson caught some frogs so that we could have fried frog legs (after they got done chasing the girls with them).

During the spring, the twins Bruce and Barry Nevius who lived across the street would catch rabbits and squirrels and bring them to Miss Hester—they had to be properly skinned (using a sharp knife cut through the skin around the hind legs), tie the legs together and proceed to pull the skin down off the legs, stripping it inside out like a glove over the body and forelegs. Remove the innards, except for the liver and heart. Soaked overnight in vinegar (we kept the rabbit foot for good luck). Grandmom would pat the rabbit dry, dredge it with flour seasoned with salt and pepper and paprika, and fry it in hot lard. The pan drippings were reserved and browned, a roux of the seasoned flour, sliced onions and cream, and fried pieces of rabbit were added and simmered slowly for about an hour until the creamy gravy was ready. Great-grandmom Ada would use the same process for cooking the squirrels the boys would catch. Once again, I remained true to my animal friends. I tasted it, but I couldn't enjoy it. I did, however, enjoy sopping up the gravy with the homemade biscuits.

All the seeds from the vegetables, watermelons (especially the seeds from little round sugar babies—Grandpop and I would go in the garden with a knife and salt shaker, pick our own watermelon, cut it in half, sit on our upside-down peach basket, sprinkle salt on it, and eat a half of watermelon each), cantaloupes, plums, peaches, and pears were saved for the next planting season. We canned everything for winter; we even made pickled watermelon rinds. We lived a self-sufficient life. Grandmom even taught me how to churn butter. She put the butter churner on the front porch, right by the front door where she could see me, and away I went moving my little hips and arms.

Poke salad (pronounced poke salet) was picked every spring. We would stop on the side of the road to pick pokeweed on the way up to the Sourland Mountain in a field on the left-hand side of the road near Hillbilly Hall. I still see it pop up every spring. My mouth waters thinking about Grandmom and the big smile on Grandpop's face when she served it. Poke was not planted but just showed up like clockwork in the early spring. On our many Sunday drives, unbeknownst to me, we would be in search of poke salad in the fields, dandelions, and creasy greens (creasies) so that we could come back to pick them. There are many different beliefs about how to cook these greens, but Grandmom boiled them first, strained them in her metal strainer, returned them to her heated black skillet with a piece of fried smoked bacon and drippings—you could hear the greens singe as they hit that hot grease— and then she added sliced onion. When the aroma filled the air, you knew you were in for a treat.

Grandpop had a grapevine that provided us with sweet juicy grapes all summer that doubled as weapons for our homemade slingshots before they were ripe.

All the children on the "Avenue" had a navy bean pea shooter. Mostly the girls against the boys when we played "The Man from Uncle" game.

On those dog days of summer nights, we all slept outside on our L-shaped porch. As soon as it got dark, we would sneak around the corner and climb the Adams Family cherry tree. We ate some and saved some for Grandmom Hester to bake us one of her scrumptious cherry pies (rainier cherries make the best pies).

One summer in the mid-1960s Ronnie had a job that I will never forget. Mr. Allison (a friend of the family that my grandmother worked for) hired him to clean and detail the Oscar Mayer Wiener hot dog truck. The truck stayed parked in front of our house for weeks. It was an attraction for the whole town to admire! What fun we had playing in that truck. Our imaginations ran wild that summer.

SPRING IS IN THE AIR

In early spring Grandpop methodically rototilled his two garden plots with a non-motorized rototiller. On Good Friday, weather permitting, we planted green beans, flat green beans, field peas, okra, onion sets, collards, turnips, squash, watermelon, muskmelons, carrots, beets, cucumbers, tomatoes, green peppers, and sweet corn. In the mail each year an order of ladybugs arrived. Grandpop would ask me to help put the ladybugs in the garden; they helped to control the invasive garden pests. (I got to play with them first—they're so cute.)

CANNING SEASON

After eating watermelon, we always saved the rinds to make Pickled Watermelon Rinds. Hester had no idea that the rinds are rich in an ingredient used to help with erectile dysfunction, or did she?

PICKLED WATERMELON RIND
(MAKES 4 OR 5 PINTS)

1 whole watermelon rind

¾ cup salt

3 quarts water

2 quarts (2 trays) ice cubes

9 cups sugar

3 cups vinegar, white

3 cups water

1 tablespoon (about 48) whole cloves

One-inch cinnamon sticks (5 or 6 pieces)

1 teaspoon lemon juice

CRAB APPLE JELLY

One of the older ladies on the third block of Columbia Avenue had a crab apple tree. After getting her permission, Ronnie and Cousin Nelson had strict orders from Hester to climb the tree and pick baskets of ripe crab apples. Grandmom would have me select the crisp small apples, remove the stems and blossoms, wash them, and then cut them into small pieces.

We would then add approximately 3 pounds to about 4 cups of water, cover, bring to a rapid boil, reduce heat, cook until tender (about 25 minutes), stirring to keep them from sticking to the bottom of the pot. We then used moistened cheesecloth placed over her metal strainer, which was resting over a bowl to reserve the juice. The jelly jars were sterilized and resting in a long pan on two burners with low flame, half filled with hot water waiting to be filled. The juice was poured into a saucepan, and at least 4 cups of sugar were added. (Hester would always say, "Baby don't skimp on the sugar, these apples are sour, your jelly will be bitter.") The apples were added into the boiling juice, stirred, and the foam was skimmed off. The hot mixture was quickly poured into the heated jelly jars but not to the top. We wiped the rim of the jars and placed the metal lids on the jars. Then we continued to heat the jars in the hot water (about 5 min.) to seal. Next step was to remove the hot jars to a waiting dish towel, add the rings, let cool. We enjoyed the scrumptious rose-colored jelly all year long.

HOMEMADE CHOW CHOW

2 quarts shredded cabbage (about one medium head). Use the grater to shred the cabbage like you are making coleslaw.

½ cup sweet onions chopped fine

½ cup chopped green or red bell pepper (optional)

2 tablespoons salt

Combine chopped vegetables and sprinkle with salt. Let stand 4 to 6 hours in the refrigerator. Drain well.

Combine the following ingredients and simmer 10 minutes. Use a large pot.

2 cups vinegar

1½ cups sugar

2 teaspoons dry mustard

2 teaspoons celery seeds

2 teaspoons mustard seed

Add vegetables to vinegar-sugar-spice mixture and simmer another 10 minutes. Bring to a boil. Then pack, boiling hot, into clean, heated canning jars; do not fill to the top. Put canning lids and rings on the heated jars—tighten. Grandmom always used Ball product canning jars and lids.

Let cool and enjoy. Serve on top of collard greens or pinto beans. (Good Lord have mercy!)

HESTER'S CELLAR

Hester's cellar was dug out by hand by Grandpop, my uncle Sonny, and any other recruits. There were two rooms. One at the bottom of the basement stairs; that area had a coal chute used for coal deliveries. It wasn't well lit; there was a lightbulb with a chain hanging from the ceiling beams. Hester needed more room for her canned goods. So, they dug out another room and added a door leading outside. That room had the walls sealed with fresh masonry cement and shelves installed; more lighting was added. Grandpop purchased a chest type freezer for the vegetables and an upright freezer for the meats.

Each area was well stocked with colorful jars of beans, green beans, beets, chow chow, jellies, field peas, watermelon rinds, peaches, pears, cherries, crab apples, and plums. I loved working with Grandmom organizing the canned goods and frozen foods, preparing for winter. Looking at the variety of bright colors of yellow, green, and different shades of red made all that hard work worth it, and also gave me a sense of security knowing there was food stored up.

There was always a feeling of an "elephant in the room" however; my older cousin Butchie died in that same basement as a child in 1955. He was playing down there, he had Uncle Ronnie with him; Butchie was about twelve years old and Ronnie was about four years old. Butchie must have been playing hide and seek and climbed into a refrigerator. The door slammed shut and he couldn't get out. Ronnie was too young to help him; Aunt Jenny-V and her husband, Uncle Buddy, who was Uncle Will's son, started the search for their son Butchie. The whole street was now involved in the search. No one had a clue as to where he was. Ronnie was so young and tried to show them; finally, after many hours of horror and panic, Earl Nevius, the neighbor across the street, joined the search party and followed the suggestion of the police to check any free-standing refrigerators. They went in the basement again; Ronnie keep pointing at the refrigerator, so they decided to open it only to make a heart-wrenching discovery when they found Butchie dead! Our family was never the same. Butchie's death caused trauma to the soul, as emotions became raw and ragged between my grandmother and her sister Geneva. Aunt Jenny-V, who happened to be one of my favorite aunts, became an alcoholic with a sadness under what was once a beautiful smile. All the beautiful colors in that basement turned gray.

ST. MICHAEL'S ORPHANAGE

A favorite summertime memory is when the nuns, dressed in their black and white habits, would bring the Black girls from St. Michael's Orphanage in Hopewell to "Miss Hester's" house to get their hair washed, braided, or straightened with a hot comb and curled with hot curlers. Hester would recruit Linda Jones, a teenager who lived in Skillman, to help with salon duties. Wash tubs were set up in the yard and we would use a tin pitcher to pour hot soapy water over their heads for shampooing and rinsing. Next there was towel drying and there would be ten to twelve girls at a time. After all the heads were washed, the girls were allowed to run and play for a while, but not too long because we didn't want them to get too sweaty! Then came the straightening comb, or hot comb, with the wooden handle that was heated on the stove. Grandmom and Linda would press and curl the girls' hair or braid it into cornrows. It was my job to put colorful barrettes at the end of each braid and to hold the mirror for them to admire themselves. I never learned how to braid hair like my sisters and because I couldn't braid Grandmom Hester thought I might have been "flickted," which meant afflicted.

It seemed as if everyone respected my God-fearing grandparents and the love they had for each other, their church, and family. Many a meal was shared with the community around their dining room table. It was used not only for family meals but also for fund-raisers for the church. Folks from all walks of life were welcomed in our home. The local doctor (Dr. O'Neill) and his wife, the priests and nuns from St. Alphonsus, the local bankers, Mr. Rockwell, owner of Rockwell Manufacturing Company, the town drunk, the local police officers Mr. Dodson and Mr. Fillebrowne, the family who seemed to be always down on their luck, cousins, and friends—all would come bathed and shaved, dressed in their fineries to support the Second Calvary Fried Chicken Dinner fund-raisers.

We used the homemade white lace tablecloth and china plates, crystal glasses, and white cloth napkins that had been starched and pressed. They meant that company was coming. The hardwood floors were polished and shined by Grandpop and Ronnie. At that time Ronnie was being trained to take over the floor stripping business that was one of Grandpop's many jobs. The food was blessed by Robert Coleman's soul-stirring grace before each meal was served.

SECOND CALVARY BAPTIST CHURCH

The money was raised to help build the church on Columbia Avenue. We all worked together preparing for the dinners; teens and young adults (girls dressed in their pedal pushers and colorful Keds sneakers) worked in the garden, picked and snapped the beans, picked the turnip and collard greens, peeled potatoes (at least 150 pounds). We also served and cleaned up. They would come in shifts to eat. We had an L-shaped porch that was turned into extra seating. My job was to clear the tables, reset them for the next crew, and keep the water and juice glasses full. I also answered the phone and took orders. (Our phone number was Ho6-0883.)

There is something about the smell of fried chicken that makes people come together, forget all about their troubles, and have a good time eating together. Segregation or religious preference was not an issue.

Year after year hundreds of dollars were raised until they had enough money for the various projects at the church. In the 1950s the church members took out a loan from Princeton Bank & Trust and hired local carpenters John Hall builders to help build the current beautiful church edifice on Columbia Avenue along with assistance from the local Black carpenters John and Norman Jones from Skillman. (Grandpop always encouraged dealing local when hiring out work.)

In 1959 we all marched from First Street Church (known as the First Colored Baptist Church-1897 of Hopewell), singing and clapping all the way to our new church (Second Calvary Baptist Church), 69 Columbia Avenue, Hopewell Borough, New Jersey.

In the late 1960s we had a spirit-filled mortgage-burning service. Chairman of the Trustee Board Robert (Bob) Bartlett Sr. stood in the front of the church congregation with a huge smile on his face and held the final loan payment papers over a metal bucket, struck a match, and burned the papers for all to see. What a time!!! What a time!! Lots of clapping, crying, singing, and shouting went on that day.

Birthdays, anniversaries, weddings, and graduations were celebrated, sewing circles, Bible studies, and luncheons to welcome the pastor and his family were shared around that table. The table decorated with a freshly starched tablecloth, cloth napkins, forks, knives, and spoons set in such proper order, crystal glasses waiting to be filled with freshly squeezed lemonade or freshly brewed iced tea with a mint leaf or lemon slice added, and of course candlesticks to match the occasion. (Emily Post would have been proud.) Grandmom used the pretty stuff when we were having company and occasionally when we were just having a casual family-style meal.

The ladies of the church were a united force (Pearl Hughes, Annie Harrison, Jennie Terry, Hester Coleman, and others). They would go door to door asking for donations for the church. After explaining their mission, local historian Bev Weidl remembers Mother Annie Harrison would say. "Don't disappoint me now." Eager not to disappoint, the wallets flew open, and the money flowed freely.

Mother Annie Harrison would make rock candy for Easter and Christmas to give to the Sunday School children. We had a large Sunday School class of twenty-five or more young adults and children.

ROCK CANDY RECIPE

Using a heavy metal saucepan, combine sugar, water, and corn syrup over medium heat.

Stir constantly until dissolved. Lower heat, cook without stirring until mixture starts to harden (about 340F).

Test by dropping a few drops of syrup mixture into cold water—should be hard and brittle threads should form.

Remove from heat—add flavoring and color (optional).

Pour into two generously greased 9-inch pans. Sit the pan of candy over saucepan containing hot water to keep it from hardening until you are ready to make the next pan of candy.

Sprinkle with powdered sugar if desired. Enjoy!

She would wrap the candy in wax paper—smiles all around when she gave us our package. I always felt so special, like she made that candy just for me.

IT'S SATURDAY—
THE DAY BEFORE SUNDAY

We actually got to sleep late on Saturday. Instead of rising at 5:30 a.m. to feed the chickens and pigs, Grandmom would let us sleep until 8:00 a.m. Grandpop did the early morning chores. Not sure when or if they ever got to sleep in.

Once we were dressed and fed, our Saturday ritual began. The big yellow croak bowl was sitting on the counter filled with rising yeast roll mixture covered with a white tea towel. When I was about five or six years old I took the notion to beat the rising yeast roll mixture like a drum—let's just say I never did that again! Hester ran a tight ship, and I had just messed up her rolls and her schedule. It's a miracle I lived to tell the story. Baking rolls for Sunday dinner and making bread for the week was part of our Saturday chores. We made bread pudding using the scraps of bread left over. Waste Not, Want Not was her motto. I managed to sneak some bread crumbs for the chickens.

Ronnie helped Grandpop with the heavy chores and shoe polishing; we had our shoes shined for church. I polished silverware, dusted furniture, ironed linens, and helped to prep the Sunday meal. Grandmom baked cakes, rolls, and pies all day. I was allowed to put icing on the cakes; even after skillful lessons, I still can't bake. Hester wasn't about to have me mess up her masterpieces.

Thank God for play time—we never returned to say we were bored. Once we were released, we took off for the "land of imagination" to play with the rest of the children on the "Avenue." I made up my own games— my favorite was the "switch game." I would chase all the kids around with a hickory switch. They would run screaming for their lives and find places to hide. (Not sure why we thought that was so much fun …)

IT'S SUNDAY MORNING

The smell of bacon, hot grits with butter and sometimes cheese, potatoes and onions, homemade hoe cakes with hot molasses, and scrambled eggs, and on special occasions we had corn fritters—the smell made it impossible to sleep!

On Sunday morning those same hard-working men, women, and children would hang up their aprons and put on their church clothes (Sunday Go-to-Meetin' clothes), hats, polished shoes, matching purses, and white gloves. The ladies had a work apron and a hostess serving apron.

The "Church Lady" hats would be derby style hats, adorned with feathers, flowers, embroidered lace fabric, and satin ribbon bands, embellished with rhinestone accents, or pillbox hats with veils, straw in the summer, wool blend in the winter. The ladies would not enter the church without their heads covered. The men wore hats also, which were immediately removed as soon as they entered the church.

Grandmom Hester usually had a long hat pin somewhere in her hat, which doubled as a weapon if needed, but mostly to hold her wig in place in case she was "slain in the spirit" (overcome with the power of the Holy Spirit). She was always prepared. My unspoken duty was to follow behind her to catch her wig, the hat, and glasses should the holy ghost cause her to come out of character and start "shoutin'."

The temperature inside the Second Calvary Baptist Church would get hot and humid once the worship service got going. The local funeral parlor owned by John (Jack) Hughes provided us with church fans. His father and mother, Ernest and Pearl Hughes, were founding members of the church. They were always so proud of his accomplishments as a Black business owner. Each fan had a picture of Black families in worship. I felt so special holding those fans; in the 1950s we didn't have many items with well-dressed Black people on them.

In the late 1950s and early 1960s one of Grandmom's many jobs was to wash, dry, and iron laundry for local White people. The ringer-type washing machine was in the pantry. We would roll it over to the sink, plug it in, fill it with water, guide the hose down the drain, and wash baskets of clothes all day long. After being lined dried, the laundry would be slightly sprinkled with water, and then using the Argo Starch in the blue box, she would make a liquid starch in the metal dishpan in which to dip the individual pieces of laundry. We would eat the chunks of starch like candy—the white lips were a dead giveaway.

The iron was heated on the coal stove. The clothes would be starched stiff and placed in the basket like pieces of artwork. Hester was a true artist.

The life skills and lessons I learned from Robert and Hester made me a confident, fearless, courageous person filled with integrity. They instilled in us a great displeasure for injustice of any form. We were repeatedly told that we were "no better than anyone else" but that we were also "no less than anyone else." My predecessors have passed on a wonderful legacy of love and hope that will be shared with pride from generation to generation.

QUEEN HESTER'S HOME REMEDIES: NECESSITY IS THE MOTHER OF INVENTION

In my home as a youth, we rarely needed a doctor. Hester believed in using God's natural remedies to make teas, broths, poultices, salts, oils, roots and tree bark, vegetables, and herbs to comfort and heal. These are tried-and-true remedies not approved or tested by the FDA.

BATHS

Here are three different baths. Oatmeal is used for poison ivy. Put oatmeal in a white sock, tie with a rubber band, dunk sock in hot water, in bathtub if possible. Use the pasty salve on the rash. Use Epsom salt baths for aches and pains. A Sitz bath is made with bay leaves for treating hemorrhoids.

POULTICES

For fevers, sprains, back pain: using a spoon, grate the inside of a white potato; place grated potato in cheesecloth or a piece of white cotton bedsheet; pour apple cider vinegar over the grated potato; apply poultice to affected area.

Musterole—introduced in 1905—mustard is the principal ingredient. It is a medicinal rub similar to VapoRub and Ben Gay. Heat it by placing capped tube into hot water. Then spread heated mixture onto flannel cloth and place with ointment side on sore muscle, sprains, or bruises (not for use on open wounds).

SALTS AND POWDERS

Epsom salts can also be used as a purgative to clean poisons from the blood. Mix a teaspoon in an 8-ounce glass of warm water. Let salt sink to the bottom of the glass. *Do not stir.* Once salt dissolves, drink the mixture.

To use as a laxative: mix a teaspoon of salts in an 8-ounce glass. Stir until salt dissolves then drink mixture—causes purging, evacuation, and cleansing of the bowels.

Stanback & BC headache powder—stir one measured packet into a glass of water or other liquid.

OILS AND TONICS

Cod Liver Oil—used as preventive medicine to keep viruses from taking a foothold in the body and causing diseases.

Castor Oil—used to prevent or relieve constipation and various diseases, like the cold and flu virus. Blend together with oranges and lemons—heat cod liver oil and castor oil mixture (do not boil). Ingest a tablespoon or so.

Ex-Lax—Chocolate Stimulant Laxative is used to relieve constipation.

Peppermint Oil—Mix one teaspoon in water to relieve stomach ailments.

Sweet Oil is used to treat ear infections. Warm it and apply one drop in each ear.

Sweet Spirits of Nitre—Mix one teaspoon of nitre in water in an orange-juice-sized glass to reduce high fever.

3 or 4 drops of **Kerosene** are dropped onto a teaspoon of sugar to treat colds and bad coughs.

666 Cough Syrup/Horehound Cough Drops. These have a distinct herbal flavor with hints of root beer, licorice, and mint.

3 or 4 drops **Oil of Turpentine** dropped onto a teaspoon of sugar was used to treat ringworm/impetigo applied directly to the wound; also used to treat and kill tapeworms, pinworms, and roundworms. A laxative made of Epsom salt (stir until dissolved) was given to dispel the tapeworms.

Dried **eel skin** is used to ease the pain of leg cramps: wrap the eel skin around your leg or arm; leave on overnight. The oil from the skin is believed to have healing qualities.

Over-the-counter **Dr. Miles** was a tonic made by Dr. Franklin Miles from Elkhart, Indiana, in the 1890s. This tonic was used to "calm nervousness."

Father John's Medicine—This cough medicine was a non-alcoholic mix made of cod liver oil that had a licorice taste.

SPICES AND VINEGARS

Ascorbic acid. Add one teaspoon in an 8-ounce glass of water to help increase Vitamin C levels.

Vinegar. For high blood pressure drink a shot glass daily to lower blood pressure (only if your stomach is not sensitive to acid). It may also be used with honey. Take a tablespoon of honey and vinegar mixture daily.

Sinus troubles. Fill a large pot with water. Add a cup of apple cider vinegar. Cover and bring to boil. Turn off flame. Place a towel over your head, remove top, and inhale steam.

Nausea. Use smashed bananas and rice cereal to prevent nausea; or a mixture of flour water; or flat Coca Cola.

TEAS/ROOTS AND SYRUPS

Black cohosh for abdominal cramps: Make a tea with black cohosh leaves. Let the tea steep until strong. Drink a cup of hot tea when needed for menstrual cramps. Also drink 2 to 3 cups of hot tea daily 8 weeks before delivery to ease the pains of during childbirth and support ease of delivery.

Camel root—Use for abdominal discomfort. Boil the roots until tender and use as a tea.

Catnip tea—Babies with colic were given catnip tea in their bottles and smoke was blown up their nostrils.

Sip flat **Coca Cola** to treat abdominal pain.

Cream of tartar—Use to treat hives. Make a paste with cream of tartar and apply to hives or insect bites.

Pectoral herbal tea—Use for bad coughs to break up the phlegm. Steep the leaves until the mixture is strong. Add honey.

Sassafras and sarsaparilla tea—Use for treating abdominal pain.

Snuff or tobacco—Make a paste and apply to bee stings.

Spearmint leaves – Pick, wrap in cheesecloth, put in boiling water. Steep leaves for half an hour.

ASTRINGENTS

Use **witch hazel** for acne, measles or other rashes, insect bites, dry skin.

Rose water and glycerin may be used as an astringent for skin treatment.

Use the inside of a **banana peel** to treat eczema.

Use **urine**—capture your own urine in a cup; apply urine with a cotton ball to affected area to treat acne or eczema, rosacea, psoriasis, or other skin ailments.

Use **Alum** (a white powder used to make pickles) to heal cuts, reduce pain after having a tooth pulled; excellent to gargle with after tonsillitis surgery or to heal mouth sores. Mix ½ teaspoon in an 8-ounce glass of water. Use a gauze pad to apply to cuts. Use as a rinse to gargle with for inside mouth ailments. *Do not use too much when mixing—it heals fast … you want it to heal the inside of the wound first.*

VEGETABLES

Garlic and onions mixture—Boil together. Make a poultice using a white sheet or a piece of flannel cloth. Apply to forehead and the bottom of your feet to reduce fever. Cover your body with heavy blankets to sweat out impurities. Discard after each use.

Onions—Use to remove toxins or flu/cold viruses from the air. Slice one large onion, place onion slices in a saucepan with water, bring to a boil, turn heat down to a slow simmer, and leave uncovered on the stove all day. Discard after use.

SOUPS

Chicken Soup: Boil chicken parts or whole chicken. Remove the bones. Add chicken meat to stock pot of water; add onions, carrots, celery (use the leaves also). Add chicken broth for flavoring. The soup helps to relieve the symptoms of cold and flu viruses.

Great Northern Beans: Soak overnight to remove outside covering of beans before cooking. Add diced vegetables such as onions, celery, carrots. Cook slowly (usually with parboiled ham hocks). This soup is used for cleansing the digestive system and removing toxins from your body.

Vegetable Soup—Sauté diced vegetables (carrots, potatoes, turnips, green beans, lima beans, celery, okra). Add water, broth, vegetables, and stewed tomatoes (use the juice also) to stock pot; add chopped green leafy vegetables when the soup is almost done.

Cream of Potato Soup—Peel white potatoes, cut into cubes; add finely chopped sautéed onions; add celery. Add to potatoes and boil until potatoes are tender. Add warm cream or milk, butter, salt and pepper. Mash a few potatoes to thicken the soup; continue to cook over medium flame for ½ hour. Stir occasionally so the potatoes do not stick to the bottom of pan. Do not bring to a boil. This recipe is used to nourish the sick, especially the elderly who have problems swallowing.

ASAFOETIDA BAG

An asafoetida bag (black resin) placed in a small sack and hung around your neck with a homemade twine necklace will help keep away the flu bug (and everything else—phew, did that stuff stink). Asafoetida resins have been around for thousands of years and have served many different purposes. Frankincense and myrrh were resins, and many of these substances were used for medicinal purposes.[2]

Asafoetida is a plant. It has a bad smell and tastes bitter. That probably explains why it is sometimes called "devil's dung." People use asafoetida resin, a gum-like material, as medicine. Asafoetida resin is produced by solidifying juice that comes out of cuts made in the plant's living roots. Asafoetida is used for such a wide variety of ailments from corns and calluses, coughs and colds, and depression to repelling dogs, cats, and wildlife.[3]

SALVES AND RUBS

Camphorated rubs were used on the chest and back to treat colds and coughs and also applied to bruises, aches, and pains.

Vicks VapoRub was rubbed on the chest and throat and under nostrils. Two fingers were used to dip a dollop of VapoRub, which was to be swallowed (contrary to directions on the box) to loosen phlegm and make the cough productive.

3 or 4 drops of **Kerosene** were dropped onto a teaspoon of sugar to treat colds.

3 or 4 drops **Oil of Turpentine** were dropped onto a teaspoon of sugar to treat ringworm or impetigo and applied directly to the wound. It is also used to treat and kill tapeworms, pinworms, and roundworms.

A laxative made of Epsom salts (stir until dissolved) was given to dispel the tapeworms.

---

[1] Robert A Gibson, *Yale-New Haven Teachers Institute, The Negro Holocaust: Lynching and Race Riots in the United States, 1880-1950, Robert A. Gibson* (New Haven: Yale-New Haven Teachers Institute, n.d.), accessed February 18, 2018, https://books.google.com/books?id=M_

[2] Poonam Mahendra and Shradha Bisht, "Ferula Asafoetida: Traditional Uses and Pharmacological Activity," *Pharmacognosy Review* 6, no. 12 (July–December 2012): 141–46, accessed February 19, 2018, https://www.ncbi.nlm.nih.gov/pmc/articles/PMC3459456/

[3] "Find a Vitamin or Supplement: ASAFOETIDA," WebMD, n.d., accessed February 19, 2018, https://www.webmd.com/vitamins-supplements/altmodmono-248-ASAFOETIDA.aspx?altModalityId=248&altModalityName=ASAFOETIDA&source=0

Dora Berry and George Renwick

CHAPTER 11

AFRICAN AMERICAN HISTORY IS AMERICAN HISTORY

by BEVERLY MILLS

Education is the most powerful weapon which you can use to change the world.

—Nelson Mandela, anti-apartheid leader and first
Black president of South Africa, 1918–2013

An Act establishing the Amistad Commission and supplementing chapter 16A of Title 52 of the New Jersey Statutes:

BE IT ENACTED by the Senate and General Assembly of the State of New Jersey[1]

1. The Legislature finds and declares that:

a. It is therefore desirable to create a State-level commission, which is an organized body, on a continuous basis, will survey, design, encourage and promote the implementation of education and awareness programs in New Jersey concerned with the African slave trade, slavery in America, the vestiges of slavery in this country, and the contributions of African Americans in building our country; to develop workshops, institutes, seminars, and other teacher training activities designed to educate teachers on this subject matter; and which will be responsible for the coordination of events on a regular basis, throughout the State, that provide appropriate memorialization of the events concerning the enslavement of Africans and their descendants in America as well as their struggle for free dom and liberty.

Sponsored by Assemblymen William D. Payne and Craig A. Stanley, on August 27, 2002, Governor James McGreevey signed the Amistad Bill. The bill was named out of respect for the African slaves who overthrew the *Amistad* in 1839. The purpose of the bill was to mandate educational awareness regarding the history and contributions of African Americans in New Jersey and to America as a whole.

"In nearly all of the English Colonies in America the institution of slavery was recognized and accepted by both government and colonists from the earliest period of settlement. In New Jersey the relation of master and slave had legal recognition at the very beginning of the Colony's political existence."[2] From the time the first colonist and slave stepped foot in New Jersey to the time the Amistad Commission was established was 337 years: from 1665 to 2002.

- Three hundred thirty-seven years to recognize the history and contribution of African Americans in New Jersey

- Three hundred thirty-seven years to take steps to change the narrative by taking African Americans out of the shadows of American history, for their story to have equal footing in our children's school curriculum

- Three hundred thirty-seven years to look at the hard truths about how New Jersey and the entire nation really came to be

This glaring omission lies at the center of our mission and work in this book and in our community—to bring vital history alive in museums, historic sites, and classrooms and curriculums throughout New Jersey's educational system. Education is about enacting real change for the future, so that young students will carry more knowledge and awareness along with an expanded point of view throughout their lives and careers. When educators reach out to bring us into their schools, we offer to take their students on tours of African American historic sites that probably were right under their noses, places they might ride past every day. We are humbled to witness the transformation in the students' eyes when they learn about history that took place right in their backyard.

Our ongoing commitment to our mission was ignited when we realized how many voices had been silenced over the centuries, beginning with the African American cemeteries we defended in our very own corner of New Jersey. Our work in the schools requires meeting blatant and more subtle omissions from our history books and educational curriculums with decades of our research and stories. What we found in every school district we have visited is the desire for more information about the significant influence African Americans have had on the development of American culture and society. My hope is that the stories in this chapter on education will give a personal face to how the institution of slavery laid the groundwork for centuries of oppression and bigotry that now still hold all of us captive. Racism is like a malignancy. Until the whole truth, from every perspective, is told, none of us are free, White or Black.

Here is one example of how a simple question led to powerful collaborations and commitment to change from multiple agencies throughout the state. After my coauthor, Elaine, toured the William Trent House, the oldest landmark in Trenton, New Jersey, she asked a single question of her tour guide, Sam Stephens. Did William Trent have slaves and did the museum staff at William Trent have a list of their names? Stephens, the treasurer of the William Trent House, showed us a list of property owned by William Trent. Included in that list of personal items were human beings. That single question led to more questions, conversations, and partnerships that ultimately resulted in three statewide symposiums attended by teachers, educators, museum curators, representatives of historic sites and libraries, archaeologists, and the public to discuss "presenting and discussing difficult topics in African American history." From these symposiums, four organizations, the Stoutsburg Sourland African American Museum, the 1772 William Trent House, the New Jersey Historical Society, and the Grounds for Sculpture in Hamilton Township, New Jersey, and Dr. Linda Caldwell-Epps, president of 1804 Consultants, formed a partnership named the Sankofa Collaborative. The name was chosen because of the meaning held by the Akan people of West Africa that the Sankofa bird, a stylized bird with its head turned to his back, is associated with "go back to the past and bring forward that which is useful."[3] At each symposium, once the green light was lit, we witnessed participants freely speaking on topics that they may have initially perceived to be too challenging or difficult.

In the beginning of this book I reopened a half-century-old door to share with you, the devastating loss of my young mother shortly after the birth of my brother—a traumatic experience that feels like yesterday. I've also recounted how Elaine and I spent over thirty-five years as stewards of the Stoutsburg Cemetery and why our work will continue to be so vital in our region. I believe our stewardship should not only be about the physical maintenance and preservation of the cemetery in Hopewell Township; it also brings a duty to continue to ensure that everyone has a clearer understanding of the African American experience in the Hopewell Valley region as well as in the state and nation. We are so encouraged that the organizations that comprise the Sankofa Collaborative share the same philosophy as Elaine and I do in their commitment to counter the lack of knowledge in our schools, historic sites, and institutions about the history of slavery and the contributions of African Americans in New Jersey. Our involvement as cofounders of the Stoutsburg Sourland African American Museum only enhances the work Elaine and I have already undertaken such as presenting in schools, historical societies, civic and church groups, libraries, and museums to present the history of Black Americans through a far wider lens. Educating our youth is vitally important to Elaine and me, and we hope that by humanizing our stories, the reader will gain a sharper focus on what transpired in the lives of local African Americans and how their experiences connected to events that happened on a larger scale. That is why we decided to title this chapter "African American History is American History."

Two examples of living American history can be illustrated with the story of two senior class trips in my own family, decades apart. Both experiences, mine and my father's, were influenced by the long-standing legacy of slavery, racism, and segregation that the Amistad Bill was enacted to correct. Each class trip exposed the deep roots of racism and the protection of "Whiteness" in which segregation and racism were not only found in the southern states but also openly practiced in New Jersey and in the capital of our nation.

When he was eighteen years old, my father journeyed with the Pennington High School Class of 1941 to go on his senior class trip to a segregated Washington, D.C. The climate of sanctioned discrimination in the early 1940s was not that far removed from the more socially conscious mood of the country twenty-seven years later when I traveled with the Class of 1968 on my senior class trip to Washington, D.C.

The world was watching as the civil rights movement, led by Dr. Martin Luther King, gripped the country. Throughout the 1960s organizers, led by King, conducted nonviolent protests in an effort to effect social change. I graduated in 1968, a scant four years after President Lyndon B. Johnson signed the Civil Rights Act of 1964 that officially banned discrimination based on race, color, religion, sex, or national origin. A year later, in August 1965, the Voting Rights Act, also signed under the Johnson administration, prohibited discriminatory voting practices that remained prevalent in many southern states. Prior to the signing of this act, Black citizens were subjected to impossible literacy tests and poll taxes that were insurmountable. The objective was to keep southern African American citizens disenfranchised and voiceless. But as I think back on the level of my consciousness at the time this landmark legislation was being signed, I was unaware of the magnitude of this bookmark in our country's history. Though I may not have been as aware of the significance of this event as I should have been, it wasn't lost on my father. If I close my eyes I can still see my father standing in the living room where the black-and-white television sat in the alcove under the stairs. He was intently watching TV and told me to be quiet and to come watch as President Johnson signed the Voting Rights Act. Dad looked at me and said, "You know what this means, don't you? Now colored people in the South can't be stopped if they try to vote." At that time my fifteen-year-old brain still didn't grasp the historical significance of what was taking place. I was living in the insulated world of Pennington, New Jersey, where no one that I knew had to worry about voting rights.

My father, also a product of the Hopewell Valley School System, went by the nickname Shud. Throughout his entire seventy years on earth people would ask the origin of the nickname, but no one knew for certain where it came from. Regardless, it stuck throughout his entire life. Dad's given name was William Wallace Smith, and he was one of ninety-two graduates of Pennington Central High School, Class of 1941. I look at his picture in the *Centralogue Yearbook*[4] and find him and one other lone African American face. It was that of Paige Hoagland, a descendant of the well-known Hoagland family. Dad was a born athlete, and his status as basketball captain was mentioned in the sports section of the yearbook where it noted, "With Wallace 'Shud' Smith as captain, Central started the season with a BANG, defeating our main rival Hamilton in the opening game by one point. Continuing fine teamwork, we won our first thirteen [my Dad corrected what was originally written] games without a loss, until a strong five from Mt. Holly [once again Dad's correction] downed us." My dad was obviously proud of his athletic accomplishments because there were apparently a couple of mistakes printed on the number of wins. I recognized his "chicken scratch" written over the stats in the yearbook as he corrected 17 out of 21 instead of 13 out of 16 scheduled games.

I turned the page to the section on the senior class trip to Washington, D.C., and I thought to myself that I couldn't recall my father ever talking about going on the trip. Interestingly, although he never mentioned it, apparently, he did go. The yearbook copy started with May 15, 1941, where it excitedly exclaimed, "What a most wonderful experience to look forward to, ninety-two excited Seniors and five chaperones boarded the train at the Pennsylvania Station at 10:30 A.M. and thus began our trip to the nation's Capital." I gazed at the picture above the copy and can clearly see my father in the group picture taken outside of Mt. Vernon, but I did not see Paige Hoagland, the other Black student. It seems as if my father was the lone African American on the trip. In the fourth paragraph it described their most "important destination," Hotel Continental, which was to be their temporary home for a couple days while visiting Washington. The entry continued with "our first thought was to get a few minutes rest and to become acquainted with our new surroundings, and then on to dinner in the Continental Room of the Hotel. We then made a tour of the city, to see what it looked like at night and also paid a visit to the Congressional Library where we were able to see the original copies of the Declaration of Independence and the Constitution of the United States."

I wondered if my father was able to accompany his classmates to enjoy the amenities of the Hotel Continental and have a relaxing dinner in the "lovely" Continental Room. I was curious because Washington, D.C., our nation's capital at that time in 1941, was a segregated city. Being in a segregated city, I wondered if my father was allowed to stay and eat at the same hotel as his classmates because I had heard from relatives that Black students had to find either lodging in a local "colored" Y or a hotel for Blacks only. Since I was unable to ask my father, who passed away in 1993, I racked my brain to think of anyone who could possibly help me answer this question. What did happen to the Black students once they entered Washington? Had they mentally prepared themselves, or was it easier to just accept the situation as it was? Would their memory of the class trip match the glowing description given by the White students?

The question surrounding my father's class trip continued to haunt me, but who was I to ask questions? The majority of people in school around the same time as my dad had either passed or moved away. While I was still conducting research, I called Betty Blackwell Davis, the owner of the Blackwell Memorial Home in Pennington, New Jersey, to ask if I could review her books of burials kept by her establishment. Betty's family has roots dating back to the 1700s in this region, and their family business has been in operation in Pennington since 1881. I playfully refer to Betty as "Cousin Betty" not only because we have enjoyed a warm friendship for years but also because we both acknowledge our connection through the Blackwell family's ownership of my 4th great-grandfather Frost. While searching through her books I asked Betty when she graduated from Pennington Central High School, to which I was told 1948. Since I've known Betty for years, I felt comfortable enough to ask her what she, as one of the White students, remembered about Black students being allowed to stay in the same hotel as the White students on the senior class trip. Without hesitation she sat down and began to tell me the story of a lone Black female classmate who was not allowed to stay at the same hotel as the White students. Instead she was to stay at a local Black YWCA. Betty clearly recalled that one of the teachers accompanied the student to her destination; however, when they arrived not only were the conditions not up to par but the teacher could not, in good conscience, leave the student to stay all alone. The plan the teacher came up with was to solicit help from Black hotel workers to sneak the student in through the back door and quickly up to a room without being detected. Because of the number of years that have elapsed Betty said that even though the student's name had escaped her, she would never forget what that young woman experienced on the senior trip.

Not long after my visit with Betty, I also remembered my father's first cousin Oliver, who was in his nineties. Prompted by Betty's story, I called Oliver to also ask him what he remembered about Black students who went on their senior class trips. "Was my dad able to stay with his classmates?" I asked Cousin Oliver His response was that he wasn't sure because age had dimmed his memory. We talked for a while. Before we hung up he said he had a clear memory of when he was in middle school, he had to be around twelve or thirteen, when his class went on a day trip to see the movie *Robin Hood* at the Lincoln Theater in Trenton. Trenton was also a segregated city in 1938, and Oliver said the theater attendants insisted that Oliver, the only Black student, was to sit in the balcony alone to watch the movie while his White classmates were to be seated comfortably downstairs. Surprisingly, he recalled, his teachers were adamant that he be allowed to sit with the rest of the class and he was not to sit alone to watch the movie. I cannot help but think how much Oliver was impacted by this experience since he could clearly remember an incident that happened some eighty years ago.

Before we wrapped up our conversation, Oliver was quick to add that he did not go on the senior trip with his class of 1944. He offered no further explanation, and I could sense from his tone that conversation on that subject was over. He seemed to warm up, though, when he fondly recalled how his older sister Bernice graduated in 1939 from Pennington High School. I didn't ask if she went on her senior class trip. Although Bernice had recently passed away, Oliver was chuckling at the memory of how his sister never had to crack a book to get As and Bs. What particularly bothered him, he said, is that he had to work so hard to get decent grades and it was effortless for Bernice. As I ended the call, Oliver was still chuckling about how his sister always academically "bested" him. After our conversation I called Bernice's son Larry to tell him about my conversation with Oliver and to find out more about his mother's performance in school. Larry was eager to talk about his mother's achievements and said she always believed a person should aim high, get good grades, and go to college. Although Larry is a soft-spoken man, I could hear pride in his voice as he told me how his mother graduated magna cum laude from Pennington Central High School and received awards in Latin and math. He told me that his mother was an avid reader and learned to play guitar from Earl Hubbard, who was a classically trained violinist who lived in Pennington. Fortunately, Bernice's academic achievements paid off because when she graduated in 1939 she received a full scholarship to Rider College. Her admission, though, was contingent upon an interview. When Bernice arrived for the interview, Larry said the admissions director expressed shock that a "Negro" had been admitted and informed Bernice that educating her would be a waste of resources since domestic or clerical work were the only jobs for which she would be eligible—and those jobs did not require a college education. So, Bernice's opportunity to attend Rider College was over and she never applied to another college. She ended up getting a job in a local factory during World War II and some years later was hired by the N.J. Division of Motor Vehicles where she worked for twenty-three years before retiring as a supervisor.

Twenty-nine years after Bernice graduated and twenty-seven years after my father, I joined my class to go on my senior class trip to Washington, D.C. It was 1968 and I picked up my grandmother at her home in Trenton so she could purchase me a suit to wear on the trip. I was told that it was of the utmost importance for a young woman to have the appropriate clothing for such a special occasion. Knowing my grandmother was always partial to navy blue, my choice was a double-breasted suit with a pleated skirt and large gold buttons on the jacket. It was navy blue and beautiful.

The day finally came when we boarded the train that was to take us to our nation's capital where we would spend three days touring Washington's historic sites and the National Zoo. When we arrived, we all stayed at the same motel and I roomed with my cousin, Marcia Clark, and friends Suzen Witcher and Jean Jackson: four Black female students out of a graduating class of 176. I recently looked at our class picture, which was taken with the Capitol as the backdrop. Our smiling faces beamed at the camera as we posed in our suits and dresses. Some even had on hats and gloves. The boys wore suits and ties, and their hair was neatly in place. Little did we know our three-day excursion was to be cut short due to the assassination of Dr. Martin Luther King.

The evening of April 3, 1968, when we went to the movies to see *Camelot*, we could have never predicted that our trip would soon come to an abrupt and unexpected ending. Recently a classmate recalled that after we came out of a tour of the National Archives, we were stunned to see machine guns mounted at the entrance as we exited. An added recollection of the day was seeing military convoys and police roaming throughout the streets. Unaware of what was going on, we then heard that Martin Luther King had been shot in Memphis, Tennessee. The only information we knew at that time was that King had been shot by a sniper and his condition was still unknown. However, it wasn't long before we received the news that King had not survived and we were going to leave Washington. Suddenly we saw convoys of soldiers roving the streets of Washington. The capital, like many major cities across the country, would erupt into flames as protesters took to the streets over the death of King. For our teachers I think the reality quickly set in that they were responsible for 176 children from Pennington, New

Jersey, who were a long way from home. Arrangements were made for us to return home as quickly as possible, so we grabbed our belongings and left our motel bound for Union Station. One of my classmates, who has a clear memory of the day's events, recalled looking out of the window of the train to see smoke that was starting to rise over Washington as we sped north.

Thinking back on my experience as a student in a predominantly White system, I remember how I begged my mother to let me go to school because my older cousins and neighborhood playmates had all gone before me. I could barely contain myself when the day finally arrived in September 1955 when it was my turn to go to school. It wasn't long, however, before my excitement turned to dread when I started to develop bouts of anxiety that plagued me only when I was in school. For reasons I cannot explain whenever I was in school I could not eat or drink at lunch or snack time. I would go all day without eating a morsel, so it wasn't long before my behavior was brought to my parents' attention. Their alarm only seemed to make matters worse.

As I moved into elementary school, I eventually grew out of my anxiety and made friends. It wasn't uncommon, however, to come to school on a Monday morning to hear about birthday parties and other social events that took place over the weekend—parties I was never invited to. One girl who I've remained friendly with since our days in kindergarten now lives part-time in Florida and the other half in Ringoes, New Jersey. When she comes back in the late spring we always get together to catch up. During one of her visits we decided to meet for breakfast. While we were chatting, I did not expect her to turn to me and say, "I think we may have talked about this before, how my mother felt so badly that you were never invited to my parties." I immediately had a mental image of her beautiful mother, who was never seen in public less than perfectly presented. She went on to tell me how her mother had wanted to invite me to the parties but felt the need to consult an older relative to seek her opinion on the matter. The consensus was that it just wasn't the right thing to do.

The significance of this story is not to condemn my friend for telling the story or her mother's decision, just the opposite. The fact that my friend was comfortable enough to talk about her mother and how she arrived at her decision was acknowledged and appreciated. The takeaway from the conversation was her mother's decision was based upon social norms that she felt compelled to uphold, regardless whether she agreed or not. I felt this was a significant conversation because it is exactly the type of dialogue and reflection that Elaine and I have encouraged in our work with the Sankofa Collaborative.

By no means have I been the lone person to experience bigotry while I was a student. Unfortunately, African Americans who were schooled in this district all have stories about racial discrimination. These stories can range from being called a derogatory name by a classmate to a teacher whose approach seemed to be vastly different in situations involving a Black student and a White student. And though my challenges seemed to lessen after I entered high school, there was a disturbing event I recall happening when I was in elementary school. It was when the special education class was suddenly populated with many of the Black kids from my neighborhood. It seemed to happen overnight, kids I knew for years, reassigned to a class that would be made up mostly of African Americans. My anxiety started to reappear because each day I wondered if I was going to be next.

Throughout the years I often wondered why this happened and what the impact may have been on these children who were placed in special education. I tried to think of how and why this could have happened and decided to invite retired school administrators with decades of employment in the Hopewell Valley School District, George Renwick and Dora Berry, to my house to have a conversation. George explained that although neither he nor Dora was employed in the district at that time, he thought it would be helpful if I read the Beadleston Act of 1954.[5] I looked at the Beadleston Act and discerned that basically there were three categories for students considered mentally retarded that included: the educable mentally retarded, the trainable mentally retarded, and those not educable or trainable. There were also multiple categories for children who were physically handicapped. Although this was not my area of expertise, I tried to glean enough information to figure out how these kids, each one whom I personally knew, fit into any of the prescribed categories. To help further clarify, George pointed out that the final determination was essentially made by an examiner who acted as the "decider in chief": essentially one person who determined whether a child should be placed in special education. George further clarified that it wasn't until later, when laws changed and child study teams were implemented, that this policy of one-voice decision making was discontinued. So, what do you think happened, I asked George. Could it be that some of the Black students were overclassified by the examiner? Dora joined in the conversation and added that as the first African American social worker in the district, she made a point to give special attention to students who appeared to have fallen into this category. As an African American, Dora said she had the ability to discern certain cultural and social differences that may have been misinterpreted by her White colleagues. So, cases that may have involved overclassification received her prompt attention.

I have chosen to tell you these stories because they have as much relevance today as they did eighty, seventy-five, and fifty years ago. All the stories I have told happened to African American students who comprised a very small percentage of the entire student body. You cannot help but wonder how these experiences impacted the lives of these students seventy-five, fifty, or even twenty years ago and how these examples can be used as teachable moments.

I started this chapter with language contained in legislation that established the Amistad Commission in 2002. The commission, implemented to promote educational awareness in New Jersey, also advised that "workshops institutes, seminars, and other teacher training activities are designed to educate teachers on the subject of the African slave trade, slavery in America, the vestiges of slavery in this county and the contributions of African Americans in building our country." Elaine and I have made numerous presentations before the middle school in the Hopewell Valley Regional School District as well as the Lawrenceville, Hillsborough, and the Montgomery school districts. We always make sure to tell the students how fortunate they are to be in a school system where their educators are encouraging learning about slavery, injustice, discrimination, and racism, particularly from people who descended from locally enslaved individuals.

*

Since 2002 when the Amistad Bill challenged New Jersey's educators to change the single narrative of how American history has been taught, some progress has been made but there is still much work to do in the state as well as the nation. In a symposium spearheaded by the Sankofa Collaborative, statistician Dr. Tabitha McKinley was invited to present on the subject of what children in the United States know about difficult topics in African American history. We were very interested to hear what Dr. McKinley had to say in her role as a state coordinator for the National Assessment of Educational Progress (NAEP). NAEP, a congressionally mandated project administered by the National Center for Education Statistics, began in 1969 to ensure that all NAEP selected schools are in compliance with federal mandates.[6]

The purpose of NAEP is to glean information about what American students know in subjects such as civics, economics, geography, mathematics, music, reading, science, U.S. history, visual arts, vocabulary, and writing. Every odd year 10,000–20,000 students from randomly selected New Jersey schools are tested, and in alternate years, national testing takes place that includes 3,000 students from various demographics from New Jersey. At the symposium there were several eye-opening moments during Dr. McKinley's presentation. What was very disturbing was her concluding slides that pointed to a glaring lack of time for teaching African American history in elementary and high school classrooms in New Jersey and the nation. In spite of the dismal statistics, Dr. McKinley advised that we cannot place the blame on students for what they are not being taught. She presented these statistics in November 2017, showing the time educators spent on teaching African American history:

- 1–2 weeks: reported by 30% of 4th grade and 22% of 8th grade instructors (2010)

- 3–5 weeks reported by 23% of 4th grade and 20% of 8th grade instructors (2014)

- 6 weeks or more reported by 7% of 4th grade instructors (2010)

- 6 weeks of more reported by 18% of 8th grade instructors (2014)

What was most revealing was that teachers with PhDs who taught twelfth graders were asked to truthfully submit the amount of time spent on analyzing and interpreting literature related to U.S. history, and 75% of these instructors admitted spending either no time at all or "a small or moderate" amount of time teaching African American history.[7]

When Elaine and I first started presenting to schoolchildren it became clear that our mission was to deliver our story to schools. The Amistad Bill has paved the way for curriculum development in New Jersey and also opens the door for further statewide collaborations and partnerships to promote African American history in the school curriculum. We applaud the work that has stemmed for this landmark legislation and wholeheartedly encourage New Jersey to continue taking the lead in promoting educational awareness of the African American story.

As we near our conclusion we bring you back to where it all began, in those early days of trampling through brambles and brush in search of a long-forgotten slave cemetery. Our mission will be to continue highlighting the lives, experiences, triumphs, and struggles of the African American people from the Sourland Mountain and surrounding region—information we want to be readily available to teachers, leaders, and members of the general public. So, as you read "Looking Forward," we ask that you read with the mind-set of a change agent who would be willing to work within your community to close the divide between how American history has long been delivered and how it should be taught. It is our belief there is danger in not acknowledging the truth, and as a society we cannot afford to continue to shut our eyes to the full understanding of our nation's history. Truth is the only healing balm that will bring about change.

1   William D. Payne and Craig A. Stanley, Assemblymen, "An Act Establishing the Amistad Commission," Pub. L. No. A1301, §16A, 52 New Jersey Statutes Annotated 86 (2002), accessed April 27, 2018, www.njleg.state.nj.us/2002/Bills/PL02/75_.HTM.

2   Cooley, *A Study of Slavery in New Jersey*, 9.

3   "About the Sankofa Bird," Southern Illinois University Department of Africana Studies, accessed April 9, 2018, http://cola.siu.edu/africanastudies/about-us/sankofa.php.

4   The Yearbook Club of the Class of 1941 of Central High School, *The Centralogue* (Pennington, Mercer, NJ: Hopewell Valley Central High School, 1941).

5   "Beadleston Act of 1954," n.d., pp. 58–59.

6   Assessment, "National Assessment of Educational Progress (NAEP)," State of New Jersey, Department of Education, 1996-2017, accessed April 9, 2018, http://www.nj.gov/education/assessment/naep/.

7   Tabitha McKinley, "Presenting Difficult Topics in African American History" (Third NJ 2017 Statewide Symposium on African American History, November 1, 2017, Hamilton, NJ).

Elaine Buck and Beverly Mills at the Timberlane Junior High School, Hopewell, New Jersey, 2018

CHAPTER 12

LOOKING FORWARD

by ELAINE BUCK and BEVERLY MILLS

It's our heritage, you see. You've got to come from somewhere.

—Albert Witcher (1921-2013), descendant of the Grover family

A decade ago, if we had had a crystal ball that would enable us to gaze into the future, would we have answered the call to devote a significant portion of our lives to this project? Would we be prepared to be a voice for scores of faceless, marginalized individuals, some of whom were our ancestors? The answer is decidedly yes. Right from the beginning we realized that cemeteries have vital stories to tell.

As we began our journey, we focused on African Americans who lived in the Sourland Mountain and surrounding region. However, this story can be repeated throughout the original thirteen colonies. New Jersey is by no means unique when it comes to our narrative, which can be replicated throughout slaveholding states. And as New Jersey is one of the original slaveholding states, we believe the time has come for the Department of Education to mandate that educators can no longer continue segregating African American history from American history—because one story cannot stand without the other.

Nelson Mandela once said that "education is the most powerful weapon which can be used to change the world." This is precisely why we wrote *If These Stones Could Talk*. It is our goal that this book be used as an instrument to open the eyes of students and adults to an understanding that there is more to American history than the single Anglo narrative. We want educators to use our book to guide discussions that will contribute to curriculum building from kindergarten through twelfth grade. We want to end the practice of having African American history only taken down and dusted off the shelf one month out of the year. We want to see a legislative mandate that African American history must be included in all American history curricula and not left up to chance. In addition, on a global level, we do not want any student to sit one more day in a classroom and be taught a single Anglo narrative lens on history. This outdated practice must cease to be perpetuated in local and national school systems. We want to be part of a raised consciousness. We will do our part to continue our work with educators, to host symposiums, and to use social media to decentralize how the African American narrative has been controlled.

It seems like just yesterday, and not over a decade, when we answered Mr. Niemeier's call for help from the Stoutsburg Cemetery Association for saving what he believed to be an old slave graveyard. We think back on how we were charged with proving the possibility of there being a graveyard there, which would require the analysis of an archaeologist. Do we consider it merely coincidence that an article about Ian Burrow, an archaeologist, appeared the same weekend we received our challenge? Do we chalk it up to irony that Al Lavery, the neighbor next door, handed us a fragment of Elnathan Stevenson's will that specifically laid out his wish to preserve the family cemetery and the adjoining land in perpetuity? We're still amazed by the fact that Elaine's classmate Joe Klett, who is the chief of the New Jersey Archives, called to say he read our story in the *Trenton Times* and retrieved a copy of Elnathan Stevenson's will that he would bring to her. Is this all happenstance or what we firmly believed—the hand of God making a way?

During the months that we worked with Mr. Niemeier, traveling back and forth to Trenton and Flemington to research documents, we were shocked and saddened to learn how pervasive slavery had been in our region. We regard this discovery as the catalyst that began our research on those interred in the Stoutsburg Cemetery. Who were these souls, and what was life like for them as Black people in a predominantly White region during colonial times, after the Civil War, and during the Jim Crow era?

So where do we go from here? While writing *If These Stones Could Talk* we were faced with the difficulty of processing what we were learning, and we were literally forced to confront our own thoughts and feelings in unexpected ways. We realized that if we ignored or cherry-picked to avoid some particularly disturbing information, the outcome might not prove to be as comprehensive in the long run. We've had to remain steadfast as facilitators and leaders to keep the door open to discussion and learning on all levels.

As we were moving forward we had to grapple with how to adequately interpret the pervasiveness of evil that enabled the American slave system to take root. How do we interpret the horrific truths that for years have been either minimized or altogether silenced? And while it's important that we continue to speak truthfully about the horrors of slavery, how do we present it authentically and meaningfully without upsetting the learner? Certainly, it is not to start with the most difficult stories. As an example, this brings to mind the "Willie Lynch Letter," a document whose origin and validity have long been questioned. It was written in the twentieth century purporting to be a blueprint on the making of a slave and how to decimate an entire race. In spite of the controversy regarding its validity, this directive very closely mirrored what actually happened on southern plantations.[1] The bottom line is that what is difficult history for one person may not be for another.

The overarching mission of writing this book is for it to be in the hands of every school-aged child in the State of New Jersey, the United States, and beyond. We strongly believe that the information we have brought to our readers has never had its rightful place in history and is long overdue. But we ask ourselves, is it enough that our book is simply read without any outcome? Not in the least. It is our hope that you, the reader, will become inspired to be an advocate for change and to challenge, if necessary, how history is taught in the school system. We want our readers to remain vigilant, to ensure that the old narrative is not repeated in their homes, communities, and schools. We also challenge our readers to think more expansively about the content of our book, and not only from a historical perspective. We want readers to understand why it was so important the individuals we highlighted were given a physical presence.

Humanizing people in stories will bring validity to those who, for the most part, were only thought of as supporting caricatures on the American stage. We believed that by bringing broader stories to our readers, we can enlist them in challenging their own beliefs or opinions. Which brings us to this question: What can the reader do to create their own opportunity to pay it forward?

As authors we will stay vigilant and continue with our mission to change how African American history is taught. We will spread our message through speaking engagements, collaborations on symposiums, and seminars and continue speaking out on the contributions and accomplishments of African Americans here and nationally. We believe it has been our duty to take on this initiative and have felt the hands of our ancestors gently guiding and leading us to a light that has been enveloped in darkness.

We invite our readers to take the opportunity to visit the region where this history took place. We recommend tours of the region we have highlighted in central New Jersey through organizations such as the Sourland Conservancy. We also invite you to visit our local historical sites as well as the Stoutsburg Sourland African American Museum in Skillman, New Jersey. Above all, we encourage you to be advocates of change, so that our educational systems are no longer comfortable teaching a single narrative that limits every student's opportunity to know a true and full story. Someone once said that we cannot repair the unknown. But can't we all be change agents once armed with the knowledge? This was our mission, the reason why we wrote *If These Stones Could Talk*.

---

[1] William Jelani Cobb, "Is Willie Lynch's Letter Real? May 2004,"
   Jim Crow Museum of Racist Memorabilia at the Ferris State University,
   May 2004, accessed March 28, 2018
   https://ferris.edu/HTMLS/news/jimcrow/question/2004/may.htm.

ABOUT ELAINE BUCK
AND BEVERLY MILLS

Elaine Buck and Beverly Mills are the founders of Friday Truehart Consultants, named after the original slave brought to Hopewell, New Jersey at the age of thirteen by his master Oliver Hart. Buck and Mills work closely with K-12 educators from school systems interested in including African American history in their lesson plans and curriculum. They are founding members of the Stoutsburg Sourland African American Museum and serve on its Advisory Board.

Buck and Mills have been Trustees of the Stoutsburg Cemetery Association for the past thirty-five years. They are both members of the National Council of Negro Women and the Sankofa Collaborative, a resource that will ensure that material and resources relating to African American history will be readily accessible statewide to a broader and more diverse audience.

Through decades of research, Buck and Mills have become more than statewide educators on a mission to open up a healthy investigation into the history of race beginning in their home state. They have also become bridgebuilders, engaging leaders in the boardrooms of museums and schools throughout Central New Jersey. Their goal is to engage readers, educate students and impact curriculum development not only in New Jersey but across the United States. Bucks and Mills have created lesson plans for schools, museums and historic sites among other venues.

Beverly Mills is the first African American woman to hold the elected position as Councilwoman, Pennington Borough, and Elaine Buck is Church Clerk for the Second Calvary Baptist Church of Hopewell.

Beverly Mills and Elaine Buck